The Challenges of Educat

The Challenges of Education in Brazil

Edited by
Colin Brock & Simon Schwartzman

Oxford Studies in Comparative Education
Series Editor David Phillips

SYMPOSIUM
BOOKS

Symposium Books
PO Box 204 Didcot Oxford OX11 9ZQ United Kingdom
the book publishing division of wwwords Ltd
www.symposium-books.co.uk

Published in the United Kingdom, 2004

ISBN 1 873927 89 4

This publication is also available on a subscription basis
as Volume 13 Number 2 of *Oxford Studies in Comparative Education*
(ISSN 0961-2149)

Typeset by Symposium Books
Printed and bound in the United Kingdom by Cambridge University Press

Contents

Preface

This collection of papers is the outcome of a series of seminars held at the University of Oxford between January and March 2003 under the auspices of the Centre for Brazilian Studies and the Centre for Studies in Comparative and International Education.

Publications on education in Brazil in English, whether articles or books, are relatively few, and so we hope that this volume will make a significant contribution to the understanding of contemporary issues in all major sectors of the country's educational provision and performance. The collection is also being published in Portuguese in Brazil, and in the best interests of both sets of readerships it was decided from the outset to invite only Brazilian contributors. To achieve this required considerable financial assistance, in respect of which we are most grateful to Professor Leslie Bethell, Director of the Centre for Brazilian Studies at the University of Oxford and the sponsors of the Centre. We would also like to express our thanks to Margaret Hancox, formerly Administrator of the Centre.

The seminars were conducted at the University of Oxford Department of Educational Studies, and, although open to all, constituted an important component of the MSc programme in Comparative and International Education, which, together with the doctoral programme, is a major area of development in this field in the United Kingdom. We are therefore also grateful to Professor David Phillips, Director of the Centre for Comparative Studies in Education, for his support of the seminar series, as well as in his capacity of Series Editor of *Oxford Studies in Comparative Education*, within which this volume resides.

Most of all we are grateful to all our contributors, who, without exception, gave considerable time and care to their preparations, and tremendous involvement and enthusiasm to their presentations. All are extremely busy professionals, and most are – or have been – practitioners within the Brazilian system, often at very senior levels. They understand all the problems, the achievements and the nuances from real experience within, and this undoubtedly lends a cutting edge to their contributions.

Given language differences and unfamiliar terminology, the editing of the various manuscripts has been a considerable task and would not have been possible without the most able and willing efforts of our Editorial Assistant, Kimberly Ochs, to whom we are most grateful.

It has been an honour and a pleasure to act as editors to what we consider to be an important contribution to the resources available for the study of education in Brazil.

Colin Brock
Centre for Comparative and International Studies in Education
University of Oxford

Simon Schwartzman
Instituto de Estudos do Trabalho e Sociedade, Rio de Janeiro; Visiting Research Fellow, Centre for Brazilian Studies, Oxford January–March 2003

The Challenges of Education in Brazil

SIMON SCHWARTZMAN

Education in Brazil has changed significantly in recent years, but is still far from satisfactory. In this introductory text, we present a broad view of the origins of Brazilian education, and, from there, we try to identify some of its key features. This should allow us to better understand the current conditions and predicaments, and open the way to discuss some of the policy options that are being tried, or may be available. Education issues are always controversial, and this chapter hopes to enhance and clarify some of the matters of contention.

The Central Issues

Until recently, there seemed to be a consensus that the problems of Brazilian education were that there were not enough schools, that children abandoned education in large numbers at early ages, and that the government did not spend enough money in education. It was deemed necessary to build more schools, to pay the teachers better, and to convince families to send children to school. It took some years of careful demographic analysis to convince policy makers and public opinion that, in fact, children do not drop out of school in significant numbers before they are 15 or so. The main problems were quality and retention – that is, the tradition of holding the children back when they do not perform as expected in school examinations, a widespread practice in Brazil (Fletcher, 1984; Klein & Ribeiro, 1991). With the slowdown of demographic expansion and internal migration in the 1980s, Brazil started to face, for the first time, problems of empty classrooms. Today, there are 43.8 million students enrolled in basic education [1] for a total population of about 36.5 million in the corresponding age bracket of 7 to 17, an unwarranted excess of more than 7 million places.[2]

As we see in Figure 1, practically all children between the ages of seven and ten are in school. Therefore, access is no longer an issue. However, as shown in subsequent figures, many students are not at the level they should be, and there are too many adults occupying the places of young drop-outs.

We see in Figure 2 that most youngsters between the ages of 15 and 17 are not in secondary education, as they should be, but are lagging behind. Because of retention, there are about 7 million students in fundamental education that are older than the reference group, and should not be there (giving a gross enrolment rate of 121%) (Figure 3). In secondary education, about half the students are 18 years or older, and should have already left school. In higher education, which still enrols only 9% of the age cohort (18-24), about half the students are aged 25 or older.

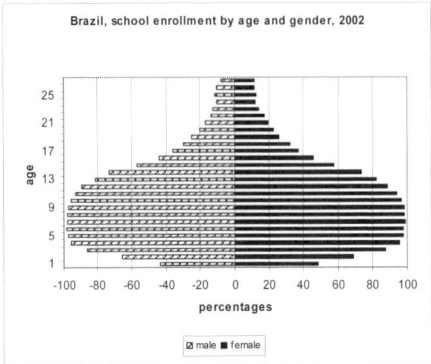

Figure 1. School enrolment by age and gender, 2002.
Source: National Household Survey, Brazilian Institute for Geography and Statistics (PNAD/IBGE), 2002.

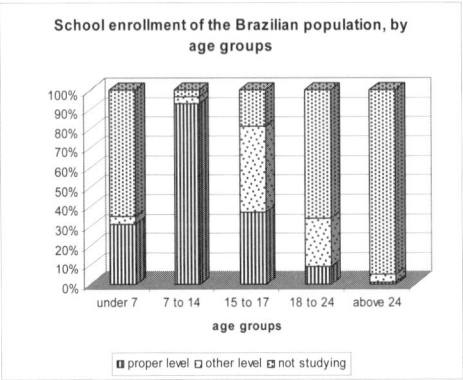

Figure 2. School enrolment by age groups.
Source: National Household Survey (PNAD), 2001.

10

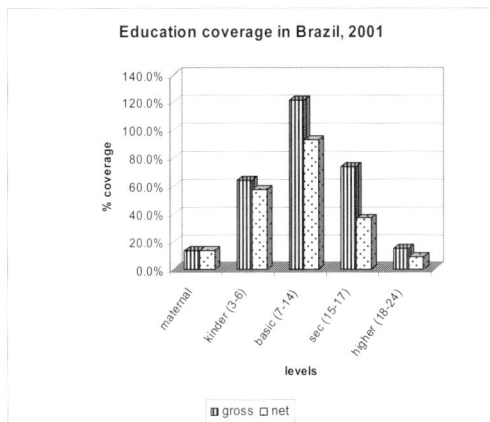

Figure 3. Education coverage by education level, 2001.
Source: National Household Survey (PNAD), 2001.

These distortions are related to a tradition of bad quality instruction that limits the student's ability to learn, as revealed by the Brazilian National Assessment of Basic Education and other evaluations (Crespo et al, 2000; Organisation for Economic Cooperation and Development [OECD] Programme for International Student Assessment, 2001), and to the high drop-out rates that occur when the young reach adolescence. In 2001, by age 16, 19% of Brazilian youngsters were already out of school; by age 18, 43%. Very simply, a large number of students go through school without learning to read and write properly. There is a very serious problem of teaching teachers how to teach (Oliveira & Schwartzman, 2002), and of reaching out to those who were left behind, to recover the time lost and to be brought to the level of their age peers.

There is also a problem of relevance of content, which affects mostly those in secondary schools, but also substantial segments of higher education. Are the students learning what they need in order to help them to enhance their personalities, and to enter the labour markets? Is Brazil graduating the specialists, researchers and innovators it needs to participate in the modern 'knowledge economy'?

The first question touches the classic dilemma of choosing between general and vocational education. It is a difficult question, because it involves both social discrimination, when students are 'tracked' to a particular education path that keeps them in lower status jobs, and the effective provision of marketable skills to persons who may otherwise not be able to find work. The international experience shows that simple content differentiation will not provide marketable skills, if there is no clear linkage between technical schools and future employees. On the other hand, when

11

these linkages are present, vocational education could provide better opportunities in a stratified job market, even at the price of long-term segmentation (Shavit & Müller, 2000). Brazil has obtained some success in vocational education for small segments of its population, with access to the training schools of the industrial and business associations, but attempts to extend these experiences more widely have not succeeded. A similar difficulty arises with higher education, where the absence of post-secondary, short-term alternatives to full university degrees ends up creating enormous waste, by persons trying and later abandoning their university careers. Here again, the simple creation of short-term course programmes, as the poor-man alternative to full diplomas, tends to be rejected, and does not prosper.

How much education does Brazil need, and for what purpose? We can readily agree that universal, good quality basic education is a requisite and a moral requirement of all modern societies, for the sake of social equity, cultural values, and economic functionality. We can also agree that governments should get involved in supporting higher education, as a source of knowledge and competence for society as a whole. However, even in advanced economies, only a segment of the job market requires highly specialised competencies, and most higher education is related to the provision of general attitudes and skills. The demands of educators and academics for more courses, better salaries, and more public subsidies at all levels tend to be endless, and it is necessary for governments and decision-makers to know what are the limits, and where to stop.[3]

The problems of equity deserve special attention. Brazil is known for having one of the world's highest levels of income inequality, and this is strongly related to education (Ferreira & Paes de Barros, 2000). Brazil is also a multiracial society, with half of its population being classified as 'non-white', and there are strong correlations between ethnic origins, income, and educational opportunities. On the whole, in 2001, the white population had 5.75 years of school, and the non-white had 4.04; the average income of white persons was twice as large as that of non-whites.[4] Today, for the younger generation, the chances of whites and non-whites to be in school are practically the same for all age groups (Figure 4). This does not mean, however, that ethnic differences do not persist. Non-whites are poorer, live in poorer neighbourhoods, and have less educated parents. Regional differences are larger still, going from 5.59 years in school in the South-east (which includes São Paulo and Rio de Janeiro), down to 3.71 in the North-east. At age 11, the chances of being in a school are practically the same in the North-east and the South-west – 97.3% and 98%. At age 16, however, the difference is already important – 77.7%, compared with 86.0%.

As a rule, public schools in poor regions, municipalities and neighbourhoods tend to be of worse quality, and school achievement depends heavily on the family's economic, social and cultural background. Middle- and upper-class families send their children to private basic and secondary schools, which are of better quality, and prepare them to be admitted to the most prestigious, public (and free) higher education institutions. Students from poorer families, if they get to higher education at all, can only enter the less prestigious courses in public universities, or go to private institutions, where the courses are also of low prestige and quality, for which they have to pay.

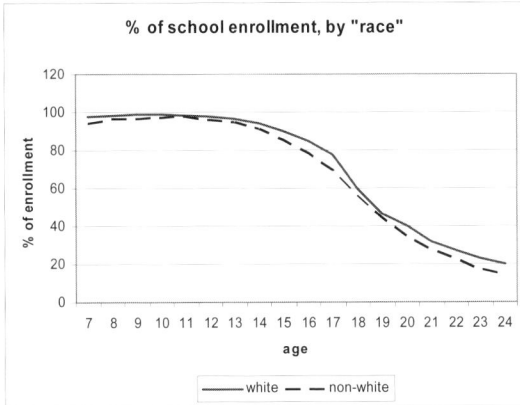

Figure 4: School enrolment by age and ethnicity, 2001.
Source: National Household Survey (PNAD), 2001.

We can summarise this overview by stating that the main problems with Brazilian education are those related to the quality and retention of students in the public systems. One major consequence of these problems is the inequity in the access to good quality education, which affects mostly the poorer segments of the population; the other is the large number of persons who leave education before getting their certificates, without acquiring the knowledge and skills they were supposed to have. Finally, the distortions created by bad quality and retention led to a huge waste of resources spent on keeping in schools older students who should not be there.

The Origins

How did education in Brazil come to its present situation?

By the early twentieth century, most of the population in western Europe, New England and Japan was already literate, while in Brazil and most other countries in the world, education reached only a tiny minority.[5] The achievement of mass literacy can be explained by a combination of different elements. The Western religions – Judaism, Christianity, and Islamism – place the reading of sacred books at the core of children's education. In the Jewish and early Protestant traditions, learning took place in the family or in small community schools, and was part of the building and maintenance of cultural identity in the face of an alien or hostile

13

environment. Throughout the Muslim world, reading the Quran was and is an essential component of one's religious and moral education. Not all these traditions, however, succeeded in converting religious reading into skills that could be used outside the religious and ritual realms.[6] For this, other conditions were necessary, including the availability of printed materials, and the need to use scriptures and figures to communicate, to keep records, to do business and to work.

Grass roots and community organisation, moreover, were not enough. The spreading of basic education and literacy schools in Europe was, at first, the work of the established churches, Protestant and Catholic, as part of the Reform and Counter-Reform movements, and became later the task and responsibility of the emerging nation states. France under Napoleon epitomises the model that so many countries tried to imitate: a nation coordinated by a strong central government that created complex institutions to involve and mobilise all citizens in an integrated and cohesive society. In its origins, a central institution of the modern nation state was universal military conscription; also important were a unified and homogeneous national language, and education institutions able not only to provide everyone with reading and writing skills, but also with the moral and civic values deemed necessary for the Nation.[7]

No modern state, however, could start this work from zero. In France, the Napoleonic state built its education institutions upon a complex network of schools created and maintained by the Church during the Ancien Régime, and on traditions of popular education that had existed in many places (Furet & Ozouf, 1977). Different nation states dealt with the Church and the diverging popular education and linguistic traditions in different ways, sometimes in conflict, sometimes in cooperation, often through cooptation. An important part of this history is the development of the teaching profession, which helped to transform the more spontaneous and traditional forms of education and learning into a network of organised and standardised schools.[8] Industrialisation and the development of the modern cities also played a part, but their role was not very obvious. David Vincent argues, for instance, that early literacy was a 'luxury' made possible by economic progress, more than a condition for it, although, once it existed, it helped in the growth of industry and trade (Vincent, 2000). In fact, there is some evidence that, in England and France, industrialisation and urban concentration led to the temporary deterioration of educational standards. Education could not develop in conditions of extreme poverty, but, once it started, it became a central ingredient in the fabric of modern societies.

Portugal, Brazil's colonial power, like Spain, was not touched by the Reformation movement. The Catholic Church, which exerted strong control on the country's universities through the Jesuit order, did not have to respond to the threat of Protestantism through the creation of schools for the common people, and this might help to explain why literacy did not spread as much in Portugal as it did in other European countries.

By the mid eighteenth century, under the Marquis of Pombal, the Jesuits were expelled from Portugal and Brazil, in an effort to bring the Portuguese empire in line with the European enlightenment. In Portugal, the reform led to the first effort to create a national system for elementary education, which marked also the beginning of the teaching profession in that country (Nóvoa, 1987). Nothing similar happened in Brazil, where the unintended consequence of the reform was the dismantling of most of the Catholic education that existed at the time.[9]

In the early nineteenth century, the Portuguese court moved to Rio de Janeiro, fleeing Napoleon, and in 1822, Brazil became independent under a Portuguese king. The first higher education institutions in Brazil are from these years – a military academy in Rio de Janeiro, two law schools in São Paulo and Recife, two medical schools in Rio de Janeiro and Bahia. In 1838, the first public secondary school, the Colégio Pedro II, was established in Rio de Janeiro.[10] Elementary education, when it existed at all, was left to the governments of the provinces, private tutors and parochial priests, except in the country's capital, where some rudiments of a system of public education began to take shape. The Church was also responsible for several religious establishments, including the famous Caraça School in the mountains of Minas Gerais, kept by Lazarist priests, which was, for many years, one of the few alternatives for young men willing to study but unable to go to Rio de Janeiro or abroad.

Colégio Pedro II, 1861, MG, Museu Mariano Procópio.

Figure 5. Colégio Pedro II, Rio de Janeiro, 1861.
Source: http://www.rio.rj.gov.br/multirio/historia/modulo02/criacao_pedroii.html

Brazil, in the nineteenth century, was a predominantly rural society, run by a centralised empire trying to adopt the trappings of European nation states, without, however, the resources to reach out to the population in the impoverished and distant provinces, where the economic cycles of sugar and gold had long since come to an end. This population was formed by a small elite of white Portuguese descendants, black slaves, the remnants of the indigenous population, and large numbers of mixed-blood, former slaves and poor free men living out of subsistence farming or squatted around the largest ports and cities of Salvador, Rio de Janeiro, and Recife (Franco, 1969; Mattoso, 1988). This demographic and cultural picture had begun to change by the end of the nineteenth century, with the influx of European and Japanese immigrants to São Paulo, Rio de Janeiro, and other southern states, first to replace the slave labour in Brazil's latest cash crop, the coffee plantations, and later to populate the country's main cities. By 1900, a third of the population in Rio de Janeiro and São Paulo had been born outside Brazil. At that time, about a third of the youngsters in Rio de Janeiro attended some kind of elementary or primary school, one in four in a private institution.

Figure 6. The Caraça School in Minas Gerais
Source: http://www.viajar.de/pages/minas/sg_minas45.html

By then, the Empire had been replaced by a Republican regime, and new educated elites started to agitate in favour of a modern nation state which would not just mimic the European institutions but could really incorporate the population into a coherent and integrated national community. In the state of São Paulo, for the first time, a new conception of public education started to take root. In the 1890s, as part of a remarkable effort to modernise the state, formerly scattered teaching units were brought together into 'school groups' (*grupos escolares*), built according to the most advanced architectural designs of the time. The students were organised according to their age and proficiency; and, for the first time, a multi-serial and sequential study programme was put in place (Souza, 1998).[11] New teacher training schools (*escolas normais*) were created and transformed, trying to introduce better teaching methods and modern contents (Nagle, 1974; Tanuri, 1979). Similar reforms were attempted or started in Bahia, Minas Gerais and the capital city of Rio de Janeiro.

In 1906 the federal government enacted new legislation for primary education, reorganising the schools, and proclaiming the virtues of vertical handwriting, supposed to be much more efficient, rational and adequate for large-scale teaching of writing skills (Faria Filho & Galvão, 1998). However, throughout the First Republic (1889-1930), primary and secondary education remained the responsibility of local and state governments, and only about 25% of the population, at most, was literate.[12] German, Italian and Japanese immigrants created their own schools, sometimes with the support of the governments of their countries of origin, or foreign priests.[13] In 1924, a Brazilian Association for Education (*Associação Brasileira de Educação*) was established in Rio de Janeiro with participants from several states and played a very important role in bringing education to the centre of the national agenda (Paim, 1981)

Figure 7. Escola Modelo da Luz (Grupo Escolar Prudente de Morais), established in São Paulo in 1895.[14]

It was only with the so-called 'Revolution of 1930', which brought Getúlio Vargas to power and started a new period of political centralisation, that education finally appeared as a national priority. The new government established, for the first time, a Ministry of Education and Culture [15], and intellectuals who had been involved in the regional educational reform and education campaigns published a famous Manifest of the Pioneers of the New Education (Azevedo, 1932), which would set the education agenda for the years to come. Movements for a 'new education' and a 'new school' had been present in European and American educational circles for several decades, with ideas taken from the works of Wilhelm Dilthey, Édouard Claparède, Adolphe Ferrière and others, and propagated by institutions like the *Ligue Internationale pour l'Éducation Nouvelle*. In the 1920s, these ideas dominated the education debates in Portugal (Nóvoa, 1987). The pioneers' proposals dealt both with the way education should take place, through the active participation of the student in the learning process, and on the way Brazilian education should be organised, through the establishment of public universities, free, universal, mandatory and basic education, and the education of teachers in university-level institutions.

There is an extensive literature on the ideas and work of these pioneers, and on what the government of Getúlio Vargas and his education ministers, Francisco Campos and Gustavo Capanema, did or did not achieve in matters of education.[16] The proponents of educational reform were deeply divided on ideological and doctrinaire grounds, from authoritarian fascists (Francisco

17

Campos) and ultramontane Catholics (Alceu Amoroso Lima) to American-type pragmatists (Anísio Teixeira), believers in the scientific powers of the new pedagogy (Lourenço Filho and Fernando de Azevedo), and Marxists (Paschoal Lemme). Part of the conflicts had to do with the pact signed between Vargas and the conservative Catholic Church, according to which Brazilian education would be reorganised under the Church's guidance and direction [17], which was strongly opposed by the more liberal reformers on the left.

In the end, what prevailed was none of those principled doctrines, but the bureaucratic and administrative instincts of Minister Capanema, infused with the nationalist and conservative values of the time. The Vargas government created a very centralised bureaucracy for higher education, and made a significant effort to shape and control basic and secondary education from above, without, however, taking the responsibility for the management and administration of the schools, which remained under the responsibility of state and municipal authorities, or in private hands. Initiatives in the period included the creation of Brazil's first research centre on education, the National Institute for Pedagogical Studies (INEP) (Mariani, 1982; Xavier, 2000), and the reform and upgrade of the old Normal School, as the new *Instituto de Educação* in Rio de Janeiro, expected to become Brazil's version of the French *École Normale*, and the model for the country. More controversial were the efforts to mobilise the young and infuse them with nationalist patriotic ideals, through religious education, the reading and singing of national and patriotic hymns [18] and, at a later stage, the forceful closure of the immigrants' schools, and the prosecution of those who taught the children in their modern tongue (Bittencourt, 1990).

In this period, primary or elementary education, which was supposed to be mandatory and universal, lasted for four years, from ages 7 to 10. It was followed by the gymnasium, then considered as secondary education, also for four years. Finally, there was a 'college' level, lasting two to three years, conceived as a preparatory course for the universities. The Capanema Ministry spent a large effort in the elaboration of the curriculum of secondary education as a European-like gymnasium or lyceum, which would provide humanistic and scientific education to youngsters aspiring to enter the universities. Most students, however, were expected to get a practical education in agricultural, industrial and commercial activities, without going into higher education. Nevertheless, there were no places to prepare and train teachers for these courses. The industrialists created their own technical schools, which were considered of good quality and adjusted to their needs, and remained outside the control of the education authorities [19]; commercial education grew in the private sector, as a second-best alternative to children coming from lower social strata, and agricultural education never developed.

On higher education, the first university legislation was passed in 1931, establishing a combination of French-style professional schools and an Italian type of 'Faculty of Philosophy, Sciences and Letters', which was supposed to be the place for research, scholarship and also teacher education for secondary schools. Here again, the federal government tried a very centralised system, with laws defining the contents of courses and careers, a National University serving the model for the whole country, and a strict system of controls and supervision of local and private institutions. However, the only national university to be created before World War II was the one in Rio de Janeiro, through the aggregation of the city's old professional schools and a new Faculty of Philosophy, Sciences and Letters. The state of São Paulo, in competition with the federal government, created its own university first, according to the same model, but with a much stronger scientific and academic content. For its Faculty of Philosophy, European professors were recruited in France, for the social sciences; in Italy, for physics and mathematics; and in Germany, for chemistry and the biological sciences. Through their work, the University of São Paulo gave origin to the most important traditions of scientific and technological research in the country, and remains Brazil's leading academic institution (Schwartzman, 1991b).

The conceptions, institutional frameworks and practices established during those 15 years of the Vargas regime, 1930-45, would shape Brazilian education for many decades. After the War, Brazil entered a period of rapid modernisation, economic growth and urbanisation, which brought with it a growing demand for education. The federal government responded by creating a network of federal universities, at least one in each state, and state governments and municipalities expanded their school systems of elementary and secondary education. Private education expanded also, catering both to the elites, with selective elementary and secondary schools, and to the lower middle classes, opening cheap alternatives for those who would not pass the entrance examinations to public universities, or wanted to combine study and work.

It would take half a century from the Manifest of the Pioneers of the New Education of 1932 for the institutional framework of Brazilian education to start changing again. During this period, Brazil became an urban society, with communications linking the whole country, and with a large industrial sector. In spite of this expansion, education was probably less a concern in the 1950s and 1960s than in previous decades. Earlier, there was the belief that education could change minds and souls, and was the road for social betterment. Later, economic growth, social conditions and politics took precedence; education, from a precondition for social change, came to be seen as an after effect. In the 1950s, President Juscelino Kubitschek led an ambitious 'targets programme' to make Brazil a modern country, through the establishment of a modern industry, the opening of roads, the building of dams and the construction of a new capital in Brasilia. However, there was only one target related to education – technical training, with less than 4% of the investment budget (Bomeny, 2002). In the same period, thanks to the international support from UNESCO and other sources, an ambitious

National Centre for Education Research (CBPE) was established in Rio de Janeiro, under the old institute for pedagogical studies. Many interesting studies came out of this institution, on urbanisation, social stratification, and social mobility – but very little on education as such (Xavier, 2000).

Some important reforms took place, however, in the 1960s and 1970s. In the late 1960s, higher education was transformed, with the introduction of US-type innovations, like the credit system, academic departments, and graduate programmes. In 1971, following international trends, mandatory education was extended from four to eight years, by adding the old four-year 'gymnasium' to the elementary school. Secondary education, now limited to school years 9 to 11, experimented with different models and links between academic and professional curricula, without much success. In 1988, after 20 years of military rule, a new Constitution was drawn up, declaring mandatory education as a 'subjective' right of every person (meaning that it was an entitlement that could be claimed in court, if necessary), establishing that all universities should be autonomous, that research, teaching and extension work were inseparable and that all public education, basic and higher, should be provided for free. For many years thereafter, Congress and interest groups debated a new Education Law, which was finally approved in 1996, giving, in principle, much more freedom and flexibility for the education institutions at all levels to set up their own course programmes and manage their affairs.[20]

Missing Links: the teaching and academic professions

From this historical background, we can try to understand why education in Brazil did not develop as in other countries. The short answer is that, by and large, Brazilian society did not have the elements that would lead its population to organise and develop its own educational institutions, and the Brazilian state, both at the national and regional levels, did not have the human and financial resources, nor the motivation, to bring the population into a centralised and vertical educational system. More specifically, two crucial links between these two spheres were missing, a well-structured and organised teaching profession for basic education, and an academic profession for higher education, which could spread, implement, and foster the values of education.

In Europe, the modern learned professions evolved from the old trade guilds into large-scale, self-regulating entities, which placed limits to the absolutist powers of governments and the erratic behaviour of the people, and carried out the day-to-day activities of rationalisation that was the cornerstone of modern societies.[21] The classic learned professions were law, medicine and, in France, engineering, but the academic and teaching professions were also very important, and have been the subject of intense scrutiny in recent years (Müller et al, 1987). In France, which was always considered the model to be followed, elite higher education remained limited to the professional *Grandes Écoles*, while the old university, closed down by the Revolution, was restored to deal mostly with teacher training and general education. As described by Randal Collins, 'the reconstituted university was in fact a bureau of the Central state making appointments to secondary schools and controlling a uniform curriculum throughout the country' (Collins, 2000, p. 234). In Prussia, a strong academic profession was responsible both for giving the country the best education at all levels in the nineteenth century, and for contributing to the disaster of the 1930s (Ringer, 1990).

In Portugal, Nóvoa shows how a teaching profession, as distinct from the academic one, was already in the making in the late eighteenth century, with its main components being brought into place – a well-defined social status, a specific savoir-faire, training institutions, common values, a legal and institutional framework. By 1794, there were 748 royally appointed professional teachers (*Mestres Reais de Leitura e Escrita*) in Portugal; in Brazil, on paper at least, the number was just 179. More important than this numerical difference was that, throughout the nineteenth and the earlier twentieth century, the teaching profession would grow and expand in Portugal, but not in Brazil. This is related, in turn, to the fact that Brazil remained a slave-based economy and did not go through a liberal revolution like the one that took place in Portugal after independence, an echo of changes that were sweeping other European nations so dramatically.

It is possible to trace, in the nineteenth century, the early attempts to bring to Brazil the notion that modern societies should be led by enlightened and educated professions. Small groups of medical doctors, lawyers and engineers tried to convince society that they had the solution for the country's problems, and sought to guarantee, at the same time, the professional privileges and autonomy they deemed necessary for their work (Schwartzman, 1991a; Coelho, 1999). Differently from Europe, the regulation of professional rights and privileges moved much more quickly than the creation and strengthening of the professions themselves. In the 1930s, the Vargas regime adopted the notion that society should be organised in well-regulated and hierarchical corporations, which included the labour unions, business associations, and the learned professions. Each profession would have its own educational prerequisite, to be provided or certified by the state, and all workers, businessmen and professionals would have to belong to a specific corporation, supervised by the state (Schmitter, 1974; Schwartzman, 1977). In practice, this attempt to organise society from above went against the movements to organise society from the bottom up, leading to weak institutions and extensive cooptation of potential leaders to political and bureaucratic power positions. For education, the consequence was the high premium given to educational credentials, creating an endless tug of war between those trying to get their credentials with the minimum possible cost and investment, and the government and professional corporations trying to control and limit the distribution of these entitlements.

21

We have seen how, in the 1930s, there were proposals to develop the teaching profession within the higher education institutions, both through the Faculties of Philosophy, Sciences and Letters, and through the academic upgrade of the old Normal Schools. This integration, however, never succeeded. Some components of a teaching profession emerged through the early efforts to modernise education in São Paulo and Rio de Janeiro. They included a generation of prestigious professional teachers in the best known secondary schools, school directors and pedagogues educated in the new Normal Schools in Rio de Janeiro, São Paulo, Minas Gerais and a few other states; qualified priests and nuns teaching in Catholic institutions; and, of course, the intellectuals that signed the Manifest of the Pioneers of New Education. These were exceptions, however, that only confirm the rule, which was the absence of a well-defined and extended teaching profession until very recently.

Two parallel trends led at last to the creation of a teaching profession in Brazil, the spreading of basic and secondary education and the development of institutions to provide them with professional qualifications and legal certification. In 2002, there were 2.4 million 'teaching functions' [22] in basic education in Brazil, about one million of which were in state networks, another million in municipal schools and half a million in private establishments. In addition, there were about half a million 'teaching functions' in secondary education (9-11). In the past, most of the teachers in the old '*grupo escolar*' (today the first four years of fundamental education) had at most a secondary degree obtained in a Normal School. Today, 25% of those have a higher education degree, and there is legislation requiring that they all should have such a degree in a few years' time. The consequence is the proliferation of all kinds of degree granting programmes in education, most given in the evening or at a distance, and of questionable quality.[23]

For a schoolteacher, the place to get a higher education degree varies depending on the level that she or he wants to teach. For pre-school and the first four years of education, the route is a school of education or pedagogy; for the remaining four years and secondary education, a degree in the subject matter is required, to be obtained in one of the old Faculties of Philosophy, Sciences and Letters or a science department. In the past, these faculties were supposed to be the place for research, scholarship, and teacher education, a combination that proved impossible to achieve. In time, the natural sciences, and most of the empirical social sciences in public universities, created their own departments and research-oriented programmes, where teacher education is not considered a prestigious activity. Teacher education remained important in the schools, faculties or departments of the traditional 'teaching' social sciences – history, geography – and in the schools of education and pedagogy, both in public and private institutions. These courses recruit students coming from poorer backgrounds who have difficulty getting into the more competitive fields, or old teachers returning to evening courses to get their newly required academic credentials.

Very few are being trained these days to teach the natural sciences, or modern social disciplines like economics or political science.

In short, Brazil did not develop a separate system for teacher education, and the attempt to develop it as part of the regular university system did not work very well. Teacher education was relegated to low prestige segments of higher education institutions and the private sector, and did not develop strong graduate and research programmes, like the ones in the natural and more academic social sciences (economics, sociology, political science). One consequence of this seclusion of teacher education and the traditional 'teaching' social sciences is that the members of this new teaching profession became, at the same time, highly organised and politically motivated, but devoid of adequate teaching competencies and knowledge in their substantive subject areas.[24] As required in these modern times, those in graduate programmes participate in congresses, conferences, academic associations, and have their publications, with a strong predominance of different varieties of Marxist and critical theory approaches. Paulo Freire, with his views on education as an instrument for political revolution, is the preferred reference. Other important names are Pierre Bourdieu, and, among Brazilians, Octávio Ianni, Florestan Fernandes and Milton Santos. They do not know much about how to teach, or what to teach, and, very often, they do not think this is very important. As they see it, society is unfair, people are exploited, governments do not care about the teachers or about education, and not much can be done before a real and deep social transformation, or revolution, takes place.[25]

The development of an academic profession for higher education started in the late 1960s, with the creation of academic departments and the expansion of public universities that took place in the following years. Before that, teaching in higher education was a minor, but prestigious activity for persons who worked mostly in their own professions, as lawyers, doctors, dentists or engineers. Except for a few medical schools and sections of the University of São Paulo, there was no research nor resources or installations for full-time academic work in universities.

Starting in the late 1960s, however, thousands of teaching jobs in higher education were opened in order to staff the new institutions being created to respond to a growing demand for enrolment coming from the middle classes. The private sector chose to work mostly with part-time instructors; in the public sector, however, full-time employment became the rule (Figure 8). Since the 1960s, about 70,000 teachers and professors have been recruited for the federal universities; by 2001, about a third had already retired, having remained active for about 22 years on average (Figure 9).[26]

This rapid and uncontrolled expansion, plus early retirements, had several important consequences. First, the financial cost of public higher education soared, placing a severe limit on the government's ability to continue to respond to the demand for higher education, and to keep the salaries above inflation. Second, only a small percentage of those hired had the necessary training and education needed for high-level academic work. To increase quality, new legislation was passed linking promotion and salary increases with higher academic degrees, leading to an inflationary expansion of specialisation and Master's programmes.

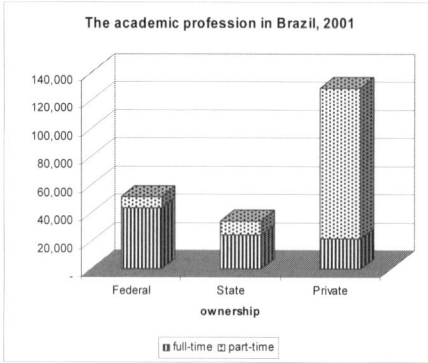

The academic profession in Brazil, 2001

Figure 8. Academic professionals, by institutional ownership.

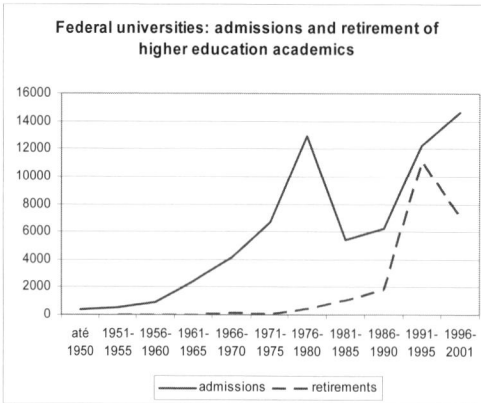

Federal universities: admissions and retirement of higher education academics

Figure 9. Admissions and retirements in federal universities.
Source: tabulated from the federal government, 'Sistema Integrado de Administração de Recursos Humanos: (SIAPE)'. I am grateful to Walterlina Brasil for making this data available to me.

Because of these developments, the Brazilian academic profession is now highly stratified. It includes a small, but significant, number of persons who are well trained in Brazilian and foreign universities, have full academic credentials, and run the main graduate departments and research centres in the best public universities. There is a large number of part-time teachers

24

working in private institutions, more identified with their specialised professions than with academic life. In between, there is a large body of full-time academics working in public institutions, without the full credentials to get the prestige and resources of advanced research, and without strong links to outside professions. Members of this segment tend to feel frustrated by their career limitations, are strongly organised in teachers' unions and associations, and play a major role in the political life of their institutions and the higher education sector (Schwartzman & Balbachevsky, 1996).

The implications of these developments are paradoxical. With the delay of a century or more, Brazil now has sizeable academic and teaching professions, which could play a crucial role in the building of well-structured and competent education institutions at all levels. But this new social actor, overall, feels alienated and dejected. It could be argued that, without their support, no improvement in education is possible. At the same time, one may wonder whether it is still possible, in the twenty-first century, to try to rebuild the old academic professions that served so well in the development of education in the European nation states.

Recent Policies

Between 1995 and 2002, for the first time since Gustavo Capanema in the 1930s, Brazil had a Minister of Education, Paulo Renato de Souza, who was not a politician, but an economist and former rector of one of the country's leading universities, the University of Campinas, and who served for two full administrations. Some of the innovations in this period were the rehabilitation of the old National Institute for Educational Research (INEP) as an office for education statistics and evaluation, and the establishment of a National Fund for Basic Education (FUNDEF), to reduce the regional differences and set a floor for state and municipal expenditures on fundamental education.

INEP became responsible for the reorganisation of Brazil's education statistics and the implementation of three large systems of education assessment – SAEB, the assessment system for basic education; ENEM, a national examination for students completing secondary education; and the national examinations for undergraduate programmes, known as '*Provão*'. Part of this development was the emergence of a new generation of education specialists, trained in statistics and psychometrics, who are providing Brazilian educators and policy makers with new and better instruments and information for their policies.

The Brazilian Constitution of 1988 determines that the federal government should spend 18% of its resources on education, and state and local governments, 25%. FUNDEF was established to make sure that this money is actually spent on education and to establish a floor, through compensations, for public expenditures per student and per teacher for the whole country. One of the effects of FUNDEF was to stimulate the

25

involvement of local municipalities with basic education, reducing the size and bureaucracy of state education administrations (Castro, 1998; Kolslinksi, 2000).

Other policies of the period included the development of new curricular guidelines for basic and secondary education, and several programmes to provide schools with managerial, pedagogic and material resources to improve their performance – schoolbooks, lunch, and cash.[27] This was also a period of unprecedented expansion of secondary education, caused at least in part by the concerted efforts to reduce retention of non-achieving students in the first years of their school life. For the poorest segments, the government created a large programme to pay families to send and keep their children at school.[28]

These actions, combined with programmes implemented by the state secretaries of education in many regions, led to an increase in enrolments in pre-school, fundamental and secondary education, more resources for teacher training and salaries, and more equipment and resources for schools. Student flow was improved through controversial policies of school promotion, sometimes accompanied by programmes to help less achieving students to catch up with their group age (the so-called 'acceleration classes'). By the end of the decade, the government was able to announce that, for the first time, practically every child in Brazil had a place and was enrolled in fundamental education.

Achievements in higher education were less significant, except for the renewed growth in student enrolment, after the stagnation of the 1980s. The Brazilian federal government is now responsible for an expensive network of 39 universities and 18 other higher education institutions, which enrol about 20% of the student population. There are also public universities owned by state governments, bringing total public enrolment to about 35% of the students. The high costs of the public institutions are caused mostly by the salaries and retirement benefits of their academic and administrative staff, all civil servants endowed with job stability and early, full-paid retirement, and by the maintenance of their teaching hospitals, which fill in, in practice, for the absence of adequate public hospitals in many places.[29]

This picture would not be complete without reference to the achievements in graduate education and the existence of many good quality professional schools, particularly in some of the leading federal and state universities. Graduate education developed in earnest in Brazil after the adoption of the American model in the 1960s, and the establishment of independent sources of support and quality control for research and graduate education in the ensuing years. In 2001, there were about 60,000 students in MA and 32,000 in doctoral programmes; about 10,000 students get their graduate degrees every year. Even discounting for some level of degree inflation, due to requisites for promotion in public universities, it is an impressive achievement, with no parallel in other countries in the region. The persistence and improvement of good quality professional education in many institutions can be explained by the early policy of not opening the public universities to unlimited admissions, as happened in countries like Argentina, Uruguay or Mexico.

Good results that do exist in basic and secondary education are more difficult to describe, because of the sheer size and complexity of these sectors. There is a strong and expected correlation between good schools and the availability of resources, and between the socio-economic conditions of the students and their scholastic achievements. The best segments of public education are likely to be found in the southern states of São Paulo, Paraná, Santa Catarina and Rio Grande do Sul, which combine reasonable levels of socio-economic development with reasonable administrative and pedagogical traditions. At the other extreme, the worst segment of Brazilian basic education is probably composed by the one hundred thousand or more rural schools, maintained by local municipalities, and enrolling about 5.5 million students, out of 35 million in basic education. These are usually one-class and one-teacher schools, with very few resources of any kind.[30]

These healthy segments of Brazilian education do not contradict the fact that the system as a whole is under severe strain, financially and institutionally, and needs to change and adjust, for more quality, efficiency and relevance. The good news is that, for these reforms, the amount of resources already committed to education is substantial; we know much more about education than we did in the past; society is more concerned with education than it has been until recently; and there are important segments of the academic and teaching professions that can participate and eventually lead.

Future Policies

From the vast array of problems and issues that can be raised, some have gained more notoriety in recent years, which does not mean, necessarily, that they address the fundamental questions. We can conclude by discussing some of them.

One recurring issue is resources. According to the experience of qualified state administrators, it is impossible to provide good, quality education in Brazil for less than one thousand reais per student per year – the equivalent of about 300 US dollars in early 2003.[31] In contrast, the latest floor established by the Brazilian government for expenditures in basic education, through the use of the national education fund (FUNDEF) was 446 reais per student for the first four years or fundamental education, and 468.3 for the other four (O Estado de São Paulo, 2003).

Brazil spends already about 5% of its GNP in education, which places it at the same level as Spain, Italy, or Japan, and above Chile or Argentina. However, this expenditure is strongly biased towards higher education. The estimation, done by INEP for 1996, was that the cost of a higher education student was 12.8 times more than of one in basic education, and 9.9 times more than one in secondary education.[32] To change this situation without reducing the expenditures for higher education would require a substantial increase in public spending, bringing it to the 7% level, similar to countries like Canada or the USA. This could be a worthy goal, but is not likely to take place in the near future, given, among other factors, the country's budgetary squeeze and the still unresolved insolvency of the pension system. In the meantime, it is necessary to put the existing resources to better use, by adjusting the system's size to the actual need, and introducing better managerial and accounting practices.

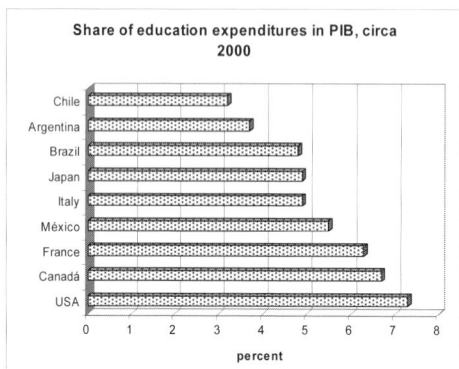

Figure 10. Share of education expenditures in PIB, circa 2000.[33]

The other important resource is commitment. No significant improvement in education can occur at any level without the active participation and empowerment of the academic and teaching professions. Education is something that takes place in the daily interaction between teacher and student or not at all, notwithstanding the recent advancements in computer education, distance education, and the like. A recent survey of education experts in Latin America showed that, thinking about the future, they are not optimistic about the chances for getting more resources for education, but expect the situation to improve through the growing commitment to education of local communities and social organisations (Schwartzman, 2001a).

Three conditions seem necessary for this commitment to take place. The first is that teachers and academics should be properly paid, and work with proper resources, within an adequate system of incentives and rewards. The second is that they perceive that governments and education authorities are working in their favour, not against them. The third is that they are competent and committed to their academic and educational tasks. The first two conditions are closely linked, and Brazil has been particularly unsuccessful on both accounts. Salaries have not kept up with expectations, and there are few or no reward systems for achievement either in basic or in public higher education.[34] Until the recent presidential election of 2002, the relationships between the federal government and teachers' unions at all levels have been hostile. This may change now, but it is not likely that there will be resources, at the national or state levels, for salary increases.

The third condition may be the most difficult of all. Without strong professional commitments, there is a tendency for political and union issues to take precedence over scientific, pedagogic and academic concerns, leading education authorities to try to increase control and supervision, and to limit the participation of teachers and academics in the management of their institutions – which generates further conflicts and alienation. The solution does not seem to be simply to transfer power to the education unions, or to give up on the need to engage teachers and academics with their work. The problem is not peculiar to Brazil, but this does not make it less relevant.

Total number and percentage of illiterates, by age, 2001

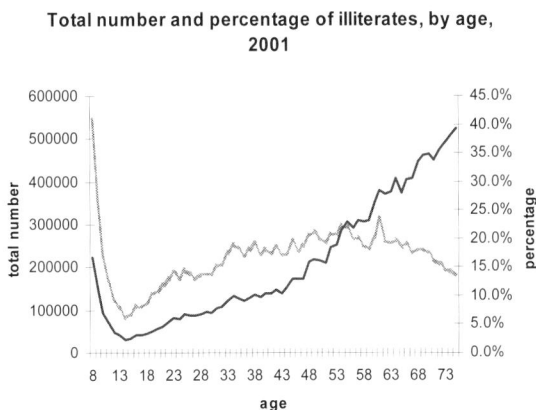

Figure 11. Illiteracy by age.
Source: Data from the National Household Survey (PNAD, 2001).

Another strategy is to create emergency programmes to deal with extreme forms of illiteracy and bad quality education, bypassing and not waiting for the complex problems of formal education to be worked out. It is very unlikely that this kind of strategy could succeed. According to the latest household survey (PNAD, 2001), 11.4% of Brazilians of 10 years of age and more declared that they were not to be able to read and write. To end adult literacy is a worthy goal, but is not very easy to achieve and probably not the first priority. Most illiterates in Brazil are older persons living in the poorest regions, and not many of them are likely to learn from literacy campaigns and incorporate reading and writing habits in their daily lives. The other large segment of illiterates is made up children that do not learn when they first get to school, but do so after a couple of years. At age 14, illiteracy in Brazil is

29

limited to 2.5% of the cohort, and it will fall naturally as the older generations wane.

There are many initiatives in the private sector, non-governmental organisations and voluntary groups to deal with the problems of low quality education, some of them very successful.[35] The main difficulty is to transfer the experience of small-scale initiatives to the regular school system.

Conclusion

As stated at the outset, the key problems for basic education in Brazil are to improve the quality of public education for the children who are already in schools and the provision of remedial education to adolescents and young adults who have dropped out or lag behind. Secondary education, which has expanded enormously in recent years, is by most accounts a disaster area. Half the students in secondary education attend evening classes, many of them work and are older than they should be, and the contents of their courses tend to be irrelevant and provided by ill prepared and unmotivated teachers. For most, the only goal is to get the education credential necessary for the job market or for some kind of higher education opportunity. Only the private sector has retained some quality, but, even there, rote learning to get into the most prestigious university courses is widespread.

Basic and secondary education are not in the hands of the federal government, and even the best policies to improve the country's schools will take years to materialise. These policies should include the intensive work or preparing teachers to deal with illiteracy; to make the schools more responsive to quality and results; to provide more resources, wherever possible; and to make sure that the resources that exist are put to the best possible use. Some hard choices will have to be made, concentrating resources in some sectors more than others – more, for instance, on fundamental education than in pre-school or at the secondary level – and asking the community to get more involved and to help foot the bill.

In higher education, the private sector is already responsible for two-thirds of the enrolment, and it would be impossible to reverse this situation in the foreseeable future. Brazilian higher education should expand much more than the current level of less than 10% participation of the relevant age group, and this can only be done through continuous diversification, pluralism, deregulation and the creation of mechanisms to curtail credentialism and stimulate quality and pertinence.[36] There are serious problems of equity in higher education, created by the selectiveness of the most prestigious public institutions, and the free tuition and other benefits given to the chosen ones. The easiest, but inappropriate, policy in this regard would be to make the institutions more open by lowering quality and standards, or establishing quotas for underrepresented segments. The best policy would be to maintain and increase the standards whenever possible, to open different paths and opportunities for students coming from different backgrounds and conditions, and, again, to ask those who will benefit from education to help pay for it. The most equitable policy of all, however, would be to provide good quality basic education opportunities to everybody.

It is not an easy agenda, but neither is it an impossible one. Brazil's educational picture is still not a good one, in spite of some bright spots; however, it shows a sense of direction and progress, which is far from uniform, and fraught with traps and false leads. But, at least, it is a movement in the right direction.

Notes

[1] A question of terminology: Brazilian education is organised today in two main blocks. The first is 'basic education', which comprises eight years of 'fundamental education', for children aged 7 to 14, and three years of 'secondary education', officially called 'middle education' (*educação media*) for youngsters aged 15 to 17. 'Elementary education' is used sometimes to refer to the first four years of fundamental education. The next block is higher education, divided into a first professional, graduate level, with course programmes lasting from three to six years, granting Bachelor's degrees; and a postgraduate level for students working for Master's and doctoral degrees (in an effort to adjust to the American terminology, the first higher education level is often translated, in English, as 'undergraduate', and the second, as 'graduate'). Besides, there is a pre-school level, for children under seven and a wide array of specialisation, non-degree postgraduate courses, lasting for a year. Post-secondary, non-university courses also exist, but in small numbers.

[2] There is a large discrepancy, however, between the information provided by the 2002 school census, carried out by the Ministry of Education, and the 2001 household survey carried out by the Brazilian Institute for Geography and Statistics (IBGE). The figures for fundamental education are, respectively, 35.1 and 31.8; and, for secondary education 8.7 and 7.6 million. These discrepancies can be explained, at least in part, by the fact that the school census takes place early in the year, and the household survey in September and later, with many students dropping out during the year; and by over-reporting by school administrations (probably), or under-reporting by families (less likely).

[3] For an assessment of the links between the supply of higher education and the demands of the labour market in Latin America in recent years, see Schwartzman (2002). For the inflation of higher education in England and its negative implications, see Wolf (2002). For the multiple functions and differentiation of higher education in Latin America and Brazil, see Castro & Levy (2000) and Schwartzman (1991b).

[4] The ethnic or race classification is obtained by asking the persons to place themselves into the categories of 'white', 'black', 'mixed' ('pardo'), 'native', and 'oriental', in the Brazilian national household surveys and censuses. This question is meant to classify the population according to one's self-described skin colour, as a surrogate for race or ethnicity (with Brazilian natives and

Orientals as subgroups within the 'yellow' category). For this tabulation, we added the blacks, about 5.6% of the respondents, with the 'pardos', 40.4%, to create the 'non-white' category. The natives correspond to 0.1% of the population, and the Orientals, mostly of Japanese descent, 0.5%. In the 2001 survey, 53.4% of respondents defined themselves as white. See, for a discussion of this classification, Telles (1998) and Schwartzman (1999).

[5] See, for Europe, Vincent (2000) and Venesky (1991). On France, see Furet & Ozouf (1977). On Japan, see, among others, Godo & Hayami (2000). On the USA, see Lockridge (1974), Monaghan (1988), and Stevens (1990).

[6] 'In Muslim countries it is quite common to be well versed in the Quran Sharif, taught in the indigenous religious schools called madrasas. Unfortunately this learning is purely rote. Hence, while students appear to be able to read the Quran Sharif with fluency, they still often cannot read the Arabic script when written elsewhere. This learning cannot be transferred to reading other books or doing math' (Samant, 1996).

[7] How much of the old nation state imagery remains, or should be maintained, in these times of globalisation, is a question that deserves a specific discussion, since its implications for contemporary education can be very significant. See, among others, Archibugi & Lundvall (2001), Lenn & Moll (2000), and Carnoy (1999).

[8] The classic reference for the analysis of these interplays between State, Church and the teaching profession in the establishment of national education systems in Europe is Archer (1979).

[9] There is no information, however, on how much education existed in Brazil in those years, the simple answer being 'not very much'. According to one source, about five hundred Jesuit priests left Brazil in 1759, closing 17 schools, 36 missions, and several junior seminaries and elementary schools (Bello, 2003). Other religious orders and secular priests remained, however. Later, the Jesuits were allowed to return, and the Church continued to play an important role in Brazilian society, including in education, in spite of constant conflicts with the country's political elite. On the Pombal reform and its impact on education in Brazil, see Maxwell (1995), Paim & Crippa (1982) and Andrade (1978).

[10] For the higher education institutions, Schwartzman (1991b); for the Colégio Pedro II, Prefeitura do Rio de Janeiro (2003).

[11] Even today, the expression '*grupo escolar*' is used in Brazil to refer to elementary schools providing the first four years of basic education. Other initiatives of the period included the creation of several higher education schools and research institutes. São Paulo was already, at that time, the world's largest coffee producer, and Brazil's richest region.

[12] The information comes from a municipal census in Rio de Janeiro of 1906, and the national census of 1900, as reported in Directoria Geral de Estatística (1916).

[13] Before the War, there were about five thousand German teachers working in a well-integrated school system spanning through the states of Rio Grande do

Sul, Paraná and Santa Catarina. In São Paulo, in 1917, there were 37 German schools, and 51 Italian ones. The Japanese started to arrive in earnest in the mid 1920s, and by 1936 there were 310 foreign schools in the state of São Paulo, of which 215 were Japanese (Bittencourt, 1990).

[14] Source:
www.crmariocovas.sp.gov.br/pdf/neh/1825-1896/1895_Escola_Modelo_ da_Luz.pdf
For a portfolio of pictures and the history of the '*grupos escolares*' in São Paulo, see Centro de Referências da Educação Mário Covas (2003).

[15] In the nineteenth century, education was the responsibility of the Minister of Interior, or the Empire. In the first Republican government, there was a short-lived 'Ministry of Public Instruction, Postal Service and Telegraphs'.

[16] See, from the pioneers themselves, Azevedo (1932), Teixeira (1968), Lourenço Filho (1967), Azevedo (1971). For an overview, see Schwartzman et al, (2000). See also Brandão (1999), Bomeny (2001).

[17] The pact signed between Getúlio Vargas and the Catholic Church for the control of the education institutions is documented in Schwartzman et al (2000). For the Brazilian Catholic Church conservative revival in those years and its role in education, see Salem (1982).

[18] This was a special project of composer Heitor Villa-Lobos, who would bring to public stadiums thousands of children in massive choirs, singing hymns and national popular music.

[19] The early attempts, and failure, of the Ministry of Education to bring Swiss teachers to create technical schools along the European traditions are described in Schwartzman et al (2000), chapter 8. Until today, the business federations maintain their own systems of technical education (Serviço Nacional de Aprendizagen Industrial, SENAI, and Serviço Nacional de Aprendizagem de Comércio, SENAC).

[20] This was the '*Lei de Diretrizes e Bases*', number 9,394, of December 20, 1996, also known as the 'Darcy Ribeiro Law'.

[21] This interpretation of the role of professions and intermediate organisations comes from Max Weber, but is also consistent with De Tocqueville's interpretation of *Democracy in America*, and its potential pitfalls.

[22] It is possible, in basic education, for one teacher to have two or more teaching contracts, or 'functions'. This means that the actual number of teachers is unknown through these statistics, collected by the Ministry of Education. The National Household Survey, however, provides independent confirmation: it found 2,378,000 teachers in basic education in 2001, 1.1 million working as public employees, a very similar result.

[23] This statement should be corroborated by an analysis of the data from the national evaluations carried out by the Ministry of Education. In some areas, like mathematics and physics, federal universities tend to fail 90% or more of their students, leading them to look for private, paid institutions where they would not have problems getting a degree. In other areas, standards are adjusted to the students' low qualifications, which are treated charitably as persons 'trying to make their first steps out of poverty'. (I am grateful to

Graziella Moraes Dias de Silva for sharing these observations from her fieldwork.)

[24] See, on the historical separation of education from the mainstream social sciences, Dias de Silva (2002). On the emergence and characteristics of the schools of education, see Bomeny (1995). On the broader issue of political participation and mobilisation of intellectuals and professionals in Brazil, see Schwartzman (1991a) and Miceli (1979).

[25] For an overview of the field of sociology of education as practised by education specialists in Brazil, which confirms these observations, see Dias da Silva & Costa (2002). On Paulo Freire, see Paiva (2000). For the perception of teachers about literacy and their own responsibility, see Oliveira & Schwartzman (2002); for samples of the ideological content of education scholarship in Brazil, see Gadotti (1996) and Saviani & Mendes (1983).

[26] The dramatic increase in early retirements around 1995 can be explained by the fear that the government would curtail the retirement privileges of civil servants. It did not happen at the time, but the issue is again on the agenda.

[27] See, for official overview, Secretaria de Educação Fundamental (2002).

[28] There is no evidence that parents would not send the children to schools if they are available and receptive; in this sense, the '*bolsa-escola*' programme is probably not very effective. In any case, it can be justified as a way of transferring some money to poor families with children. For an overview and evaluation of one such programme in the city of Recife, see Lavinas et al (2001).

[29] Costs are also increased by the absence of criteria or incentives to reduce the expenditures per student and the student/teaching ratio in the universities, which can vary by a factor of five or more, from one institution to another. Because of this, and the uniform, nationwide careers and salary scales, the costs for the government are high, but salaries paid to the best qualified staff are well below the expectations, generating frustration and dissatisfaction on both sides.

[30] Data from the 2002 school census. In the last several years, these schools have been receiving substantial support from a World Bank supported project, Fundo Escola, whose outcomes are still unclear.

[31] Alcyone Saliba, former state secretary of education of the state of Paraná, personal communication.

[32] http://www.inep.gov.br/imprensa/noticias/outras/news00_20.htm

[33] Sources: For Brazil, Argentina and Chile, INEP, '*Gastos do Brasil são mal distribuídos entre os diferentes níveis de ensino*'; http://www.inep.gov.br/imprensa/noticias/outras/news00_20.htm. For the other countries, Gouvernement du Québec, Government of Canada, Institut de la statistique du Québec, Organisation for Economic Cooperation and Development, Population Reference Bureau, Statistics Canada, US FedStats. http://www.stat.gouv.qc.ca.donstat/econm_finnc/conjn_econm/compr_inter/educpib_an.htm.

[34] Contrary to common belief, salaries for teachers in state administration, and for professors and academics in higher education, are not below the average

income of persons with similar levels of education. Expectations, however, are more important than sheer numbers.

[35] Among them the *Fundação Abrinq pelos Direitos da Criança*, the *Fundação Ayrton Senna* and the *Fundação Bradesco*.

[36] It could be argued that credentialism is not an issue any longer, since a large proportion of students go today to general fields like administration, and later to jobs that do not require a specific diploma. However, the premium paid by a higher education degree in Brazil in the job market is still very high, suggesting that the diplomas still have an important value (I am grateful to Cláudio de Moura Castro for raising this issue).

References

Andrade, A.A.B.d. (1978) *A reforma pombalina dos estudos secundários no Brasil*. São Paulo: Edição Saraiva.

Archer, M.S. (1979) *Social Origins of Educational Systems*. London: Sage.

Archibugi, D. & Lundvall, B-A. (2001) *The Globalizing Learning Economy*. New York: Oxford University Press.

Azevedo, F.d. (1932) *A reconstrução educacional no Brasil, ao povo e ao governo. Manifesto dos Pioneiros da Educação Nova*. São Paulo: Companhia Editora Nacional.

Azevedo, F.d. (1971) *Brazilian Culture; an introduction to the study of culture in Brazil*. New York: Hafner.

Bello, J.L.d.P. (2003) *História daeducação no Brasil 2003*. Available at: http://www.pedagogiaemfoco.pro.br/heb01.htm

Bittencourt, C.M.F. (1990) *Pátria, civilização e trabalho: o ensino de história nas escolas paulistas, 1917-1939*. São Paulo: Edições Loyola.

Bomeny, H. (1995) Faculdades de Educação, Cursos de Pedagogia e Crise do Ensino. *Ensaio. Avaliação e Políticas Públicas em Educação*, Rio de Janeiro. Fundação Cesgranrio, 3, pp. 87-112.

Bomeny, H. (2001) *Os intelectuais da educação, Descobrindo o Brasil*. Rio de Janeiro: J. Zahar.

Bomeny, H. (2002) Quando os números confirmam impresses: desafios na educação brasileira, in *Texto escrito como subsidio à elaboração do Relatório Nacional do SAEB 2001*. Rio de Janeiro.

Brandão, Z. (1999) *A intelligentsia educacional: um percurso com Paschoal Lemme por entre as memórias e as histórias da escola nova no Brasil*. Vol. 3, *Estudos CDAPH*. Bragança Paulista: Universidade São Francisco.

Carnoy, M. (1999) *Globalization and Educational Reform: what planners need to know. Fundamentals of Educational Planning*. Paris: UNESCO, International Institute for Educational Planning.

Castro, C.d.M. & Levy, D.C. (2000) *Myth, Reality, and Reform: higher education policy in Latin America*. Washington: Inter-American Development Bank. Distributed by Johns Hopkins University Press.

Castro, J.A.d. (1998) O Fundo de Manutenção e Desenvolvimento do Ensino e Valorização do Magistério (FUNDEF) e seu impacto no financiamento do ensino fundamental, in *Texto Para Discussao*. Brasília: IPEA – Instituto de Pesquisa Economica Aplicada. Available at: http://www.ipea.gov.br/pub/td/td.html

Centro de Referências da Educação Mário Covas. *Memorial da Educação 2003*. Available at: http://www.crmariocovas.sp.gov.br/neh/php?t=001a

Coelho, E.C. (1999) *As Profissões imperiais: advocacia, medicina e engenharia no Rio de Janeiro, 1822-1930*. Rio de Janeiro: Editora Record.

Collins, R. (2000) Comparative Historical Patterns of Education, in *Handbook of the Sociology of Education*, ed. M. Hallinan. New York: Kluwer.

Crespo, M., Soares, J.F. & Mello e Souza, A. (2000) The Brazilian National Evaluation System of Basic Education: context, process, and impact, *Studies in Educational Evaluation*, 26(2), pp. 105-125.

Dias da Silva, G.M. (2002) *Sociologica da sociologia da educação: caminhos e desafios de uma policy science no Brasil (1920-79)*, *Estudos CDAPH*. Bragança Paulista: Universidade São Francisco.

Dias da Silva, G.M. & Costa, M. (2002) Amor e desprezo – o velho caso entre sociologia e educação no âmbito go GT-14. Paper presented at Grupo do Trablho em Sociologia da Educação, 25a Reunião Annual da ANPED – Associação Nacional de Pós-Graduação e Pesquisa em Educação, Caxambu, Mg. 2002, at Caxambu, Minas Gerais.

Directoria Geral de Estatistica (1916) *Estatistica da instrucção*. Rio de Janeiro: Directoria Geral de Estatistica.

Faria Filho, L.M.d. & Oliveira Galvão, A.M.d. (1998) *Modos de ler, formas de escrever: estudos de história da leitura e da escrita no Brasil*. Belo Horizonte: Autêntica.

Ferreira, F.H.G. & Barros, R.P.d. (2000) Education and Income Distribution in Urban Brazil, 1976-1996., *CEPAL Review*, 71, pp. 41-61. Available at: http://www.eclac.cl/publicaciones/default.asp?idioma=IN

Fletcher, P.R. (1984) *Primary School Repetition: a neglected problem in Brazilian education: a preliminary analysis and suggestion for further evaluation*. Stanford: Stanford University Press.

Franco, M.S.d.C. (1969) *Homens livres na ordem escravocrata*. São Paolo: Instituto de Estudos Brasileiros Universidade de São Paulo.

Furet, F.& Ozouf, J. (1977) *Lire et écrire: l'alphabétisation des Français de Calvin à Jules Ferry, Sens commun*. Paris: Éditions de Minuit.

Gadotti, M. (1996) *Pedagogy of Praxis: a dialectical philosophy of education*. Albany: State University of New York Press.

Godo, Y. & Hayami, Y. (2000) Catching-up in Education in the Economic Catch-up of Japan with the United States, 1890-1990, *Economic Development and Cultural Change*, 50(4), pp. 961-978. Available at: http://www.fasid.or.jp/cgibin/byteserver/fasid/english/activ/research/pdf/disc_2000-004.pdf

Klein, R. & Ribeiro, S.C. (1991) O censo educacional e o modelo de fluxo: o problma da repetência, *Revista Brasileira de Estatística*, 52(197), pp. 5-45.

Kolslinski, M.C. (2000) O processo de implementação de politicas sociais descentralizadas: o estudo do FUNDEF. Dissertação de mestrado, Departamento de Educação, Universidade de Campinas, Campinas.

Lavinas, L., Barbosa, M.L. & Tourinho, O. (2001) *Assessing Local Minimum Income Programmes in Brazil: ILO – World Bank Agreement.* Geneva: International Labour Office. Available at: http://www.ilo.org/public/english/protection/ses/info/publ/

Lenn, M.P. & Moll, J.R. (2000) *The Globalization of the Professions in the United States and Canada: a survey and analysis.* Washington, DC: Center for Quality Assurance in International Education.

Lockridge, Kenneth A. (1974) *Literacy in Colonial New England; an enquiry into the social context of literacy in the early modern West,* 1st edn. New York: Norton.

Lourenço Filho, M.B. (1967) *Introdução ao estudo da escola nova; bases, sistemas e diretrizes da pedagogia contemporânea,* 9 ed. São Paulo: Editora Melhoramentos.

Mariani, M.C. (1982) Educação e ciências sociais O Instituto Nacional de Estudos e Pesquisas Educacionais, in S. Schwartzman (Ed.) *Universidades e instituições científicas no Rio de Janeiro.* Brasília: CNPq, Coordenação Editorial.

Mattoso, K.M.d.Q. (1988) *Família e sociedade na Bahia do século XIX, Baianada, 6.* São Paulo: Corrupio.

Maxwell, K. (1995) *Pombal, Paradox of the Enlightenment.* Cambridge: Cambridge University Press.

Miceli, S. (1979) *Intelectuais e classe dirigente no Brasil (1920-1945), Corpo e alma do Brasil.* São Paulo: DIFEL.

Monaghan, E.J. (1988) Literacy Instruction and Gender in Colonial New England, *American Quarterly,* 40 (1, Special Issue: Reading America), pp. 18-41.

Müller, D.K., Ringer, F.K. & Simon, B. (1987) *The Rise of the Modern Educational System: structural change and social reproduction, 1870-1920.* Cambridge: Cambridge University Press.

Nagle, J. (1974) *Educação e sociedade na Primeira República.* São Paulo: Editora Pedagógica e Universitária.

Nóvoa, A. (1987) *Le temps des professeurs: analyse socio-historique de la profession enseignante au Portugal (XVIIIe-Xxe siècle). 1 a ed. 2 vols.* Lisboa: Instituto Nacional de Investigação Científica; Distribuição Imprensa Nacional – Casa da Moeda.

O Estado de São Paulo (2003) MEC define reajuste do Fundef em 6,7%. *O Estado de São Paulo,* January 27.

OECD Programme for International Student Assessment (2001) *Knowledge and Skills for Life – first results from PISA 2000 – Education and Skills.* Paris: OECD.

Oliveira, J.B.A. & Schwartzman, S. (2002) *A escola vista por dentro.* Belo Horizonte: Alfa Educativa Editora.

Paim, A. (1981) *A UDF e a idéia de universidade, Biblioteca Tempo universitário.* Rio de Janeiro: Tempo Brasileiro.

Paim, A. & Crippa, A. (1982) *Pombal e a cultura brasileira.* Rio de Janeiro: Fundação Cultural Brasil-Portugal; Tempo Brasileiro.

Paiva, V. P. (2000) *Paulo Freire e o nacionalismo-desenvolvimentista*. São Paulo: Graal.

Prefeitura do Rio de Janeiro. *A criação do Colégio de D. Pedro II*. Secretaria Municipal de Educação 2003. Available at: http://www.rio.rj.gov.br/multirio/historia/modulo02/criacao_pedroii.html

Ringer, F.K. (1990) *The Decline of the German Mandarins: the German academic community, 1890-1933*. Hanover: University Press of New England.

Salem, T. (1982) Do Centro D. Vital à Universidade Católica, in S. Schwartzman (Ed.) *Universidades e instituições científicas no Rio de Janeiro*. Brasília: CNPq, Coordenação Editorial. Available at: http://www.schwartzman.org.br/simon/rio/tania.htm

Samant, U. (1996) Literacy and Social Change: from a woman's perspective. Mi Shiknar: I Will Learn. Paper presented at Proceedings of the 1996 World Conference on Literacy. Available at: http://literacyonline.org/producs/ili/webdocs/ilproc/ilprocus.htm

Saviani, D. & Mendes, D.T. (1983) *Filosofia da educação brasileira, Coleção Educação e transformação*. Rio de Janeiro: Civilização Brasileira.

Schmitter, P.C. (1974) Still the Century of Corporatism? in F.B. Pike & T. Stritch (Eds) *The New Corporatism: social-political structures in the Iberian world*. Notre Dame: University of Notre Dame Press.

Schwartzman, S. (1977) Back to Weber: corporatism and patrimonialism in the seventies, in J.M. Malloy (Ed.). *Authoritarianism and Corporatism in Latin America*. Pittsburgh: University of Pittsburgh Press. Available at: http://www.schwartzman.org.br/simon/malloy.htm

Schwartzman, S. (1991a) Changing Roles of New Knowledge: research institutions and societal transformations in Brazil, in P. Wagner, Carol Hirschon Weiss, Bjorn Wittrock & Hellmut Wollman (Ed.) *Social Sciences and Modern States: national experiences and theoretical crossroads*. Cambridge: Cambridge University Press. Available at: http://www.schwartzman.org.br/simon/ newknow.htm

Schwartzman, S. (1991b) *A Space for Science: the development of the scientific community in Brazil*. University Park: Pennsylvania State University Press. Available at: http://www.schwartzman.org.br/simon/space/summary.htm

Schwartzman, S. (1999) For a de foco: diversidade e identidades étnicas no Brasil. *Novos Estudos CEBTAP* 55, pp.53-96. Available at: http://www.schwartzman.org.br/simon/pdfs/origem.pdf

Schwartzman, S. (2001a) *The Future of Education in Latin America and the Caribbean*. Santiago, Chile: UNESCO, Regional Office of Education for Latin America and the Caribbean. Available at: http://www.schwartzman.org.br/simon/futuro_unesco.htm

Schwartzman, S. (2001b) A revolução silenciosa do ensino superior, in E.R. Durham & H. Sampaio (Eds) *O Ensino Superior em Transformação*. São Paulo: Universidade de São Paulo, Núcleo de Pesquisas sobre Educação Superior. Available at: http://www.schwartzman.org.br/simon/pdfs/ nupes2000.pdf

Schwartzman, S. (2002) Higher education and the demands of the new economy in Latin America. Background paper for the LAC Flagship Report. Washington, DC: The World Bank. Available at: http://www.schwartzman.org.br/simon/flagship.pdf

Schwartzman, S. & Balbechevsky, E. (1996) The Academic Profession in Brazil, in P.G. Altbach (Ed.) *The International Academic Profession: portraits of fourteen countries*. Princeton: Carnegie Foundation for the Advancement of Teaching. Available at: http://www.schwartzman.org.br/simon/profess.htm

Schwartzman, S., Bomeny, H.M.B. & Costa, V.M.R. (2000) *Tempos de Capanema*, 2 ed. São Paulo; Rio De Janeiro: Paz e Terra, Editora de Fundação Getúlio Vargas. Available at: http://www.schwartzman.org.br/simon/capanema/introduc.htm/

Secretaria de Educação Fundamental (2002) *Políticas de malhora da qualidade da educação: um balanço instructional*. Brasília: Ministério da Educação.

Shavit, Y. & Müller, W. (2000) Vocational Secondary Education, Tracking and Social Stratification, in M. Hallinan (Ed.) *Handbook of the Sociology of Education*. New York: Kluwer.

Souza, R.F.d (1998) *Templos de civilização: a implantação da escola primária graduada no Estado de São Paulo, 1890-1910*. 1 a. ed., *Coleção Prismas; Variation: Coleção Prismas (Editoria UNESP)*. São Paulo, SP: Editoria UNESP Fundação.

Stevens, E.W. Jr. (1990) Technology, Literacy, and Early Industrial Expansion in the United States, *History of Education Quarterly*, 30(4, Special issue on the History of Literacy), pp. 523-544.

Tanuri, L.M. (1979) *O ensino normal no Estado de São Paulo, 1890-1930*. São Paulo: Universidade de São Paulo, Faculdade de Educação.

Teixeira, A. (1968) *Educação não é privilégio*. 2. ed. rev.e ampl ed, *Coleção Cultura, sociedade, educação*. São Paulo: Companhia Editora Nacional.

Telles, E.E. (1998) Does it Matter Who Answers the Race Question? Racial Classification and Income Inequality in Brazil, *Demography* 35(4), pp. 465-474.

Venesky, R.L. (1991) The Development of Literacy in the Industrialized Nations of the West, in R. Barr (Ed.) *Handbook of Reading Research*. New York: Longman.

Vincent, D. (2000) *The Rise of Mass Literacy: reading and writing in modern Europe, themes in history*. Cambridge: Polity Press.

Wolf, A. (2002) *Does Education Matter? Myths about Education and Economic Growth*. London: Penguin.

Xavier, L.N. (2000) *O Brasil como laboratório: educação e ciências sociais no projeto do Centro Brasileiro de Pesquisas Educacionais CBPE/INEP/MEC, 1950-1960, Estudos CDAPH, .7*. Bragança Paulista: Centro de Documentação e Apoio à Pesquisa em História da Educação Instituto Franciscano de Antropologia Universidade São Francisco: Editora da Universidade São Francisco.

Expansion and Inequality in Brazilian Education

JOÃO BATISTA ARAÚJO E OLIVEIRA

Expansion

It is never untimely to remember that Brazil is a land of contrasts, and that these contrasts are closely associated with educational policies and practices. It combines a system of private education roughly comparable with that of the industrialised countries, catering for little over 10% of the population, with a low-performing public educational system offered to the majority. It holds the most productive system of postgraduate education and academic research among emerging economies [1], yet 20 million of its 100 million adult population is illiterate, and over 75% is functionally illiterate. It developed a system of educational statistics and testing on a par with industrialised countries, yet its eight-grade system of primary education has been unable to teach the majority of primary school children how to read and write effectively.

Expansion has been and still is the trademark of Brazilian education. In the early 1950s, Brazil had a population of about 50 million inhabitants, 70% of which lived in rural areas. At that time, the total population was comparable to that of France or England, but very few Brazilians – less than 30% of the population – were enrolled in schools of any type. Meanwhile, European countries had already completed universal coverage of primary education and were about to complete the expansion and universalisation of secondary education.

Beginning in the 1950s, Brazil experienced an extraordinary rate of growth in educational provision. While the population grew over 3.3 times, to 170 million in the year 2000, formal education enrolments reached 57.9 million students, which correspond to 34% of the total population. This is the equivalent of enrolling about 19 cohorts – a world record. In the last 50 years, Brazil increased its educational system by about 1 million students per year on average. Table I presents the evolution of enrolments in the 1996-2002 period. As happened in the previous 50 years, growth has been steady, with some slumps occurring due to changes in priorities.

To notice, on Table I:

- Education grew at all levels, but secondary and higher education grew in higher proportions, as a natural result of expansion at lower levels.
- Primary education [2] reached a peak in 1999 and started to slow down after that year.
- Literacy classes were progressively absorbed into primary education, given the stimulus of FUNDEF – a resource redistribution fund encouraging primary education enrolments.
- Acceleration classes started in 1998, reached a peak in the year 1999, and then began to decrease.

Level	1996	1997	1998	1999	2000	2001	2002	Growth
Infant	N/A	348,012	381,804	831,978	916,864	1,093,347	1,152,511	231.17%
Pré-School	4,270,208	4,292,208	4,111,120	4,235,278	4,421,332	4,818,803	4,977,891	16.57%
Literacy	1,443,927	1,426,694	806,288	666,017	674,044	652,866	607,815	-57.91%
Primary	33,131,270	34,229,388	35,792,554	36,059,742	35,717,948	35,298,089	35,258,089	6.42%
Secondary	5,739,077	6,405,057	6,968,531	7,769,199	8,192,948	8,398,008	8,710,584	51.78%
Special education	201,142	334,507	293,403	311,354	300,520	323,399	337,897	67.99%
Equivalence	2,752,214	2,881,770	2,881,231	3,071,906	3,401,830	3,777,989	3,779,593	31.16%
Vocational/ Technical	-				462,258	565,046		
Higher	1,759,703						3,070,774	74.51%
TOTAL							57,895,154	
Acceleration classes	-	-	1,189,998	1,207,593	1,203,506	1,125,665	1,072,648	-9.86%

Table I. Evolution of enrolments, 1996-2002.
Source: MEC-INEP – Censo Escolar – Sinopse Estatistica.
% Growth: 2002/first year for which there were available data.

In addition to growing enrolments, other signs of growth and expansion can be detected in the following policies and initiatives implemented since the 1960s:

- Primary school was expanded from four to eight years in the late 1960s.
- The school year was expanded from 180 to 200 days in 1997.
- Technical education was postponed for the end of secondary education in 1998.
- Primary school teachers were required to complete higher education (15 years) as opposed to normal schools (11 years) of education.
- Schooling opportunities were extended to pre-scholars and the over 3.7 million adults.
- Several school districts attempted to expand the school day (full-time school).
- Since the 1960s several adult literacy campaigns have been launched. The latest of these campaigns, *Alfabetização Solidária*, claims to have reached 3.6 million illiterates.[3]

The government which took office in January 2003 continued with the expansion rhetoric and promised to:

- offer universal coverage from year 0 to primary school;
- expand primary and secondary education to full as opposed to part time;
- expand enrolment in secondary education;
- double enrolment in universities;
- eradicate adult illiteracy, officially reaching 20 million Brazilians.

Expansion has always been the typical policy response to what governments perceive as 'demand' – regardless of the age or ability level of students. The title of Table II suggests how government supply corresponds to an idiosyncratic concept of 'demand'.

First grade enrolment, 2002	5,978,272	7-year-old age cohort	3,300,660
Fourth grade graduates, 2001	3,699,857	Fifth grade enrolments, 2002	4,714,111
Eighth grade graduates, 2001	2,707,683	Ninth grade enrolments, 2002	3,481,556
Eleventh grade graduates, 2001	1,815,913	New college entrants, 2002	1,036,690

Table II. Additional evidence on education inflation.
Source: MEC/INEP – Sinopse Estatistica 2001 and 2002.

Table II shows some examples of over-enrolment resulting from the inflationary expansion model of educational planning and management characteristic of Brazil. In the case of fifth and ninth grades, over-enrolment is due to high rates of repetition, but also to the entrance of over-age students. In the case of colleges, the number of entrants is primarily composed by the backlog of over 4 million applicants held back by the entrance examinations. Expansion is thus not due to lack of places for age-level students. Since the mid 1970s, the total number of places offered in primary education has been superior to the size of the 7-14 year-old age cohort (Fletcher, 1983; Klein, 2003).

Table III presents unequivocal evidence of educational inflation by comparing student flows in 1996 and 2002. As a reference, the table also includes information on the year 2000 age cohort, based on the national census. Age cohorts have been increasing slowly in the 1990s and started to decrease after the year 2000. In that year, the three first age cohorts were stabilising at about 3.2 million per year.

Table III illustrates that:

- School age cohorts have stabilised at around 3.3 million children, but enrolments have continued to increase.
- There has been a marked increase in the upper grades – more students are finishing eighth grade. Even though those reaching grade 8 are

much older than expected, the total enrolment at that grade is equivalent to one entire cohort. Nonetheless, only 1.8 million students graduated from eighth grade in 2002.

- Part of the gap between first and second grade enrolment is due to enrolment of children under seven years of age. However, the greater part is due to excessive repetition rates.
- Enrolment in secondary school is almost equivalent to the size of three cohorts.

Above all, Table III illustrates the education pyramid of schooling in Brazil. Assuming a stable age cohort distribution during this period, there were about 6.3 million over-age students in 1996 and almost 10 million over-age students in the year 2002. Major efforts were undertaken in the late 1990s to 'universalise' primary education to ensure that all 7-14 year-olds were in schools. In fact, the increase in enrolments did not attract many students in that age bracket. Data from INEP's census show that in fact the new policies attracted mostly over-age students, thus contributing to increase the absolute and relative number of over-age students. The new 7-14 year-olds came mostly from the literary classes, attracted by the funding from FUNDEF.[4] Thus, virtually 100% of the extra enrolment was due to the enrolment of new over-age students.

Grades	Enrolment 1996	Enrolment 2002	Corresponding grade cohort
1	6,404,406	5,818,308	3,300,664
2	5,193,631	4,264,962	3,245,677
3	4,493,865	4,492,856	3,230,301
4	3,935,398	4,394,217	3,367,200
5	4,397,913	4,814,111	3,433,809
6	3,489,249	3,963,573	3,524,814
7	2,873,863	3,657,202	3,461,413
8	2,343,014	3,338,529	3,560,831
Total Primary	33,131,270	35,258,089	26,794,232
9	2,527,580	3,481,556	3,521,881
10	1,727,171	2,575,801	3,497,668
11	1,274,933	2,239,544	3,682,950
Total Secondary	5,735,077	8,710,581	10,702,499

Table III. The education pyramid, 1996-2002.
Source: Educational census for years 1996 and 2002; IBGE population census 2000 for grade-level cohort of 7-17 year-olds. Secondary school enrolments do not include about 121,000 students in 1996 and over 200,000 students in 2002 enrolled in 4-year secondary schools.

Overall, the aforementioned data suggest that the surplus of supply is not due to demand from age-level students, but mostly to:

- excessive repetition and grade-retention, which will be discussed below;

- excessive numbers of students leaving schools during the academic year to return next year;
- admission of over-age students in primary schools, due to lack of targeting for FUNDEF and of policies limiting entry age.

According to official estimates, primary school students stay in schools for an average of 8.5 years. It takes a little over 11 years to complete primary school and a little over 50% of those starting first grade will be able to complete the full primary school cycle.

Clearly, the culture of expansion is deeply embedded in Brazilian educational politics and policies. Instead of focusing on the quality and inefficiency aspects of the problem, virtually all politicians, educational administrators and a majority of researchers believe and claim that there is still demand, need and room for educational expansion in Brazil.

The next three sections analyse the quality, efficiency, and equity implications of educational policies based on never-ending expansion and over-enrolment.

The Costs of Educational Inflation: quantity versus quality

It is virtually impossible to talk about the impact of quantity on quality due to the fact that only in the early 1990s did educational authorities start to collect information on the achievement of students. Moreover, curricula and the conditions of schooling have changed, thus precluding any *direct* measurement of the impact of expansion on quality.

Nonetheless, there are several sources of information about the quality of education in Brazil. There is the SAEB – *Sistema de Avaliação Básica* – for fourth, eighth and eleventh grade, ENEM – *Exame Nacional do Ensino Médio* – for secondary schools, and ENC – *Exame Nacional de Cursos* – for higher education. Brazil also participated in international assessments such as those sponsored by UNESCO's Regional Office for Education in Latin America and the Caribbean (OREALC) and the Organisation for Economic Cooperation and Development (OECD).

Table IV presents the results of the assessment of basic education for Portuguese language and for mathematics, for grades 4, 8 and 11. The figures at the top of each column correspond to the minimum standards expected for each subject and grade. Compared with this minimum, the results show a pattern of very low quality.

	SAEB results, Language					
	Fourth Grade		Eighth Grade		Eleventh Grade	
	200		250		325	
	1997	1999	1997	1999	1997	1999
Brasil	186	179	259	232	283	266
Municioal	177	164	241	230	–	–
State	183	167	243	226	271	256

	SAEB results, Mathematics					
	Fourth Grade		Eighth Grade		Eleventh Grade	
	225		325		400	
	1997	1999	1997	1999	1997	1999
Brasil	190	181	250	246	288	280
Municioal	181	174	239	240	-	-
State	187	177	241	239	271	267

Table IV. SAEB results, language and mathematics.

Overall, SAEB results show that:

- the majority of public school students do not reach the minimum standards. In each grade and subject, from 60 to 80% fail to do so;
- the achievement of state and municipal schools is virtually identical;
- the achievement of private schools is consistently and significantly superior to that of public schools;
- there is a slight decrease in overall scores in the last two rounds of SAEB tests (1999 and 2001, the latter not shown on Table IV), suggesting a decreasing trend in achievement;
- there is a large difference between the regions. The average achievement of an eighth grade student from states in the north-east compares with the achievement of a fourth grade in a southern state.
- in short, public education is failing to contribute to diminish out-of-school inequalities. At the same time, as shown by Soares (2004), private schools add more value, especially for students coming from higher socio-economic levels, and less value to lower SES (socio-economic status) students – thus contributing to increase the equity gap.

Some analysts claim that standards set by the SAEB experts are unrealistically high. International comparisons suggest otherwise. The assessment done by UNESCO's Office for Education in Latin America and the Caribbean of student achievement in the Latin American region shows that the average achievements of Brazilian students are comparable to those of Argentina and Chile, but more than one standard deviation below the performance of students in Cuba (UNESCO, 2000). If Cuban students can achieve much higher scores, it is unlikely that Brazilians or Argentines cannot. The OECD's PISA evaluation (OECD, 2001) showed that over 56% of 15 year-old Brazilians at seventh or eighth grade did perform at or below level 1 in the Language Test. Level 1 is the bottom level of a five-point scale. These results suggest that it takes Brazilians 7 to 8 years of schooling to barely decode, but not understand, what they read. The mathematics results were even lower. Overall, the achievement test results of Brazilians on national and international assessment suggest that the educational system has not been able to prepare the majority of students for life and for further studies.

Some analysts claim that achievement tests may reflect distorted views of education about the real skills acquired by students in schools. Some even argue that more years of education – as supported by the expansionist inflationary policies – are more important than quality. In fact, labour market data tend to suggest otherwise. Figures 1 and 2 present data on the relationship between education and income in the years 1992 and 2001.

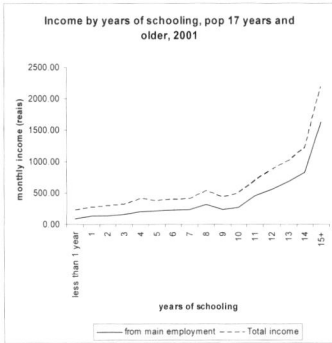

Figure 1. Income, by years of schooling, 2001.
Source: IBGE, PNAD 2001.

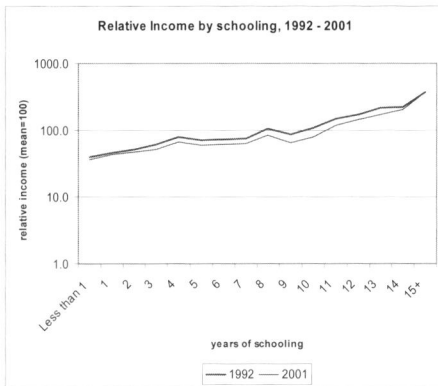

Figure 2. Relative income by schooling, 1992-2001.
Source: IBGE, PNAD 1992 and 2001.

Figure 1 shows the wage variations according to years of schooling, and Figure 2 compares the income distribution around the mean in 1992 and 2001. Figure 2 shows that while in 1992 it took about 7-8 years of schooling to reach the national mean wage, in 2001 it took about 10-11 years to do so. Since the mean value did not change much during the period, it means that workers need to study more years to earn the same salaries.

Table V presents data on the levels of schooling of the workforce. It shows that Brazilians start to work at a relatively early age – almost one-third of the 15 year-old cohort is already in the labour force. However, it also shows that labour force participation interferes significantly with years of study only for those in the 10-14 age group. The reason is twofold. First, most of the jobs are incidental and part time, and active participation does not necessarily mean a job. Second, a significant number of 15+ age students go to evening schools.

Age	Economically active		Economically inactive		Total	
	Years of study	Total	Years of study	Total	Years of study	Total
10	2.7	276,246	3.3	3,012,104	3.2	3,288,350
11	3.2	398,634	4.0	2,972,838	4.0	3,371,472
12	3.9	521,827	4.8	2,957,031	4.7	3,478,858
13	4.6	704,621	5.5	2,712,529	5.3	3,417,150
14	5.3	914,290	6.2	2,490,443	6.0	3,404,733
15	6.1	1,181,077	6.9	2,212,810	6.6	3,393,887
16	6.8	1,581,868	7.5	1,878,570	7.2	3,460,438
17	7.3	1,826,175	8.2	1,634,906	7.7	3,461,081
18	8.0	2,057,625	8.5	1,295,901	8.2	3,353,526
19	8.4	2,197,035	8.5	1,011,520	8.4	3,208,555
20	8.5	2,286,607	8.5	848,151	8.5	3,134,758

Table V. Age and years of study, active and inactive population.
Source: PNAD, 1999.

Figure 3 presents data on education and unemployment. These years were chosen because most of the structural adjustment of the Brazilian economy to face international competition and 'globalisation' was completed in the early 1990s. To understand these data, and what they may mean, it is important to know that over 60% of the wage earners in Brazil have eight or less years of education, about 20% have between 9 and 11 years, and less than 20% have higher education degrees.

Table VI presents the years of schooling and the number of workers in the labour force in 1992 and 1999. This table shows:

- a decrease in the number of workers with four or less years of education and a steady increase thereafter. This may reflect either a substitution of less for more schooled workers or the impact of the new entrants in the labour market;
- the eleventh year of education group (complete secondary education) experienced the highest rate of growth in the period, followed by those with college degrees;

- overall, more than 66% of the places offered in the labour market do not require more than eight years of education – contrary to the popular view that only those with secondary education can find jobs.

In fact, holders of secondary school diplomas constitute only 16% of the total labour force. As shown in Figure 3, unemployment grows from 6 to 10% for this group of workers.

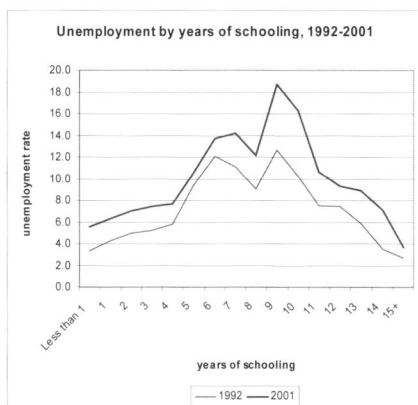

Figure 3. Unemployment by years of schooling.

Years of schooling	1992	1999
< 1	8,364,936	6,754,744
1	1,736,233	1,512,197
2	3,162,357	2,885,688
3	4,509,457	4,056,879
4	8,653,390	8,200,487
5	4,246,647	4,625,562
6	2,298,196	2,679,296
7	2,264,408	2,828,120
8	4,727,754	6,028,120
9	1,112,669	1,671,745
10	1,310,879	2,015,066
11	6,362,067	10,061,278
12	738,408	929,297
13	481,539	619,812
14	774,707	745,140
15+	3,178,558	4,497,233
Total	53,822,005	60,155,790

Table VI. Labour force by years of schooling, 1992 and 1999.
Source: IBGE-PNAD, 1999.

Taken together, these four tables show that:

- the correlation between education and income is positive, as predicted by traditional human capital theory;
- in Brazil, the wage differentials are fairly large, disproportionately larger for holders of higher education diplomas;
- relative salaries have been decreasing for all but the holders of higher education diplomas. The decrease has mostly affected those with 5-11 years of schooling. This probably means that being literate (four years of education, the old primary school) makes a difference;
- completing the eighth and eleventh grades still commands a higher salary (signalling), but significantly less than in the past. Labour markets rely on screening effects of education, but seem to compensate for greater supply of graduates and, possibly, lower skills. The labour market may value other non-cognitive abilities (Autor et al, 2001) that schools have been unable to impart;
- holders of incomplete secondary education degrees fare worse in the labour market than those finishing primary education;
- winner takes all. Finishing college commands a high premium.[5]

Contrary to common belief, it seems that labour markets are not particularly interested in students with (low quality) complete or incomplete secondary education. This group is the one with major relative salary losses and higher unemployment rates. The myth that 'globalisation' works equally in all countries and that 'globalisation' requires everyone to hold a secondary school diploma is just that – a myth – at least as far as the labour markets of the world's ninth economy are concerned.

Overall, educational policies based on indiscriminate expansion do not contribute to establish a system of education with minimum standards of quality – be it measured in terms of academic or labour market skills. More years of poor education do not improve the academic and labour market situation of the less advantaged.

The Costs of Inflation: quality versus efficiency

Does inflationary educational expansion foster efficiency? If conventional concepts of efficiency are considered (output/input) the answer is obviously negative. However, the inefficiency of educational policies based on unchecked expansion may be even worse than conventional economics may suggest.

There are several sources of inefficiency in the Brazilian model of education based on unlimited expansion. We have already considered the effects of additional numbers of students per grade, and of the time it takes a student to complete primary or secondary education. Table VII summarises what happens in a typical academic year in Brazil.

This table presents two indicators of inefficiency: number of students failing and total loss. The difference between total loss and students failing is accounted for by students who enrol at the beginning of the year, leave the school during the year for some reason, and return next year. The evidence that most students remain is based on the relationship between total enrolment and the size of age cohorts – virtually 100% of 7-14 year-olds are enrolled and more than 85% of 15-17 year-olds are also enrolled.

Grades	Initial enrolment	No. of students passing	Total loss	% loss	No. of students failing
1	5,978,272	4,407,236	1,571,036	26.3	901,878
2	4,782,389	3,374,254	1,408,135	29.4	649,518
3	4,625,014	3,761,420	863,594	18.7	437,138
4	4,342,009	3,699,857	642,152	14.8	389,401
5	4,763,018	3,453,792	1,309,226	27.5	573,902
6	3,963,575	3,209,582	753,993	19.0	389,787
7	3,622,550	2,849,036	773,514	21.4	286,136
8	3,221,262	2,754,818	466,444	14.5	248,407
Total primary	35,298,089	27,909,995	7,388,094	20.9	3,876,167
9	3,438,523	2,282,490	1,156,033	33.6	352,478
10	2,479,473	2,043,951	435,522	17.6	187,986
11	2,138,931	1,815,913	323,018	15.1	106,246
12	62,182	54,312	7,870	12.7	2,192
Total secondary	8,398,008	6,196,666	2,201,342	26.2	648,902

Table VII. A portrait of the inefficiency of Brazilian education.
Source: MEC-INEP: Censo Educacional 2001 and 2002.

The SAEB results and those of international comparative assessments suggest that repetition and losses are strongly associated with low student performance – rather than excessive rigour of teachers. If teachers applied the same criteria of experts responsible for external assessments, repetition rates would be in the 60-80% level in each grade.

Losses are greater in certain grades – first, fifth and ninth, reflecting specific difficulties schools have in teaching children to read and write in the first grade and in other *transition* years. Total loss in the ninth grade may also suggest the inadequacy of a unified secondary school system with no options left for students.[6]

Other important sources of inefficiency include the existence of two major public school systems in virtually all municipalities – creating inefficiencies in school zoning, school size and staffing. Higher than necessary enrolments create the need for additional schools and staff. There are now, in Brazil (data from the 2001 SAEB questionnaires):

- 214,188 schools;

- 1,581,044 primary school teacher equivalents;
- 1,189,650 classrooms for primary education (sufficient for over 60 million students in double shifts);
- almost 500,000 secondary school teachers.

Another important indicator of inefficiency is teacher salary. If teacher salaries are below market levels, it is difficult to recruit qualified persons for the job. The FUNDEF legislation in Brazil requires school systems to spend at least 60% of total educational expenditures on teacher salaries. With this ceiling, the salaries for teachers with secondary school degrees are competitive, but the salaries for teachers with higher education, required by the new legislation, are not, as shown in Table VIII. It shows that teachers with 11 years of education, teaching in the first four grades, generally earn wages similar to the average of other employees with similar levels of education. These salaries may be adequate to attract average-level students to the teaching profession.[7]

Teaching level	Teacher's schooling			Premium for higher education	No. of teachers
	<11 years	11-14 years	15+ years		
Secondary	445	634	968	52.7%	348,831
Primary	339	476	770	61.8%	521,268
Primary 1-4	219	416	713	71.4%	881,623
Primary 5-8	190	487	946	94.3%	104,765

Table VIII. Monthly teacher wages (reais, 2001).[8]
Source: IBGE-PNAD-2001.

In the case of primary education, and given limited budgets, additional policies contribute to reduce the total amount of resources available to pay teachers, thus lowering the wages of teachers: reducing teacher loads, increasing primary education from eight to nine grades or increasing the number of hours students spend in schools. In many municipalities, expanding pre-schools puts additional burdens on education budgets, thus lowering the amount of resources available to pay primary school teachers. On the other hand, non-expansionist policies such as reducing the total number of students from 35.3 million to 26.7 million 7-14 year-olds could improve teacher salaries anywhere from 50 to 100% depending on other efficiency measures.

The above data and discussion demonstrate that inflationary expansionist education policies do not contribute to efficiency. Such policies do not contribute to raise academic standards or to increase social or individual rates of return, nor do they attract or maintain a qualified teaching force.

The Cost of Inflation: quantity versus equity

Expanding educational systems is justified by public authorities as beneficial to the poor. The majority of the population believes that this is so – given their daily experience with the fact that people with higher levels of schooling tend to earn higher salaries so equality of access becomes synonymous with equality of opportunities.

However, as classic political economy points out, there is a difference between '*la volonté générale*' and '*la volonté de tous*': what is good for everyone is not necessarily good for all. Expanding education offers more opportunities to the poor. The poor can now come to pre-schools and primary schools, and have almost universal access to secondary schools. There is no doubt that expanding favours inclusion. However, the net benefits of inclusion without quality must be examined. Since resources are scarce, it remains to analyse which investments would mostly foster equity.[9]

Historically, public investments in education in Brazil have been growing and levelled at around 5% of the GDP. An official publication, *Geografia da Educação Brasileira* (Instituto Nacional de Estudos e Pesquisas Educacionais, 2001), estimates that total public investment in education in 1998 reached 47 billion reais, roughly equivalent to 5.2% of GDP. In 2002 that would roughly correspond to 20 billion dollars, which is roughly distributed as illustrated in Table IX. The disproportionate amount of per capita resources devoted to higher education is part of the overall picture of educational inequities.[10]

	Total investment (billion of dollars)	Number of students	Investment per student
Infant	1	4,200,000	238.00
Primary	11	32,500,000	338.40
Secondary	3	7,500,000	400.00
Higher education	5	800,000	6,250.00
Total	20	47,000,000	425.00

Table IX. Public investment in education.[11]

Within prevailing circumstances, expanding pre-school in the municipalities systematically involves diluting resources, which would normally be invested in primary education. There is no evidence that pre-school opportunities are targeted to the most needed. There is also no evidence that students going to pre-schools in Brazil have any gains, short-term or lasting, as far as drop-out, achievement or other benefits are concerned.[12]

Most of the equity impact of inflationary expansion policies on primary education has already been shown:

- Poorer students take longer to complete a grade and are less likely to leave schools after 8.5 years of schooling – the average school leaver takes about 11 years to graduate.

- Older students get lower grades in the SAEB exams at all levels and subjects. Merely relating students does not contribute to improve learning. However, automatic promotion policies have not demonstrated that they contribute to improve learning or earning, even though they might improve the chances of completing a degree.
- Additional years of poor education lead to relatively lower salaries.

We have seen that, when they reach age 14, students – mostly the poorer – begin to become active in the labour market. One-third of 15 year-olds and almost two-thirds of 17 year-olds are working or looking for jobs. The majority of these youngsters remain in schools. Schools in Brazil are part time and more than 50% of secondary schools are evening schools. However, they enter the labour market with less years of education, hence with lower wages and inadequate skills. Apprenticeship programmes are not valued in the country, and technical education is reserved for those completing secondary education.

Overall, inflationary expansion policies clearly undermine quality, efficiency, and equity. The next part examines what happens to educational policies that take a different view.

Attempts to Improve Quality, Efficiency and Equity

Amidst an overarching framework which fosters unending expansion and ignores quality, efficiency and equity implications, several attempts have been made to improve quality and efficiency at the federal, state and municipal levels.

Regarding *quality*, the educational reform in the state system of education of Minas Gerais in the early 1990s is a case in point. The reform was based on existing international and national evidence and experience with 'what works' and included simultaneous pedagogical, managerial, and financial reforms at the school level. Over about eight years of sustained effort, it managed to improve the achievement of students, as shown in the results of SAEB through the 1990s. However, this is the only documented case in which educational reforms have contributed to improve quality, but even this effort has not proven to be sustainable in the long run (Oliveira, 1998, 2002). In spite of many efforts, there is no public evidence from other states or municipalities concerning effective, significant, and sustainable quality gains. No state or municipal system of education in Brazil can offer evidence that it offers education of minimum quality to the majority of its students in any way, much less in a sustainable way.

Various strategies have been undertaken to address *efficiency*. In most cases, the attempts were focused on specific topics, with no overall impact. FUNDEF – the National Fund for Primary Education – for example, significantly contributed to transparency in the use, and probably an initial increase, in the amount of resources devoted to primary education. However, many of its effects were overridden by counter-efficiency measures, the most important of which was the continuous growth of supply, in spite of demographic changes: more than two million over-age students were enrolled, thus diluting possible efficiency gains of FUNDEF.

Table X illustrates how FUNDEF contributed to increase the number of older and under-age students, rather than 7-14 year-olds in the primary education system.[13]

Region	Years	Total	7-14 years of age	15 years and more	% 15 years and more
Brazil	1996	33,131,370	25,909,860	7,221,510	21.8
	2002	35,150,362	27,572,578	7,577,784	21.6
Bahia	1996	3,553,446	2,315,394	1,238,052	34.8
	2002	3,629,276	2,2511,200	1,378,076	38.0
Ceará	1996	1,843,948	1,312,969	518,268	28.1
	2002	1,863,625	1,397,306	466,319	25.0
Goiás	1996	1,135,948	801,191	334,757	29.5
	2002	1,099,223	823,200	276,023	25.1
Paraná	1996	1,808,149	1,508,496	299,653	16.6
	2002	1,693,577	1,533,161	160,116	9.5
São Paulo	1996	6,394,838	5,312,782	1,082,058	16.9
	2002	5,993,885	5,300,860	693,035	11.6

Table X. Over-age student population, 1996-2002.

The table shows that for a total increase of 2 million students between 1996 and 2002 there was an increase of 1.6 million 7-14 year-old students, which were presumably out of the reach of schools. However, the majority, about 1 million of these 'new' 7-14 year-olds, were previously enrolled in the so-called literacy classes – they only moved from one to another classification, they were not out of school. Overall, only about 600,000 7-14 year-olds came to schools for the first time; the majority of new students were already over 15 years. In many states there were distortions. In the state of Bahia, for example, the actual number of 7-14 year-olds decreased, while the number of overage students actually increased.

FUNDEF was also intended to improve efficiency by increasing teacher salaries. However, the major impact of FUNDEF was on improving the salaries of lay teachers in the regions where salaries were very low. It can be easily demonstrated that this is a consequence of the fact that FUNDEF made it mandatory to spend 60% of total funds on teachers. In the majority of states, these expenditures were already superior to 60% of total education expenditures. In fact, FUNDEF contributed to increase salaries of non-qualified teachers. However, even – as some government authorities claim – if salaries were increased, no relationship was shown between better salaries and better performance of students.

A major block to improving *efficiency* is and continues to be the existence of two public systems, state, and municipal. Dual command dilutes responsibility, makes local educational planning even more difficult, and generates excessive supply of schools and teachers. FUNDEF was supposed to serve as the instrument to promote municipalisation, by allocating funds to where students were.

Table XI shows the evolution of state versus municipal enrolment in this period. The net transfer of students from states to municipalities was of 3.9 million students, about 20% of total state enrolment. In practice, almost half, 1.8 million of this total, occurred in the state of São Paulo, where no previous municipalisation efforts had occurred. In 2002, São Paulo still holds the largest (77%) network of state schools in the country. The relative participation of municipalities – from 10.9 to 17.6 – is mostly due to new enrolments of over-age students and to changing the status of literacy classes into first grade. Except for the state of São Paulo, only a maximum of 2 million students were actually transferred from state to municipal systems in this eight-year period.

Region	Year	Total enrolment	State schools	Municipal schools	% of Municipal schools
Brazil	1996	33,131,370	18,168,772	10,921,053	33.0
	2002	35,150,362	14,236,020	17,653,143	50.2
Bahia	1996	2,887,940	1,309,045	1,318,205	45.6
	2002	3,629,276	1,124,330	2,313,273	63.7
Ceará	1996	1,641,289	526,322	807,507	49.2
	2002	1,863,625	324,916	1,338,780	71.8
Goiás	1996	1,086,875	648,845	307,081	28.3
	2002	1,099,982	550,617	440,344	40.0
Paraná	1996	1,781,853	877,637	762,037	42.8
	2002	1,693,577	760,690	802,320	47.4
São Paulo	1996	6,572,322	5,078,539	726,704	11.1
	2002	5,993,885	3,285,418	1,936,175	32.3

Table XI. Rates of municipalisation, selected regions, 1996-2001.

Other efforts to improve efficiency at the state, municipal and school levels have been undertaken – various authorities and organisations implemented managerial and training programmes of various kinds. Organizations such as CONSED – the Council of State Secretariats for Education – and the Ford Foundation have implemented programmes of that sort. The state of Bahia implemented a massive programme to help municipalities to improve management practices associated with a programme to increase school authority (Fundação Luís Eduardo Magalhães 2000). This programme was later implemented in 54 municipalities all over Brazil under the auspices of the Instituto Ayrton Senna and Fundação Banco do Brasil.[14] Overall, however, most attempts to improve efficiency were either undocumented or failed to produce or to publish any significant gains.

The remainder of this chapter deals with one specific issue directly related to dealing with the *inflationary model* and how to deal with student flows.

Dealing with Student Flows

Even though expansion was and still is the dominant trend, several attempts have been made to deal with the problem of student flows since the mid 1990s, and they include: automatic promotion, longer cycles and acceleration programmes. In some systems, more than one strategy has been implemented at the same time. Tables XII, XIII and XIV present some data on these issues.

Grade	Passing	Failure	% Fail	Passing	Failure	% Fail
		1995			2001	
1	4,099,833	1,252,284	23.4	4,407,236	901,878	17.0
2	3,518,677	973,365	21.7	3,374,254	649,518	16.1
3	3,286,297	582,169	15.0	3,761,420	437,518	10.4
4	3,016,629	383,081	11.3	3,699,857	389,401	9.5
5	2,683,124	821,145	23.4	3,453,792	573,902	14.2
6	2,347,412	532,083	18.5	3,209,582	389,787	10.8
7	1,999,183	331,168	14.2	2,849,036	286,136	9.1
8	1,720,196	176,985	9.3	2,754,818	248,407	8.3
Total 1-8	22,671,349	5,052,280	18.2	27,509,995	3,876,547	12.4
9	1,395,086	335,579	19.4	2,282,490	352,478	13.4
10	1,145,688	145,597	11.3	2,043,951	187,986	8.4
11	1,093,886	59,678	5.2	1,815,913	106,246	5.5
Total 9-11	3,634,610	540,854	13.0	6,142,354	646,710	9.5

Table XII. Passing and failure rates, 1995-2001 – Brazil.
Source: MEC-INEP – Sinopse Estatistica, 1996 and 2002.

Grade	Passing	Failure	% Fail	Passing	Failure	% Fail
		1995			2001	
1	756,569	21,228	2.7	724,534	24,422	3.3
2	765,884	207,250	21.3	711,441	29,836	4.0
3	697,388	103,045	12.9	701,025	15,354	2.1
4	688,411	52,419	7.1	677,391	66,103	8.9
5	681,483	147,689	17.8	652,620	37,468	5.4
6	637,609	113,327	15.1	709,516	39,380	5.3
7	569,753	61,256	9.7	701,008	39,429	5.3
8	511,225	31,831	5.9	668,035	60,233	8.3
Total 1-8	5,308,482	738,045	12.2	5,545,570	312,225	5.3
9	446,112	87,003	16.3	609,428	69,622	10.3
10	360,198	36,433	9.2	544,672	47,097	8.0
11	359,689	13,375	3.6	503,683	28,696	5.4
Total 9-11	1,165,995	136,811	10.5	1,657,783	145,415	8.1

Table XIII. Passing and failure rates, 1995-2001 – São Paulo.
Source: MEC-INEP – Sinopse Estatistica, 1996 and 2002.

	1996						
	Enrolment	Pass	Fail	% Pass	% Fail	Total loss	% Loss
Brazil	33,131,270	24,069,956,	4,639,990	72.7	14.0	9,065,314	27.4
Bahia	2,887,940	1,851,475	481,994	64.1	16.7	1,036,461	35.9
Ceará	1,641,289	1,089,793	191,081	66.4	11.6	551,496	33.6
Goiás	1,086,875	725,488	142,706	66.7	13.1	361,387	33.3
Paraná	1,781,853	1,337,334	253,667	75.1	14.2	444,519	24.9
São Paulo	6,572,322	5,578,746	568,595	84.9	8.7	991,576	15.1

	2001						
	Enrolment	Pass	Fail	% Pass	% Fail	Total loss	% Loss
Brazil	35,258,089	27,909,995	3,666,564	79.2	10.3	7,384,094	20.9
Bahia	3,706,887	2,475,575	567,828	66.8	15.3	1,231,312	33.2
Ceará	1,855,939	1,512,666	167,432	81.5	9.0	343,323	18.5
Goiás	1,099,982	845,608	142,706	76.9	12.9	254,374	23.1
Paraná	1,691.131	1,403,359	163,443	83.0	9.6	287,772	17.0
São Paulo	6,092,455	5,545,570	312,225	91.0	5.1	546,885	9.0

Table XIV. Evolution of repetition and loss, 1996-2001.
Source: for enrolment, 1995 education census; for pass and fail rates, 1996 education census.

Overall, these tables show that:

- there was a marked decrease in the rate of repetition between 1996 and 2002. National rates fell from 22.2 to 13.8% for primary education and from 14.8 to 10.5% for secondary education. First grade failure decreased from 30.5 to 20.4%;
- decreases were even more significant in the state of São Paulo, where automatic promotion practices have been adopted: from 13.9 to less than 1% for primary education and from 11.7 to 8.7% for secondary education;
- in spite of decreased rates of repetition, overall loss (repetition plus drop-out) remained very high. For Brazil as a whole, it fell from 27.1 to 20.0% between 1996 and 2001. In states like Caerá and Goiás, there was a marked reduction in drop-out rates, even though failure rates did not drop significantly.

Next, we analyse the effects of specific policies.

Automatic Promotion

The most dramatic evidence of automatic promotion policies comes from the state of São Paulo, as shown on Table XIII. Automatic promotion has been widely implemented in the state system, and, to a lesser extent, in municipal systems. In less than 10 years the total loss has been reduced to less than 9% and enrolments in different grades have become of similar size, as shown in

Table XV. At least in the state system, the introduction of automatic promotion was accompanied by policies and directives concerning how to deal with students running behind the academic programme. There is no evidence about the actual implementation of those directives.

Grade	Enrolment in 2001	Age	Cohort size in 2000
1	771,421	7	607,350
2	756,580	8	565,229
3	730,831	9	639,361
4	759,301	10	630,929
5	729,518	11	703,376
6	788,908	12	749,682
7	784,743	13	718,541
8	771,153	14	669,650

Table XV. Enrolments and age cohorts, state of São Paulo.

Yet, in the first four grades, enrolments are typically 20% or more above the size of the age cohort. In the same period, SAEB and state-held examinations called SARESP show no major improvement or decrease.

The impact of automatic promotion policies in a case like São Paulo illustrates that:

- even in the case of automatic promotion, adjusting student flows does not yield immediate results; it may take additional years for the system to operate more smoothly;
- automatic promotion does not improve the quality of the educational system, as reflected in the state and national external examinations (SARESP and SAEB);
- younger students are reaching fourth and eighth grades in greater proportions than before. In the past, lower fourth and eighth grade averages were attributed to older, multi-repeater students. Present results suggest that younger students, promoted automatically, replaced those older students at the lower levels of performance. If automatic promotion does not decrease averages, it certainly decreases the levels of students in fourth grade. This suggests that automatic promotion entails significant equity implications.

The case of São Paulo is probably the most careful and elaborate attempt to introduce automatic promotion in Brazil. Even though it may be too early to evaluate its impact – as it breaks traditional behaviours – there is no evidence that it does any good to students in educational systems. Efficiency gains, if obtained because of smoother student flows, have not been converted into quality gains.

Cycles

Academic cycles of two, three or four years have been introduced in various municipal and state educational systems in Brazil. There are two basic differences between cycles and automatic promotion. First, curricula are generally designed to be taught during the cycle – not necessarily within a given grade. Second, promotion at the end of the cycle depends on students achieving certain standards.

Studying the effect of cycles on promotion is very difficult, since official statistics are not available to researchers in Brazil.[15] Data would need to be obtained on a case by case basis. Observing data from individual municipalities clearly indicates that at the end of the cycle repetition rates tend to increase. Overall, as shown in the 1996-2001 comparison, the overall repetition rates have decreased, thus suggesting that cycles (and automatic promotion) are associated with a decrease in repetition and retention rates.

As with the case of automatic promotion, there is no evidence that cycles improve student learning. A thorough review of the existing literature on cycles and automatic promotion in Brazil (Souza et al, 2003) or books such as those published by Franco (Franco, 2001) or the series of discussions on the topic published by the Brazilian Congress (Câmara dos Deputados and Comissâo de Educaçâo Cultura e Desporto, 2002) failed to produce a single consistent, empirical, much less definitive study of those issues.

Differently from automatic promotion, cycles are based on the assumption that teachers will have more time to 'work' with the specificities of students, and that students will have more time to learn the mandated curricula for the cycle. The lack of specific curricula, teaching strategies and other resources to differentiate or individualise instruction makes it hard to believe that such practices per se may contribute to student learning. Rather, the increase in repetition rates at the end of the cycle suggest that such practices may have negative efficiency and equity implications – as it would take longer to 'notice' that students are not learning.

Acceleration Programmes

From the mid 1990s, a number of initiatives have been undertaken in different municipal and state systems. The initiatives vary from purely nominal changes to carefully designed attempts to address the student flow problem. Most initiatives were focused on offering special programmes that would allow students to skip grades. Some programmes included special pedagogic materials and strategies. In addition, a few programmes were clearly focused on using acceleration programmes as a means to smooth student flows. In other words, some programmes were merely nominal, some were pedagogic innovations to deal with problem students, and some were more strategically focused on the issue of student flows. As shown on Table I, between 1998 and 2002 over one million students have been enrolled in acceleration programmes of different kinds. Given the variety of strategies and interventions, it is possible to compare the differential or overall effects of such programmes.

Some such programmes have been subject to external evaluation, as in the case of the *Accelera Brasil* in the State of Bahia and the State of Tocantins (Oliveira, 2001; Fundação Carlos Chagas, 2002; Fundação Cesgranrio, 2003).[16] Together, these programmes reached several million students and account for over 60% of the total number of students enrolled in acceleration programmes in Brazil; the state of Bahia accounted for over 50% of the total national efforts after the year 2000. These programmes share a number of characteristics:

- They are part of a larger programme of educational reform and of a political commitment to normalise student flow.
- They use specially designed materials for students.
- Teachers receive direct supervision throughout the academic year.
- The programmes are closely monitored and externally evaluated.
- Students are promoted by their own teachers, on the basis of performance.
- These programmes represent a major financial commitment and cost from 20 to 25% in addition to regular annual student costs.
- The purpose of these programmes is to help 1-4 students to achieve fourth grade level and continue on to the fifth grade; in the case of the 5-8 programme, students have two years to achieve eighth grade level.

In all published reports mentioned above, and consistently along the various years of implementation, the average of students in the acceleration programmes was roughly equivalent to the average of regular fourth and eighth graders in the same school system. In the 2002 evaluation in the state of Tocantins, for example, the averages in Portuguese for fourth grades were 145 and 153 for the regular and the acceleration group, using an SAEB-equated scale. Quality and year of implementation may account for local variation in results – in general, scores are higher in the first years and tend to slow down as the acceleration programmes become routine and reach for more difficult students.

Other acceleration programmes were also implemented in various states and municipal school systems – the state of Ceará has been particularly active in implementing such programmes.

The existing evidence suggests that given certain circumstances, acceleration programmes contribute to quality – at least in the sense of ensuring that older, multi-repeater students can reach averages compatible with those of regular students. Under normal circumstances, as repeatedly shown in SAEB results, these are the students achieving the worst results. These quality gains also mean important equity gains, first, because those students were able to receive a better-quality education, and second, because by skipping grades, they may be in a position to stay more years at school and eventually finish primary education – as opposed to dropping out after successful years of repetition in lower grades.

Regarding efficiency, some cost–benefit studies on some such programmes have demonstrated the economic gains of successful completing grades – as opposed to automatic promotion (Oliveira, 2001). Table XVI shows that acceleration of students older than 15 years in 23 municipalities involved in *Accelera Brasil* programmes is 2.8% of total enrolment, as opposed to 7.8% for the country as a whole.

Overall, and with few exceptions, acceleration programmes failed to achieve dramatic changes in the student flow profile. A thorough review of the literature on cycles and automatic promotions (Gomes, 2003) suggests no conclusive evidence on the possible benefits of either cycles or automatic promotions in Brazil. As mentioned by authors in countries where such practices are adopted, there are a number of other practices which may ensure that students manage to learn at least the minimum requirements associated with each grade.

Municipality	Students > 15 years	Total First to Fourth Grade enrolment	% students over 15 years of age
Rio Branco	34	6,613	0.5
Eunápolis	2,142	11,153	19.2
Ilhéus	1,069	15,362	7.0
Irecê	41	4,635	0.9
Pereiro	41	2,082	2.0
Sobral	120	18,774	0.6
Anápolis	393	19,370	2.0
Pastos Bons	28	1,638	1.7
São João Batista	149	2,645	5.6
Montes Claros	36	9,737	0.4
Sabará	20	7,244	0.3
Virginópolis	0	562	0.0
Campo Grande	1,915	35,072	5.5
Santarém	626	34,631	1.8
Campos	152	20,543	0.7
Macaé	66	11,963	0.6
Mossoró	172	8,352	2.1
Campo Bom	3	3,637	0.1
Sapiranga	11	4,307	0.3
Itajaí	5	8,732	0.1
Joinville	45	24,691	0.2
Palmas	90	9,272	1.0
Porto Nacional	107	1,544	7.0
Total	7,265	262,548	2.8
BRASIL	1,542,936	19,727,684	7.8

Table XVI. Older students in municipalities under acceleration programmes.

Moreover, in the majority of countries where such practices are adopted, there is an implicit or explicit early tracking of students – as early as the fifth grade in most countries. Ultimately students in these countries may simply get a certificate of completion of studies. In Brazil all certificates are formally equivalent. Thus, in many or most cases, automatic promotion may easily become associated with false diplomas.

The cases of Bahia and Goiás are instructive, since these have been two states with very strong rates of participation in acceleration programmes. The data from Table X show that in the case of the state of Bahia, the actual number of students increased, and the number of students over 15 years of age also increased. In the case of Goiás, the decrease in total numbers has been modest, but the decrease in older students has been relatively large. States which adopted other policies such as cycles, automatic promotion and which undertook fewer 'acceleration classes', such as Ceará, Paraná and São Paulo, achieved more remarkable results in reducing the total number of enrolments and the number of older students.

The explanation probably lies in the fact that, particularly in the case of Bahia, public authorities failed to limit the entrance of older students, thus contributing to worsen, rather than to improve, the age–grade correlation. In the case of Goiás one possible explanation is the reluctance of municipalities to involve greater number of students in acceleration programmes.

Overall, the analysis of the three strategies, automatic promotion, cycles and acceleration programmes, seems to show that:

- none of these efforts, per se, is sufficient to correctly address the student flow problem;
- cycles and automatic promotion do not contribute to quality, but probably increase inequity;
- well-designed and implemented acceleration programmes may contribute quality, efficiency and equity gains, but at least thus far, have not been able, by themselves, to redress the student flow problem;
- in the case of municipalities, one of the reasons may be the co-existence of state and municipal systems of education – students keep moving from one to another system and thus compromising the effort;
- in other cases, and especially in Bahia, the lack of strong rules to limit the admission of older students is responsible for the increased age–grade distortions.

In all cases, three common problems remain:

- First, dealing with age–grade distortion requires a strict collaboration between state and municipal education systems. It is likely that only when all education is municipal the problem will be solved – since municipalities will have full control of FUNDEF and receive the benefits of greater capital per enrolled student.
- Second, age–grade distortions are part of a larger complex of issues, which include the definition of school programmes, expectations and

responsibilities of schools and principals, structure of incentives, etc. Unless these issues are addressed simultaneously, direct attempts to deal with student flows will only yield limited results. Until expansion predominates as the motto of educational policy, schools and teachers will feel no incentive to improve or ensure quality.

- Third, the bottom line is student learning. Student learning in public schools in Brazil is severely limited by the incapacity of schools to teach first grade students to read and write. Without a firm basis and fluency in these basic skills, students will have difficulty in further schooling – independently of retention or automatic promotion policies. Unless and until all schools guarantee that all students learn to read and write with adequate fluency at the end of first grade, education in Brazil will see the gap widen between richer and poorer students.

The recent experiences of countries such as the USA (National Reading Panel, 1998; Snow et al, 1998) are illustrative of the need and possibilities of change. In these countries, and particularly in the UK, average reading scores have not changed significantly in the last 50 years, but the number of students failing to achieve minimum standards was as low as 45% in the mid 1990s.

Government initiatives such as the UK's National Literacy Strategy (Office for Standards in Education, 1996; Beard, 2000; Department for Education and Employment, 2000a; Riley, 2001; Stuart, 2003) have contributed to increase the proportion of students reaching the Level 4 minimum standard from 55% in 1996 to over 75% for both reading and writing, and over 80% for reading alone. The Fullan report (Fullan, 2000) is particularly eloquent in the analysis of the factors that make such reforms both possible and effective. They require an updated understanding of what literacy is, a state-of-the-art knowledge of the contributions of cognitive psychology to the teaching of reading and writing, the specification of adequate curriculum guidelines (Department for Education and Employment, 2000b), study programmes, teacher education, instructional materials, assessment, and external evaluation linked to increasingly high performance targets.

If public policy has any purpose, it must be to serve the poor, and ensure equal or at least less unequal opportunities of access, permanence, success and completion of schooling. Issues of equity have to be addressed on their own merits, but they cannot be solved unless quality and efficiency issues are simultaneously addressed. Given resource scarcity, equity can only be served if choices are made – concerning priorities and the allocation of political, administrative, technical and financial resources.

Historically, Brazilian society has never learned to promote equity through social policies – improvements benefiting the poor have so far been the consequence of overall economic growth. Largely, and for the majority of the population, education has failed both to promote and to be used as an instrument to promote social mobility and less inequality. Until and unless

Brazilian society understands that limitless expansion of education does not foster the cause of equality, the scenario of magic realism will prevail. In *100 Years of Solitude*, Gabriel Garcia Marques depicts the successive generations of Arellanos, Amarantas, Ursulas, Jose Arcadios running in circles around a never-ended repetition of hopeless, crude reality. In the same way, Brazil and Brazilians are likely to continue to assist new Ministers of Education proposing endless expansions and extensions that will only contribute to perpetuate the prevailing state of affairs.

Notes

[1] See the article by Elizabeth Balbachevsky in this volume.

[2] Primary education is used in this chapter to refer to the first eight years of education. Acceleration classes refer to special programmes geared towards older, typically multi-repeater students.

[3] According to Instituto Montenegro (Instituto Paulo Montenegro, 2001), only 33% of Brazilian adults can adequately read normal, daily texts. This figure would put the functional illiterate population above 100 million Brazilians. Information on Educação Solidária available at the website of the institution: http://www.ipm.org.br

[4] FUNDEF is a fund created for the purpose of improving the efficiency and equality in the distribution of resources for primary education. Resources are distributed to states and municipalities according to the number of students. In the absence of an age limit, school systems inflated enrolments by attracting older students.

[5] Yet, there are major wage differentials according to the type of degree. In addition, there are also major differences in the candidates for different degrees – the highest paying degrees are associated with major performance students and higher entry requirements in the respective colleges.

[6] Brazil is the only country the author knows in which there is no curriculum differentiation either within or between schools, forcing students – the majority of whom have a weak academic background – to follow the same, college-oriented curricula, which may entail not only high inefficiency, but even higher inequity (Oliveira, 1996, 2001). As shown in the previous section, Brazilian labour markets do not seem to put a premium on extended, low quality and low-skills education.

[7] Legislation passed in the late 1990s required all teachers to complete higher education. As a result, those teachers who presently get market-level salaries will acquire four more years of education and decrease their relative salaries by 30-50%.

[8] An official publication, *Geografia da Educação no Brasil* (Instituto Nacional de Estudos e Pesquisas Educacionais, 2001, p. 59) shows average salaries of 425 reais for first to fourth grade teachers, 605 for fifth to eighth grade teachers and 700 for eighth grade teachers, for an average load of 20 contact-hours per

week. There are great regional variations running from 221 to 1,364 reais for basic education teachers (pre-school to secondary school level).

[9] One difficulty of discussing equity issues in Brazil is the fact that most people do not 'believe' in the simple fact that resources are scarce. The majority of people believe that the government has any amount of resource that may be required; it only lacks the 'political will'. Regarding the level of public investment in education, the best estimates from Secretaria do Tesouro Nacional has been varying from 5.1 to 5.5 of the GNP. That corresponds to about 20 billion dollars in 2002.

[10] Public higher education is free in Brazil. Over 70% of students in these institutions come from secondary private institutions. Given the high rates of return to higher education, this probably is the single most important contribution to income concentration in Brazil.

[11] Public investment based on 1998 data from the Geografia da Educação Brasileira (2001) and adapted by the author. Numbers of students in public schools have been rounded. These figures are compatible with World Bank estimates in Report 24413, 2002, Table 2.1. The author's estimation is that expenditures in infant education are probably higher, perhaps around 2 to 2.5 billion; that part of the resources for primary education are diverted for secondary education, which has less direct funds than reported; and that higher education costs more.

[12] There is some evidence from the USA that excellent pre-school provision may give a head start to otherwise disadvantaged students. The advantages are less academic and mostly behavioural: increased probability to stay in schools, lower crime rate, etc. (Carneiro et al, 2002; Krueger, 2002).

[13] The increase in the number of younger students is largely due to the inclusion of the old 'literacy classes' in the first grade of education. See Table I.

[14] This programme is named Escola Campeã, started in 2001, and is expected to last until the end of 2004. Specific efficiency targets are established and are monitored and evaluated, such as reductions in transportation costs, optimisation of school buildings, increasing teacher salaries as a result of better management practices, etc. No report has been published of this data, but this seems to be a promising approach to the extent that it integrates a number of actions in a consistent way – as opposed to the typical 'Christmas tree' approach to educational innovation characteristic of Brazil and many other countries, in which disconnected projects are put together more or less at random.

[15] A 2002 World Bank report noted that 'confidential' data collected by the Bank in Brazil had been provided to the Brazilian government but would not be released to other researchers in Brazil. The lack of public access to public data is a major barrier to improving the quality of research and debate about educational policies in Brazil.

[16] The states of São Paulo and Paraná also commissioned but never published the external evaluations of their programmes.

66

References

Autor, D., Levy, F. & Murnane, R. (2001) The Skill Content of Recent Technological Change: an empirical exploration. *Working Paper*. Cambridge, MA: National Bureau of Economic Research.

Beard, R. (2000) *National Literacy Strategy. Review of Research and Other Related Evidence*. London: Department for Education and Employment, Standards and Effectiveness Unit.

Câmara dos Deputados and Comissão de Educação Cultura e Desporto (2002) *Solução para as não-aprendizagens: series ou ciclos. Brasília: Câmara dos Deputados, Comissão de Educação, Cultura e Desporto, 2002.* Brasília: Câmara de Deputados.

Carneiro, P., Heckman, J. & Manoli, D. (2002) Human Capital Policy. *Alvin Hansen Seminar*, April 25. Cambridge, MA: Harvard University.

Department for Education and Employment (2000a) *The National Literacy Strategy.* London: Department for Education and Employment.

Department for Education and Employment (2000b) *The National Curriculum for England.* London: Department for Education and Employment.

Fletcher, Philip R. (1983) O MOBRAL e a alfabetização: a promessa, a experiência e alguma evidência dos seus resultados. Stanford, CA: Jonhson Library of Government Documents, Stanford University Libraries.

Franco, C. (2001) *Avaliação, ciclos e promoção na educacão.* Porto Alegre: Artmed.

Fullan, M.G. (2000) The Return of Large-Scale Reform, *Journal of Educational Change*, 1, pp. 5-27.

Fundação Carlos Chigas (2002) *Relatório da avaliação de desempenho dos municípios do Projeto Escola Campeã.* São Paulo: Fundação Carlos Chigas.

Fundação Cesgranrio (2003) *Relatório de avaliação do desempenho do sistema estadual de Educação do Estado de Tocantis.* Rio de Janeiro: mimeo.

Fundação Luís Eduardo Magalhães (2000) *Programa de gestão municipal da educação.* Salvador: Bahia: Fundação Luís Eduardo Magalhães.

Gomes, C.A.C. (2003) *Dissertação escolar: alternativa para o sucesso?* Vol. versão preliminar, ed. M.C. Gonçalves & A.L.d.S. Pereira. Brasília: Universidade Católica de Brasília.

Instituto Nacional de Estudos e Pesquisas Educacionais (2001) *Geografia da educação brasileira.* Brasília: Ministério da Educacão.

Instituto Paulo Montenegro (2001) *Indicador nacional de alfabetismo funcional – Um diagnóstico para a inclusão social pela educação.* São Paulo: Instituto Paulo Montenegro.

Klein, Ruben (2003) Por uma educação de qualidade' *Ensaio*, 11(37), pp. 225-118.

Krueger, A.B. (2002) Inequality, Too Much of a Good Thing. *Alvin Hansen Seminar*, April 25. Cambridge, MA: Harvard University.

National Reading Panel (1998) *Report of the Sub-groups.* Washington, DC: National Academy of Sciences.

Office for Standards in Education (1996) *The Teaching of Reading in 45 Inner London Primary Schools*, vol. 27, 96, DS. London: Office for Standards in Education.

Oliveira, J.B.A. (1998) *Reforma do estado e pacto federativo.* Belo Horizonte: Secretaria de Estado de Planejamento.

Oliveira, J.B.A. (2001) Custos e benefícios de um programa para regularizar o fluxo escolar no ensino fundamental: novas evidências, *Ensaio,* 9, pp. 305-342.

Oliveira, J.B.A. (2002) *Novo estudo sobre educação em Minas Gerais.* Belo Horizonte: Banco de Desenvolvimento de Minas Gerais.

Organisation for Economic Cooperation and Development (2001) *Knowledge and Skills for Life – First Results from PISA 2000 – Education and Skills.* Paris: OECD Programme for International Student Assessment.

Riley, J. (2001) The National Literacy Strategy: success with literacy for all? *The Curriculum Journal,* 12, pp. 29-38.

Snow, C., Burns, S. & Griffin, P. (1998) *Preventing Reading Difficulties in Young Children.* Washington, DC: National Academic Press.

Soares, Francisco (2004) Quality and Equity in Brazilian Basic Education: facts and possibilities, in this volume, pp. 69-88.

Souza, S., Alavarse, A., Steinvasher, D.J. & Arcas, P. (2003) Ciclos e progressão escolar: indicações bibliográficas, *Ensaio,* 11, pp. 99-114.

Stuart, M. (2003) Fine Tuning the National Literacy Strategy to Ensure Continuing Progress in Improving Standards of Reading in the UK: some suggestions for change, paper presented at the DfES Phonics Seminar, March 17. London: University of London Institute of Education.

UNESCO (2000) *Relatório de avaliação de desempenho dos alunos de países da América Latina y el Caribe.*

Quality and Equity in Brazilian Basic Education: facts and possibilities

FRANCISCO SOARES

Introduction

Brazilian education is organised in five levels: Infant, Fundamental, Secondary, Higher and Postgraduate Education. The first three are often referred to as Basic Education, and the last two as Higher Education. This unique terminology, particularly the one adopted for the three first levels, often gives rise to confusion when comparisons are made with other countries.

Basic education is compulsory for children aged 7 to 14 and free at all public institutions, including for those who did not have access to school at the appropriate age. Although access to basic education schools has largely been achieved, the very high rates of grade repetition, as well as of truancy and school evasion show that for the majority of the population, the system is not providing the education required for responsible citizenship and entry into the formal workforce. The main purpose of this chapter is to present a description and a critical appraisal of the status of this level of education.

Today data of good quality are available to describe every level of the Brazilian educational system. Castro (1999) gives a comprehensive overview, where both the national evaluation efforts and the information systems of the National Institute of Educational Studies and Research (INEP), an agency of the Ministry of Education (MEC), are described. This chapter uses data from 2001 cycle of the National System for Evaluation of Basic Education (SAEB) to describe the Brazilian basic education and to provide evidence supporting the enacting of some school policies that could help improve the quality and equity of this level of education in Brazil.

The Basic School: its outcomes and problems

Even before the 1988 Brazilian Constitution ensured the principle of free access to compulsory education as a citizen's right, the federal, state and municipal governments were prioritising programmes to build schools and to hire teachers to work with children aged 7-14. As a result Brazil has today a large system of basic education.

Table I shows the number of schools and Table II the enrolment, based on the 2002 Educational Census. Relating these data to the 2000 population census, it can be seen that almost all Brazilian children aged between 7 and 14 are enrolled in basic school. Actually, there is a much higher number of children enrolled at basic school than the number of children in this age group, 35 million against 28 million. This is an evidence of not only the high repetition rate, but also of late entry, evasion and student drop-out. It should be observed that most students go to public schools. However, it is the private system, which responds to only 9% of the students, that receives almost all students from higher socio-economic status. Another aspect to be taken into consideration is the large number of small rural schools, and their geographic isolation.

School type	Educational level	
	Fundamental	Secondary
Public	159,228	13,916
Private	18,552	6,304
Urban	70,410	19,399
Rural	107,370	821
Total	177,780	20,220

Table I. Number of schools by school type.
Source: INEP-MEC, Educational Census, 2002.

Students' categories	Educational level	
	Fundamental	Secondary
Male	18,017,980	3,826,466
Female	17,280,109	4,571,542
Public	32,089,803	7,283,528
Private	3,208,286	1,114,480
Urban	28,864,106	8,269,981
Rural	6,433,983	128,027
Morning	31,891,584	4,093,373
Evening	3,406,505	4,304,635
Total	35,298,089	8,398,008

Table II. Enrolment numbers.
Source: INEP-MEC, Educational Census, 2002.

Access to school, although essential, is not enough to fulfil every educational need. For that the child must attend a good school on a regular basis. Therefore the quality of an education system should be first assessed through indicators of attendance, evasion, promotion to the next grade, and the conclusion of basic education.

There is no reliable data describing the present situation concerning attendance at basic education schools despite the fact that the law establishes compulsory presence for at least 75% of the school days. Some anecdotal evidence suggests that the absence rate is high. The situation has been made worse due to recent misguided implementations of projects to reduce grade repetition. Some of those projects sent the wrong message to students, i.e. they will be promoted no matter what they do. Since Brazilian society often values grade completion more than learning, school attendance and involvement lost priority, since the diploma was secured by the new rules.

To measure grade repetition, evasion and conclusion, there is reliable data obtained through the Educational Census. By law, every school should fill in the educational census questionnaires. The National Institute of Educational Studies and Research (INEP) processes the data collected and produces useful indicators. While these indicators describe the basic conditions necessary for an educational system, they cannot be taken as real indicators of quality in education.

There is a national education law, known as the 'National Educational Guidelines and Framework Law', that provides elements to understand what the legislator understands as quality education. It establishes that the basic education will aim at the basic formative stage of the individual through:

- the development of learning capability by means of a comprehensive ability to read, write and calculate;
- the understanding of the natural and social environments, the political system, the technology, the arts and the values on which the society is based;
- the development of the learning capability, having in mind the acquisition of not only knowledge and skills, but also the attainment of attitudes and values;
- the strengthening of family ties, human solidarity and mutual understanding on which social life is based.

The legislator very clearly points out that education should provide the student with opportunities to achieve goals related to cognitive, vocational, social and personal aspects of his/her life. When this is achieved it is said that the student had access to 'quality education'. In order to verify the supply of a 'quality education', the federal government created an evaluation system: the National System for Evaluation of Basic Education (SAEB), which, however, collects data related only to the cognitive aspects of the education system. Besides the difficulty of collecting data on the other aspects of education, this option is justified by the fact that the other goals cannot be attained if the students do not acquire the reading and mathematical abilities. The other goals of education are not the responsibility of the school system alone, but also of the families, and other social organisations.

SAEB – National System for Evaluation of Basic Education

SAEB is the national system for evaluation of basic education in Brazil. It is based on a rigorous sample methodology. It began in 1990 and has been carried out on a bi-annual basis since 1993. SAEB evaluates students from the last year of each cycle at both basic and secondary levels. The levels evaluated are the fourth and eighth year of basic education and the senior third year of secondary education.

The students are tested on Portuguese language and mathematics. In addition to the tests, they also complete a questionnaire, which collects data on socio-economic status, learning attitudes and parents' participation in educational activities. Teachers also answer questionnaires on teaching practices, management and socio-economic background. The information collected on individual students and schools is confidential and results are only published at national, regional and state levels of aggregations.

The test aims at evaluating cognitive processes rather than mere content. It examines the abilities expected from the students at each level of education. The test specifications are based on the National Curricular Parameters (PCN) and the National Educational Guidelines and Framework Law (LDB). These specifications are the result of a thorough national consultation with teachers, researchers and specialists.

To guarantee the inclusion of items related to all the cognitive processes, SAEB tests are organised in such a way that different students take different tests, but with common items. This precaution and the use of item response theory (IRT) ensure that the students' proficiencies for the different cycles and grades are on the same scale. Obviously, senior high school students are expected to do better than fourth grade ones. The proficiency methodology is described in Klein & Fontanive (1995). In terms of proficiency measurement, SAEB is a particularly well-designed tool.[1]

In this chapter we use data from SAEB 2001, mainly the eighth grade mathematics results. This option reflects the known fact that proficiency in mathematics depends more on school quality than language proficiency. All analyses presented are based on the data from 50,300 students, 5,986 classes, and 2,818 schools from the state, municipal and private sectors from every Brazilian state and the federal district.

Brazilian Basic Education Quality

The proficiency evaluated by the SAEB assesses adequately the level of cognitive skills and competence considered necessary for a basic education student.

Figure 1 depicts the mathematics proficiency histograms for the three grades tested. Firstly, it should be noted that the three graphs overlap, demonstrating that in all grades there are students whose ability levels are compatible with more or less advanced classes. It should be particularly noticed that there is a large overlap between the results of the eighth grade (basic education) and those from the secondary education senior year. This indicates that the secondary education is adding little, in cognitive terms, to the students.

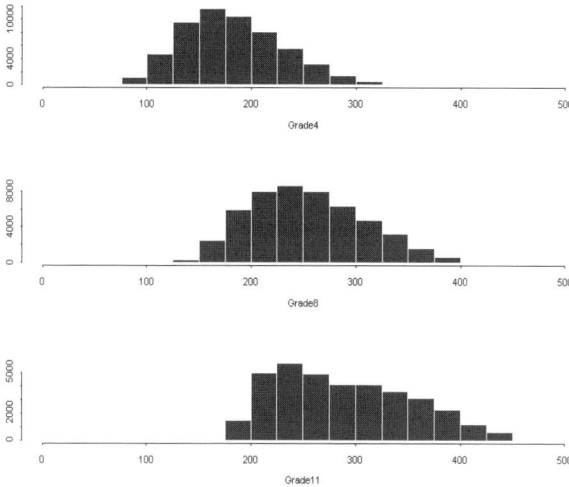

Figure 1. Mathematics proficiency by grade.

Table III, taken from the SAEB 1997 official report, shows, for each grade, the expected levels of performance for each school year. Although the methodology used to establish these levels has not been properly described, this is the only reference available. As can be seen in Figure 1, students' overall performance is much below the values considered appropriate. It means that the vast majority of Brazilian students have not acquired the cognitive skills expected for their grades. Therefore, the Brazilian educational system has problems not only with student flow, as indicated above, but also more serious issues in relation to the quality of what the students learn.

Levels	Grade
100	Not significant
175	End of Basic School's Grade 2
250	End of Basic School's Grade 4
325	End of Basic School's Grade 8
400	End of Basic School's Grade 3

Table III. Expected proficiency levels by grade.
Source: INEP-MEC SAEB 1997 Final report.

73

In the remaining sections of this chapter we are going to consider mainly the eighth grade mathematics results, which are shown in the second histogram of Figure 1. The standard deviation value of this distribution is 50 points. This gives us a reference against which to measure the impact of these factors. A 25-point effect is equivalent to a proficiency distribution shift of half a standard deviation, something comparable to one school grade.

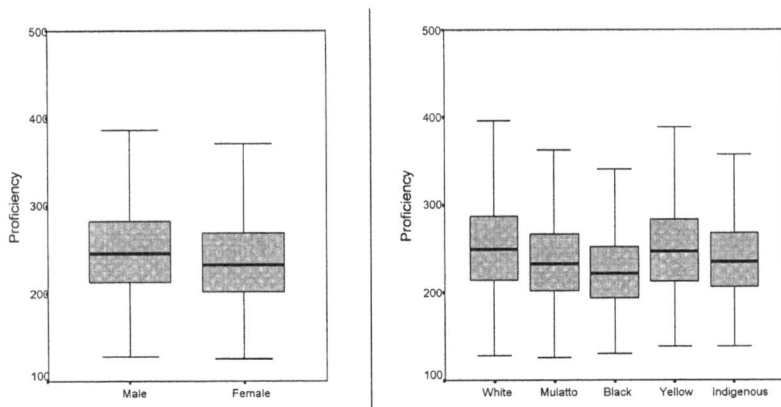

Figure 2. Mathematics proficiency by students' sex and skin colour.

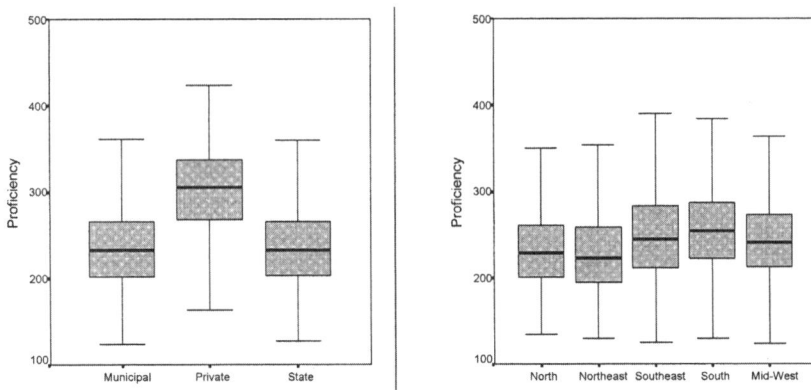

Figure 3. Mathematics proficiency by school type and country region.

Figures 2 and 3 show the box plot [2] results for students categorised by gender, geographical location, colour and school systems. There are big differences to be noticed. The boys have a little better median proficiency that the girls, blacks fall behind students from other colours, including the mulattos. Reflecting known Brazilian regional differences, the South-east and

South have higher median proficiencies than the other regions and, finally, the private schools have a very large advantage in relation to either the state or municipal schools. All those differences have been reduced in several other societies and so the same can occur in Brazil.

As in any society, but in a special way in Brazil, the student's family socio-economic status has an effect on his/her school performance. For this reason, it is impossible to understand the system without taking into account the students' socio-economic level. In the next section we introduce the indicator of socio-economic status to be used in the remaining sections of this chapter.

The Measurement of Socio-economic Status

There is no agreement on the best way to measure socio-economic status (SES) for use in educational studies. On the one hand, it is agreed that the index should include family wealth, parents' education and occupational status. On the other, it is not clear how these constructs should be dealt with. Besides, it is not easy to collect the necessary data in the educational context, where it is the students, who frequently do not know well details related to their parents' lives, that answer the questionnaires. In this chapter we use an SES measure which incorporates the recommendations of Buchman (2002) and was developed by the same methodology used in the Programme for International Student Assessment (PISA) (Organisation for Economic Cooperation and Development [OECD], 2001).

Initially, four indicators of socio-economic and cultural positions were built: social exclusion, parents' educational level, family wealth, and home educational resources. Then these factors were combined, through factor analyses, in a single indicator.

The so-called *social exclusion factor* was built taking into account the availability of running water, electricity and paved streets in the students' houses and locale. The education factor is the maximum of the number of years of schooling of students' father and mother. The family wealth indicator was built based on three items: number of people per room in the house (assuming that richer families will have a smaller ratio); the existence of a housemaid, and the number of automobiles owned by the family. To measure the home educational resources, the following items were synthesised through an IRT model: calm place to study, access to daily newspapers, magazines, encyclopaedias, atlases, dictionaries, calculator and the Internet.

Socio-economic Gradient

The socio-economic gradient is defined as the best line to summarise the relationship between the students' measure of socio-economic status and his/her proficiency. See, for example, chapter 2 of Willms (2002). In order to find this line, a plot with a point for every student is first constructed. The exact location of this is determined by both his/her socio-economic index and proficiency. Figure 4 presents the socio-economic gradient for the students tested in the SAEB 2001, in eighth grade mathematics. The point, representing each student, is affected not only by the quality of the educational system they belong to, but also by social, economic and cultural factors. However, it can be clearly observed that students from families with higher socio-economic status have also higher proficiencies on average, while there are high variations about this general structure. Finally, since the gradient is defined as a straight line, the marginal benefit of the socio-economic advantage is the same in any point of the social position.

To increase proficiency levels and lessen the effect of socio-economic status in academic results should be the aim of any educational system. In simple terms, the objective is to raise and level the learning bar. This is especially relevant in Brazil, where the relationship between educational achievement and social position proficiency is so strong.

Figures 5, 6 and 7 show the gradients for students classified by gender, colour, school type and country region. It is clear from those plots that, over and above the differences in proficiency that can be associated with gender colour, region, and system, improvement in performance is associated with higher inequality. This is shown by the steeper gradients for students who are males, whites, from the South-east and from private schools. These educational inequalities appear in a recurrent manner in the various evaluation cycles, as demonstrated in many studies that analysed the SAEB results (Barbosa et al, 2001; Barbosa & Fernandes, 2001; Soares et al, 2001; Soares & Alves, 2002).

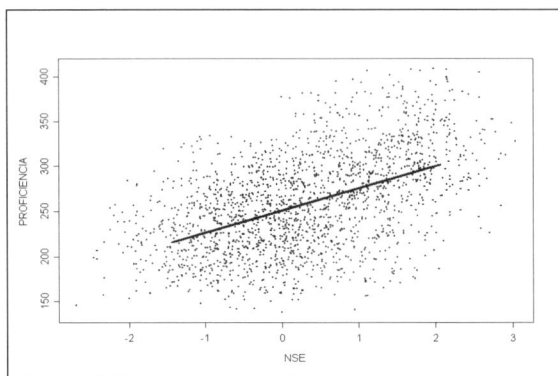

Figure 4. Relationship between student performance and social-economic background for the Brazilian students as a whole.

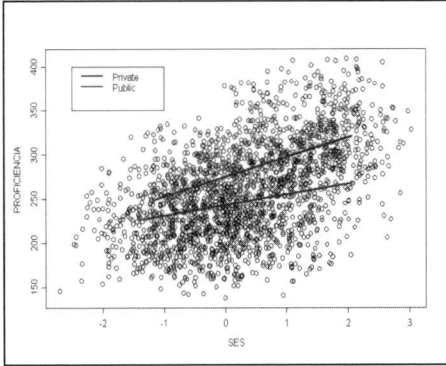

Figure 5. Relationship between student performance and social-economic background for the Brazilian students by school type.

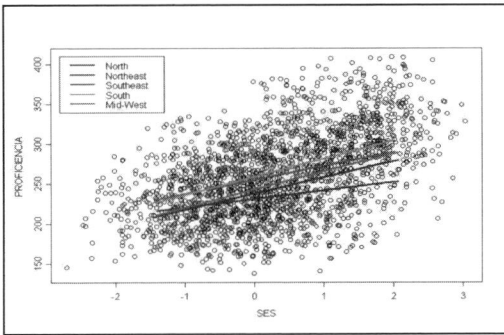

Figure 6. Relationship between student performance and social-economic background for the Brazilian students by region.

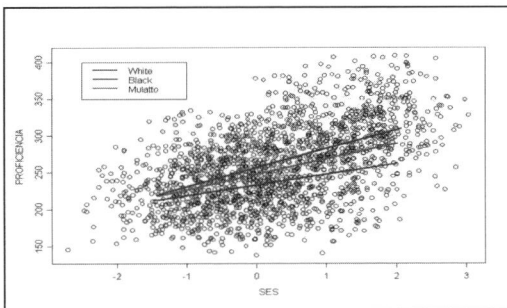

Figure 7. Relationship between student performance and social-economic background for the Brazilian students by race.

These data plots show that education quality is not evenly distributed among the social classes and even worse, equity is observed only at the very low levels of proficiency.

One of the basic theses of this chapter is that both problems, i.e. quality and equity, should be approached concomitantly. In the next section, we examine the possible role of social, school, and family elements to overcome these problems. International examples show that this can be accomplished. The 2000 PISA results show that Korea, Canada, Finland, Iceland, and Japan present both a high degree of equality and quality in their educational systems. Particularly in Korea, the number of students with high academic performance, whose parents come from a low socio-economic and cultural background, is so high that the relationship between socio-economic position and academic performance is almost non-existent. The same phenomenon is observed in Cuba, as shown by the evaluation of the Latin American education organised by the UNESCO Regional Bureau for Education in Latin America and the Caribbean and analysed by Willms & Sommers (2001). Yet, the question remains: could Brazil be successful in giving access to a good quality education without going through the present stage of inequality?

Improving Student Performance and Overcoming Inequalities

In this section we study, using the SAEB data, the impact of the three social dimensions – the students' socio-economic status, cultural backgrounds of their families, and the school they attend – on their cognitive performance.[3]

In order to do this we use a statistical model with two hierarchical levels, students being level 1, and the school, level 2. For the level 1 model we have expressed each student's performance as a base value moderated by influences due to gender, colour, socio-economic level and age–grade gap. For level 2 models we measured the impact of school characteristics on the basic students' performance level and on the variation of the effect of the model 1 level variables.[4] There are several presentations of hierarchical models for social scientist audiences, for example, Lee (2000).

Following Willms's recommendations (Willms, 2000), we have included among the school characteristics the average of its students' SES and age–grade gap as proxies for the school SES and ability of the whole group of students. Willms justifies the use of these factors citing studies from several countries which show that schools or classrooms with students with high social class or high ability intakes tend to have several advantages. On average these schools are more likely to have greater support from parents, fewer disciplinary problems, and a school climate oriented towards higher performance and they are more likely to attract and retain talented and motivated teachers. The literature uses the expression 'peer effects' to describe what occurs in schools when bright and motivated students work together.

By including these school characteristics in our level 2 model, we neutralise statistically their effects when measuring the importance of other school processes. This procedure produces a very stringent test on the association of the factors with cognitive achievement, which, however, can be unfair to some schools (Bryk & Raudenbush, 1992, p. 128) that have privileged students but also good teachers.

The relationships among the multiple factors associated to cognitive performance are complex. Any intervention on social, school or family factors has in impact not only on students' performance but on the other explanatory factors as well. For example, a change of policy coming from the State Secretariat for Education and backed by the schools can lead to more work satisfaction, higher teachers' participation and changes in the whole chain of factors. Because of these complexities, we choose a conservative analysis. The models fitted to the data included all the control variables and only one educational process variable at a time. These models allow us to verify the *existence* of an impact due to a factor, but do not produce good measures of its effect, which, we feel, cannot be obtained only with sectional data as produced by SAEB.

The results reported here should not be used for an automatic decision-making process. The expectation that we could look at the data to see which schools are performing below standards, then identify the variables causing low performance, and finally prescribe a corresponding remedy, is what Torgenson appropriately called 'the positivist's dream', where knowledge replaces politics (Torgenson, 1986).

Social Policies

The students' socio-economic status, mainly when it is considered at school level, is by far the factor with the biggest impact on their school results. It is a real, extra-school constraint which can help or hinder the learning process and that directly affects the functioning and organisation of schools and classes. Therefore policies that reduce the disparities between the socio-economic and cultural background of the students of a given educational system have an impact on cognitive results, even if not immediately.

Table IV shows our results describing the influence of social factors on the basic level of proficiency and on the increase of reduction of equity related to gender, colour, SES and age–grade gap. The presence of a statistically significant association, which increases the quality or the *inequity*, is depicted in Table IV and in all other tables by the symbol ▲. If this association is only marginally significant we use the symbol △. Analogously, if the factor is associated with a decrease in the quality or reduces inequity we use the symbols ▼ or ▽. When there is no association between the factor being considered and quality or equality we use the symbol –.

Processes	Impact on the basal level	Impact on inequity due to:			
		Gender	Colour	SES	Age–grade gap
School type	▲	-	▼	-	-
School SES	▲	-	▲	▼	▲
Student SES	▲				

Table IV. Influence in performance basal level and inequalities due to gender, colour, socio-economic position and age-grade gap related to social factors.

The students' social position, as much as that of their school, is strongly associated to the students' performance level. The influence of an individual's social position on his/her cognitive achievement has been recognised at least since the publication of the Coleman report (Coleman et al, 1966). However, the influence of the school SES, i.e. the average SES for all students of that school, must be specifically highlighted.

Basic education in Brazil is very segmented. Most students with high socio-economic status attend private schools. Their highest privilege is that their schoolmates have similar academic motivations. The interaction between the school type and the average socio-economic background of the schools is significant and shows the special privilege enjoyed by those few Brazilians who attend private schools where the average socio-economic level is high. We must further observe that, even after the stringent socio-economic equalisation used here, the proficiencies of students from private schools are higher than that of students from state schools.

The last four columns of Table IV summarise the influence of these factors on equity. The socio-economic gap is smaller in schools with higher socio-economic status. In other words, poor students do better in schools where they are the minority. Private schools reduce the gap between students of different colours. This is sad since most black students attend public schools where no similar effect is observed. However, schools with higher socio-economic status increase the colour gap. This apparent paradox is explained by the different patterns of behaviour of the colour gap in private and public schools, a finding which deserves more research. Finally, schools with high SES increase the differences between students with high and low age–grade gaps. While not shown in the table, the gender gap disappears in private schools that have students with high SES.

All these observations are of limited relevance to policy makers and educational systems managers, given that socio-economic conditions are not affected on a short-term basis by educational policies.

School Policies

The aim of this section is to answer the following questions: What school policies and practices improve levels of schooling outcomes? And what school policies and practices reduce the inequalities described above?

Before answering specifically, it is useful to quantify the extent of the potential impact of all the school factors taken together. The hierarchical linear models can be used to do this, since they partition the variance in proficiency into the two components, the first associated with students and the second with schools. However, since the schools in Brazil are very much divided along socio-economic lines, we use the results of a model that controls the proficiency by socio-economic variables to present the partition of variance result.

The important result to report is that, for eighth grade mathematics, the set of all school factors account for 12.3% of the total proficiency variance. This value shows that the major part of performance variance must be attributed to intrinsic variations among students different from their socio-economic differences, bearing in mind that these have been controlled in the model. However, the remaining value, which is compatible with international literature on the subject, is high enough for us to recognise that there is a variation between schools that cannot be attributed to social factors only, or to random fluctuations. It means that we can assert, beyond reasonable doubt, that the Brazilian basic schools, by themselves, do make a difference in students' lives and that their influence must, therefore, be optimised through school policies and practices. This has a resonance with Rutter's famous study, *Fifteen Thousand Hours*, in England (Rutter et al, 1979).

Teachers' characteristics	Impact on the level of reference	Impact on inequity due to:			
		Gender	Colour	SES	Age—grade gap
Degree in Mathematics	▲	-	▲	-	-
Teachers' expectations	▲	-	-	-	-
Content already developed	▲	-	-	-	-
Traditional pedagogical option	-	-	-	-	-
Relationship with the principal	▲	-	-	-	-
Relationship with the team	▲	-	▲	-	-
Perception of school external problems	△	-	-	▽	-
Perception of school internal problems	▲	-	-	-	▲
Commitment	-	▽	-	-	△
Dedication	-	-	-	▲	-
Salary	▲	-	△	-	-
Gender	▽	-	-	-	-

Table V. Effect of the processes associated with the teachers on cognitive performance and on the gaps related to gender, SES and age–grade gap.

Table V presents a summary of the effects of the teachers' characteristics that affect proficiency and the gaps associated with gender, race, SES, and age–grade. Firstly, it should be noticed that not all factors associated with the teachers and listed in the school effectiveness literature are included, the reason being that the SAEB data is collected through a questionnaire answered by the teachers of the tested subjects on the day in which the test is being given. Therefore, many factors cannot be assessed. For a review of the teacher characteristics and attitudes associated with a better performance, see Darling-Hammond (1999). However, since it is reasonable to assume that there is association between the measured and not-measured factors, the table constructed with the collected data is not biased.

While most of the factors considered impact positively on the proficiency level, few have an impact on equity. A possible explanation is that the schools today do not see overcoming inequalities as a problem and thus this is not a concern for the teacher. This hinders the presence of successful experiences that would be registered in the data and captured in our analysis. It should be noted that the few factors showing impact on equity are *increasing the gap* due to colour, SES and age–grade gap. For example, in schools with qualified teachers all students gain; however, the white students gain more. This explains why this variable has a ▲ sign in the student colour column.

School characteristics	Impact on the basal level	Impact on equity due to:			
		Gender	Colour	SES	Age–grade gap
Equipment	▲	-	▲	-	-
Safety	▲	-	△	▽	▼
School maintenance (cleanness)	▲	-	△	-	-
School maintenance (classes)	▲	-	▲	-	-
School maintenance (building)	▲	-	-	-	-
Pupil selection	▲	-	-	-	-
Principal vision on teachers' commitment	▲	-	-	-	-
Perception of school external problems	▲	-	-	▽	-
Perception of school internal problems	▲	-	-	-	▲
Principal with postgraduate degree	-	-	-	-	▽

Table VI. Effect of school processes on the cognitive performance and on the difference related to gender, SES and age–grade gap.

The influence of school processes is presented in Table VI. Each of the school factors included is measured either by items either in the principal's questionnaire or in the school conditions questionnaire, filled in by the SAEB site coordinator. Important characteristics such as school climate could not be measured since only the teachers of the evaluated classes answered the questionnaire. For a more complete description of school factors, see Lee et al (1993) and Sammons et al (1995). The results are very similar to the ones observed in the teacher factor; i.e. several factors impact the level and the few ones that impact equity do so in the direction of increasing the gaps.

The School of the Disadvantaged

In order to have a more general view of schools' and teachers' factors we combined the positive characteristics identified in the last two sections in only two factors. The method of aggregation used was the simplest one. We just counted the number of positive characteristics. Table VII shows the average of these factors for subgroups of the students identified by the variables, gender, skin colour, socio-economic background and age–grade gap, the same factors that generated the differences presented earlier.

	Number of positive teacher characteristics	Number of positive school characteristics
Gender		
Male	3.61	1.45
Female	3.59	1.40
Skin colour		
White and Yellow	3.82	1.66
Others	3.37	1.17
SES		
Low	3.95	1.90
High	3.35	1.05
Age–Grade gap		
Yes	3.91	1.72
No	3.25	1.10

Table VII. Average number of positive characteristics in the students' subgroups generated by, sex, skin colour, SES and age–grade gap.

The quality of the teachers and the school that enrols boys and girls is the same. Therefore, the differences in performance between boys and girls cannot be attributed to the different characteristics of the school they attend. However, for the skin colour, SES and age–grade gap, it can be said that students who have a weaker performance are also those with lower values in the teacher and school factors. In other words, the school of the students with the worst performance is also worse than the school of the students with the best performance. Then the most obvious policy in order to overcome these differences is to allocate the best teachers and schools to non-white students with low socio-economic background and a bigger age–grade gap. This study does not intend to discuss the viability of such a proposal. We show in the following sections that this policy alone would not eradicate the differences mentioned.

Family Contribution

The family impacts student achievement through the transmission of cultural capital, or the formation of study habits or by expressing high expectations of academic success. SAEB questionnaires have some indirect information on these factors, and Table VIII presents the results.

Student processes	Impact on the level of reference	Impact on equity due to:			
		Gender	Colour	SES	Age-grade gap
The student likes to study	▲	-	▲	▲	▲
Books available at home	▲	-	▲	▲	▲
Homework	▲	▽	▲	-	▲
Reading habits	▲	-	-	▲	▲
Parents' involvement	△	-	-	-	-

Table VIII. Influence in the reference level and in performance discrepancies due to gender, colour, and socio-economic position and age–grade gap related to student and family factors.

This set of factors is the one with more clear effects on the level of students' performance. Therefore every school should try hard to involve the parents in the education of their children by reading to them, supervising their homework and developing their motivation for studying. However, a rise in the level of those factors is associated today with greater gaps. In other words, the data is showing that today only by reducing the proficiency level, a very unfortunate outcome indeed, is it possible to reduce the gaps. It is reasonable, however, to assume that by the time the Brazilian families have more economic and capital resources, the relation between these variables and the student proficiency will be different.

Conclusion

Policy recommendations should be backed by solid evidence. The evidence presented here is not definitive, since it was obtained through data analyses based only on the results from an eighth grade SAEB 2001 mathematics test. Stronger evidence would be obtained with similar analysis based on the other grades' results as well as the other subjects and cycles of the SAEB. In addition, it should be emphasised that the SAEB sample design is not the most appropriate to analyse the effect of social and school factors on achievement. Longitudinal designs would be more appropriate and experiment designs the gold standard. For a very clear presentation of the limitation of educational surveys like SAEB, one could read Podgursky (2001).

SAEB not only generates information about the quality of Brazilian basic schools, but also provides very useful information on how to improve them. The analysis presented in this chapter along with others shows that the determinants of quality in Brazilian basic schools are very similar to those of other countries. Therefore all international literature in the area is relevant to the Brazilian basic education system. Since Brazilian education is often too self-centred, the importance of this simple finding must not be minimised.

The transformation of all the results presented in this chapter into educational policies requires studies different from the one presented here. This will be done, eventually. Nevertheless, it must be clear that policies to change the despairing scenario of basic education in Brazil would require the participation of all the sectors involved. The solution will not come only as a result of governmental policies imposed on schools, as some people believe. It will be a slow transformation based on small victories. However, just as access was obtained, quality and equity in education can also be reached with time.

Acknowledgements

The author acknowledges the financial support of the Ford Foundation, which funded the research described in this chapter and thanks Juliana Mambrini for the help with the data preparation and statistical analysis.

Notes

[1] There is an increasing literature on SAEB. To understand the sampling aspects used, look up the survey sample plan in Andrade et al (2001). Franco (2001) puts together a collection of critical reflection articles on SAEB 1999. Bonanimo's book (2002) is the most comprehensive one, giving a historical evolution synthesis, a description of the methodologies used and the impact of this system (SAEB 2001). Planning can be found in Locatelli (2002), along with the final report main results, published by INEP. SAEB's two first cycles are evaluated in Crespo et al (2000).

[2] Box plots (often called 'box and whisker' plots) are a way of presenting the shape, central value and variability of the distribution of scores of a group of students. The *median* is such that half of all students get a score higher than the median, and 50% get a score lower. The median splits the data into two parts. The median of the lower half of the data is the *first quartile*, i.e. point at which 25% of the patients score lower (and 75% score higher). The median

of the upper half of the data is the *third quartile*, i.e. the point at which 75% of the students score lower (and 25% score higher). The 'box' in a box plot shows the median score as a line and the first and third quartile of the score distribution as the lower and upper parts of the box. The *'whiskers'* shown above and below the boxes represent the largest and smallest observed scores that are less than 1.5 box lengths from the end of the box. In practice, these scores are about the lowest and highest values one is likely to observe.

[3] A particularly appropriate class of statistical models has been used to investigate these educational topics. These models are called hierarchical regression models. Although they have a wide application scope, they are particularly suitable for educational data analysis because of their clear hierarchical structure, i.e. a structure which groups students into classrooms, classrooms into schools, and schools into educational systems or geographical regions. This statistical technique is very useful since it enables one to identify the complex relationships existing between the factors at each level and how the various levels influence each other. Bryk & Raudenbush (1992) and Goldstein (1995) describe the technical details of these models.

[4] The author will send the mathematical expression of all the models used in the analysis presented in this chapter to anyone interested. Please email francisco-soares@ufmg.br

References

Andrade, D., Silva, P.L.N. & Bussab, W.O. (2001) *Memorando técnico: o plano amostral do SAEB 2001.* Technical report submitted to the Instituto Nacional de Estudos e Pesquisas Educacionais, Brasília, Ministério da Educação.

Barbosa, M.L.d.O. & Fernandes, C. (2001) A escola brasileira faz diferença? Uma investigação dos efeitos da escola na proficiência em Matemática dos alunos da 4a série, in C. Franco (Ed.) *Promoção, ciclos e avaliação educacional*, pp. 155-172. Porto Alegre: Artmed.

Barbosa, M.E.F., Beltrao, K.I., Fariñas, M.N., Fernandes, C. & Santos, D. (2001) *Modelagem do Saeb – 99. Relatório Técnico.* Technical report submitted to the Instituto Nacional de Estudos e Pesquisas Educacionais, Brasília, Ministério da Educação.

Bonamino, A.M.C. (2002) Tempos de avaliação educacional; O SAEB, seus agentes, referências e tendências. Rio de Janeiro: Quartet Editora & Comunicação Ltda.

Bryk, A.S. & Raudenbush, S.W. (1992) *Hierarchical Linear Models: applications and data analysis methods.* Newbury Park: Sage.

Buchmann, C. (2002) Measuring Family Background in International Studies of Education: conceptual issues and methodological challenges, in A.C. Porter (Ed.) *Methodological Advances in Cross-National Surveys of Educational Achievement*, pp. 150-197. Washington, DC: National Academic Press.

Castro, M.H.G.d. (1999) *Education for the 21st Century: the challenge of quality and equity.* Brasília: MEC Instituto Nacional de Estudos e Pesquisas Educacionais INEP.

Coleman, J.S., Campbell, E.Q., Robson, C.F., McPartland, J. & Mood, A.M. (1966) *Equality of Educational Opportunity.* Washington, DC: Department of Education.

Crespo, M., Soares, J.F. & Mello e Souza, A. (2000) The Brazilian National Evaluation System of Basic Education: context, process and impact, *Studies in Educational Evaluation*, 26, pp. 105-125.

Darling-Hammond, L. (1999) *Teacher Quality and Student Achievement: a review of state policy evidence.* Seattle, WA: Center for the Study of Teaching and Policy, University of Washington. Available at: http://depts.washington.edu/ctpmail/DFs/LDH%5F1999.pdf

Franco, C. (2001) O SAEB: potencialidades, problemas e desafios, *Revista Brasileira de Educação*, 17, pp. 127-132.

Goldstein, H. (1995) *Multilevel Statistical Models.* London: E. Arnold; New York: Halsted Press.

Klein, R. & Fontanive, N.S. (1995) Avaliação em larga escala: uma proposta inovadora, *Em Aberto*, pp. 29-35.

Lee, V.E. (2000) Using Hierarchical Linear Modelling to Study Social Contexts: the case of school effects, *Educational Psychologist*, 35, pp. 125-141.

Lee, V.E., Bryk, A.S. & Smith, J. (1993) The organization of effective secondary schools, in J.A. Banks & L. Darling-Mammond (Eds) *Review of Research in Education*, pp. 171-276. Washington, DC: American Educational Research Association.

Locatelli, I. (2002) Construção de instrumentos para a avaliação em larga escala e indicadores de rendimento: o modelo do SAEB, *Estudos de Avaliação Educacional*, 25, pp. 3-21.

Organisation for Economic Cooperation and Development (OECD) (2001) *Knowledge and Skills for Life – first results from PISA 2000 – Education and Skills.* Paris: OECD Programme for International Student Assessment.

Podgursky, M. (2001) Flunking ETS, *Education Next Summer*, pp. 75-78. Available at: http://www.educationnext.org/20012/75.html

Rutter, M., Maughan, B., Mortimore, P., Ouston, J. & Smith, A. (1979) *Fifteen Thousand Hours: secondary schools and their effects on children.* Cambridge, MA: Harvard University Press.

Sammons, P., Hillman, J. & Mortimore, P. (1995) *Key Characteristics of Effective Schools: a review of school effectiveness research.* London: Office for Standards in Education; Institute of Education, University of London.

Soares, José Francisco & Alves, Maria Teresa Gonzaga (2003) Desigualdades Raciais no Sistema Brasileiro de Educação Básica, *Revista da Faculdade de Educação (USP)*, 29, pp. 147-165.

Soares, J.F., César, C.C. & Mambrini, J. (2001) Determinantes de desempenho dos alunos do ensino básico brasileiro: evidências do SAEB de 1997, in C. Franco (Ed.) *Avaliação, ciclos e promoção na educacão.* Porto Alegre: Artmed.

Torgenson, D. (1986) Between Knowledge and Politics: three faces of policy analysis, *Policy Sciences*, 19, pp. 33-59.

Willms, J.D. (2000) Monitoring School Performance for 'Standards-based Reform', *Evaluation in Education*, 14, pp. 237-253.

Willms, J.D. (2002) *Vulnerable Children.* Edmonton: University of Alberta Press.

Willms, J. D. & Somers, M.A. (2001) Family, Classroom, and School Effects on Children's Educational Outcomes in Latin America, *International Journal of School Effectiveness and Improvement*, 12(4), pp. 409-445.

The Reform of Secondary Education and the Implementation of ENEM in Brazil[1]

MARIA HELENA GUIMARÃES DE CASTRO & SERGIO TIEZZI

Introduction

Until recently, secondary education was considered to be the most forgotten education level in Brazilian public education policy. Regarded as a passage to higher education, until the mid-1980s secondary schooling was historically geared for the education of the elites. The expansion of secondary-level education was impeded by high repetition and truancy rates. As late as 1994, the backwardness of education was still immense in Brazil. Given the prevailing culture of repetition, little more than 50% of students completed the mandatory eight consecutive years of basic education, taking an average of 12 years to do so.

It can be said that the 1990s inaugurated a new cycle in Brazilian education with the democratisation of access to basic education and the extraordinary expansion of secondary-level education. This expansion was accompanied by the implementation of a far-reaching evaluation system and curricular reform. As all reform processes tend to be slow and progressive, it is still too early to assess the real impact of the changes introduced after 1999. The challenge ahead is to improve the quality of basic education, as shown by the results of assessments implemented in 1995-2002, particularly the National Secondary Education Examination (*Exame Nacional do Ensino Médio*, ENEM) discussed below.

It is worth noting that when a new government was inaugurated in 1995, more than 70% of the 4.9 million students enrolled in secondary school were attending night schools, as there was a greater supply of vacant classrooms in basic education schools for night-time studies. More than 50% of all enrolled students attended professional courses at secondary schools, although in reality these neither promoted professional development nor provided a good general education. In the good schools secondary education consisted of courses to prepare students for higher education entrance examinations, the *vestibular*. This was the great assessment 'exam' in Brazilian secondary education, and was practically restricted to the middle and higher classes. In general, Brazilians did not know what their students were learning or what capacities they were developing.

What Brazilians did know can be summarised thus: the curriculum was excessively encyclopaedic and elitist; schools were not prepared to face the new demands posed by the modern world; secondary school finalists were literally survivors of an exclusive selection process that was completely out of tune with the process of democratisation of knowledge required by the deep changes in contemporary society.

Placing secondary education on the agenda of educators and public policy makers was a task that could be put off no longer. The democratisation of access to secondary education, an aim already achieved by almost all other Latin American countries, became one of the key aims in the government's agenda. Equally important was the urgent need to elaborate a reform that, in addition to rethinking the curriculum, would also propose a new framework for education systems dominated by the individual states, in accordance with the federative principles that govern the Brazilian state.

A new Law of Guidelines for Education had been in the National Congress since the promulgation of the 1988 Federal Constitution. Its passage was slow and generated intense debates and polemics. At the end of 1996, after redemocratisation and a year of government under Fernando Henrique Cardoso, the country finally approved the general education law.

The Federal Constitution states as a principle 'the progressive universality of access to free secondary education'; in other words, secondary education should be progressively extended to all those who end primary education, even though attendance is not mandatory. Secondary education becomes part of the process that the country deems essential for the exercise of citizenship and for access to productive activities, including study for personal development; that is to say, education in its own right. Constitutional principles gained new meaning with the LBD (Law 9.394) approved in 1996, by making secondary education the last phase of basic education in Brazil, and giving young people the opportunity of gaining higher levels of education. The idea of universal education, which consisted of mandatory basic education, or primary education as it is called in many countries, went on to include nursery school and secondary education in accordance with the commitments adopted with the 1990 Declaration of Jomtien. The LBD incorporated the aims of Education for All, gave rise to the Education Decade and made Brazil one of the rare countries in the world that dared to incorporate the commitments of Jomtien into general education law.

Thus, a new panorama began to emerge in Brazil in the 1990s: as basic education became universal and consolidated, large contingents of finalists began to seek new future paths. Enrolment in secondary education is increasing, the supply of places in the public sector has increased at an extraordinary rate, the number of young people attending night school is falling, a new curriculum is taking hold, preparatory and professional secondary education (not the subject of this chapter) is being restructured and reorganised, and finally, a new system of evaluation, the ENEM, and the new curricular guidelines in particular, are now guiding the reform process.

This chapter looks at the implementation of the reform of secondary education and uses ENEM results to analyse the frontiers and challenges that must be addressed to attain completely universal access to basic education and to ensure the necessary level of quality.

Context

It must be remembered that at the beginning of the 1950s only 650,000 students out of a total population of more than 50 million people were enrolled in secondary school. In the 1960s, there was a timid expansion as a result of the implementation of a system to recognise the equivalency of secondary-level studies to aid professional and academic studies. However, it was only a formal equivalency, and did not create the conditions necessary to aid the professional development of students who might not want to engage in further study.

At the beginning of the 1970s, the law for the organisation of the Brazilian education system established that mandatory education would consist of eight sequential years, which added the first phase of secondary education to the already mandatory primary education. Thus, the legal opportunities for more years in basic education improved for the population as a whole as secondary education became a second cycle of schooling leading to professionalisation. In practice, the interpretation of the law and resulting arrangements ended up creating two types of secondary education: one to prepare people for professional life, and a propaedeutic one.

These changes led to a first wave of growth of secondary education by eliminating the examination taken to pass from the old primary level to the first cycle of secondary education. Thus, between 1970 and 1980, more than a million new students enrolled in secondary education. This growth was not sustained in the 1980s, however, and it was only in the 1990s that increased enrolment was observed again. The main causes for the interrupted growth of secondary education are the implementation of an erroneous secondary education model and the low quality of mandatory education, which resulted in high rates of repetition and a concomitant break in student flows. For the lowest income sectors, the big challenge was simply to reach the end of basic education successfully and few managed to achieve this.

The new wave of growth in enrolment in secondary education in the 1990s far outstripped the rate of growth observed in the 1970s. In 2002, there were more than 8.7 million students. At the peak of the first wave of growth in the 1970s, the participation of private schools in enrolment rates reached its highest level, accounting for more than 46% of the total enrolment. In 2000, the participation of the network of private schools fell below 15%, which shows that expansion was mainly a result of public sector efforts (see Table I).

Year	Total	Public					Private	%
		Total	%	Federal	State	Municipality		
1971	1,119,421	632,373	56.5	44,604	536,695	51,074	487,048	43.5
1980	2,819,182	1,508,261	53.5	86,125	1,324,682	97,454	1,310,921	46.5
1991	3,772,698	2,753,324	73.0	103,092	2,472,964	177,268	1,019,374	27.0
1995	5,374,831	4,210,346	78.3	113,312	3,808,326	288,708	1,164,485	21.7
1998	6,968,531	5,741,890	82.4	122,927	5,301,475	317,488	1,226,641	17.6
1999	7,769,199	6,544,835	84.2	121,673	6,141,907	281,255	1,224,364	15.8
2000	8,192,948	7,039,529	85.9	112,343	6,662,727	264,459	1,153,419	14.1
2001	8,398,008	7,283,528	86.7	88,537	6,962,330	232,661	1,114,480	13.3
% 1971/2001	650.2	1,051.8		98.5	1,197.3	355.5	128.8	
% 1995/2001	56.2	73.0		-21.9	82.8	-19.4	-4.3	

Source: Ministry of Education/INEP

Table I. Evolution of initial enrolments in secondary education by administrative dependency – Brazil 1971/2001.

Two factors can explain the extraordinary expansion of secondary education over the last decade. On the one hand, the progressive decline in high repetition rates led to improved student flows in basic education, generating a new demand for secondary-level education. On the other hand, the technological innovations of recent decades have introduced constant innovations in the production of goods and services and led to the emergence of very technologically advanced productive sectors. Products and processes become obsolete very quickly. New disequilibria linked to technical knowledge applied in the productive process are generated, which radically change the demands that society places on the education sector.

In order to ensure good conditions for education it is necessary to adapt constantly to rapid technological evolution. The rearticulation between education, work and technology constitutes a new challenge that demands more institutional flexibility, innovative partnerships and regularly updated teaching content.

In this context, secondary education becomes a central issue in current debates about education systems the world over, in the attempt to articulate the aims of preparing students for further and higher education, the exercise of citizenship, work and personal development.

The education model that shaped a certain limited period of people's lives is no longer useful today; education has to be frequently revisited and become a permanent process to develop new knowledge: a lifelong education. A general basic education is the new paradigm. All young people must develop the ability and competence to 'learn to learn' or to develop the capacity to think logically and critically and contextualise all acquired knowledge.

According to this new view, professional training must become a complement to basic education and be organised in a flexible way that permits constant updating to keep up with technical progress. Education cannot remain purely academic when one is dealing with students, many of whom do not enter higher education. The permanent education called for by society demands that education systems fulfil two basic conditions: universal secondary schooling and a wide-ranging and diversified system of post-secondary professional education that is flexible and open to everybody. This was the gist of the Brazilian reform.

Much has been done over the last decade to overcome the backwardness in Brazilian education accumulated by decades of negligence. Today, 97% of children between the ages of 7 and 14 are in school, and illiteracy rates have been falling rapidly. However, while basic education became practically universal, the same cannot be said of secondary education, as shown by the data presented below.

The biggest problem is the quality of education, which does not ensure basic learning levels. Part of the problem lies in the entry of new social groups to the school system. Teachers are often insufficiently trained to deal with students whose parents had little or no schooling or who come from broken homes. However, part of the problem is also a result of the lack of incentives to embark on a teaching career or to undergo initial and continued teacher training, as such courses are often inadequate for the promotion of improved standards of quality.

It is not only the federal government that is responsible for education, however. According to the constitution, the states and municipalities are also responsible for basic education: they are required to spend 25% of their budgets on education. As a whole, these resources are superior to those available to the federal government. Thus, a realistic policy must be based on a joint effort by these three spheres of government.

In Brazil, secondary education has always oscillated between two basic alternatives: providing education which is final and prepares people for professional life, or providing propaedeutic education that prepares people for higher education. This second option is further subdivided according to the course of graduate study that students want to follow. For those who have already passed the normal school-attending age, the only way to attain a higher level of education was through supplementary basic and secondary education, which effectively closed the door for professional or technical education.

The reform directed by the Ministry of Education in the period between 1995 and 2002 aimed to improve and expand secondary education in tune with the demands of the productive sector and with the developmental needs of the country, society and citizens. Unlike the vision that underpinned the 1971 LDB, the new LDB views secondary education as a way to ensure continuity of basic schooling, and aims to promote a general culture that focuses on understanding the world today, maintaining technical courses after or alongside propaedeutic education to meet the demands of a clientele that is already largely made up of workers.

The model inspiring the Brazilian education reform implemented by the new LDB passed on 20 December 1996, and other later decrees, was the new education paradigm that began to orient most secondary or professional education reforms around the world in the 1990s. Laws do not change reality, but they undeniably call for and guide change.

Level education/year	Initial enrolments	Completions	Gross enrolment rate	Net enrolment rate
Secondary education				
1970	1,119,421	–	–	–
1980	28,191,824	545,643	33.3	14.3
1991	3,772,698	666,334	40.8	17.6
1994	4,932,552	917,298	47.6	20.8
1998	6,968,531	1,535,943	68.1	31.8
2002	8,710,584	1,853,343*	74.8	32.6

*completions 2001.

Table II. Growth in secondary education.
Source: Ministry of Education/INEP.

In Brazil, technical-professional education was historically undertaken by middle-class sectors with the intention to enter higher education rather than the job market. Because the best technical schools were federal institutions, which offered free general as well as technical education, they ended up becoming preparatory courses for higher education. Thus, they lost the students that were really interested in learning a profession, and the job market found it difficult to find qualified professionals.

A very substantive element of the reform was that professional education became independent of secondary education and a complementary part of basic education; in other words, professional education no longer replaces or competes with basic education.[2] The LDB also established that secondary education could be undertaken alongside technical professional education. This called for and continues to demand an enormous governmental and social effort to increase options for post-secondary studies.

Thus, the secondary level education reform, whose implementation began in 1999, is based on a set of policies that focus on four key aims:

- expanding the system to attain universality progressively;
- redefining the role of secondary education in the education process as a whole;
- improving supply; and
- improving the quality of education.

The Growth of Secondary Education

Secondary education in Brazil has expanded immensely over the last decade, after almost two decades of vegetative growth that directly accompanied the expansion of higher education. It was the level of education that grew the most, overtaken only by secondary-level supplementary education.

The numbers are eloquent: according to the School Census of the Ministry of Education, in 2002, around 8.7 million students were enrolled in secondary education, more than double the number of students enrolled at the beginning of the 1990s. Between 1994 and 2002, there were 3.7 million new enrolments in regular secondary education, after 14 years of vegetative growth. From 1980 to 1994, only 1.8 million new enrolments were added to those already in existence. The number of students completing this level of education also increased. From 1991 to 1994, the number of finalists had increased by 40%, from 660,000 to 917,000. From 1994, the system promoted better student flows, so that by 2001 there were 1.8 million finalists.

However, an even greater number of students found it difficult to conclude their secondary-level studies. Over the last few years, students who are behind in their studies and over 18 years old, and those who had to abandon their studies, are increasingly seeking youth and adult education. According to the law, by taking an official examination, a young person can obtain a finalist's certificate by undertaking a faster, more condensed version of preparatory courses (the so-called supplementary or *supletivo* courses). Different courses to educate young people and adults were put on offer mainly by civil society, non-governmental organisations, religious communities and businesses.

Enrolment for this kind of education practically tripled in 1995-2001. The number of successful finalists also increased. In 1995, student flow calculations estimated that 71 out of every 100 people leaving school were successful finalists. The estimates for 1999 indicate an expected rate of 78 per 100 school-leavers.

Increased demand is a result of the progressive increase in basic education finalists on the one hand, and on the other, a job market that is ever more limited and demanding in terms of required educational qualifications, and pushes youths and their families to prolong investment in education, particularly in large urban centres and in the more developed states of the country.

The data on education in Brazil in 2001 published by the National Institute of Educational Studies and Research (Instituto Nacional de Estudos e Pesquisas Educacionais, INEP), already makes it possible to identify a tendency for improved student performance in basic, including secondary, education. There was a positive evolution in the rate of student passes, from 71.6 to 75.8% between 1996 and 2000, and a decline in the number of failures from 9.5 to 7.5% over the same period. The number of students who abandon their studies has also declined, falling from 18.9 to 16.7% over the

95

same period. Although the improvement reflects an increase in the number of successful basic education finalists, entering secondary level education is still a big challenge for most young people (Abramovay & Castro, 2003, pp. 25-26).

Another important element to highlight is that the increase in school attendance occurred mainly in the public municipal or state-level school network. In 1985-97, the rate of growth of both was 174% and 161%, respectively, while for the private school network it was 26.2%.

In addition to the pressure exerted by a job market that now requires secondary-level education as a qualification for entry, this expansion can be explained by four main factors:

- the positive results of a set of policies linked to the improved functioning of basic education;
- an emphasis on programmes to combat repetition rates and improve student flows;
- the reform of secondary education and policies implemented to strengthen secondary education as a final stage of basic education;
- the implementation of ENEM from 1998 onwards.

The new LDB of 1996 proposed the development of new curricular guidelines and an assessment system to evaluate the education system as instruments to assist the implementation of a richer and more analytical kind of education. This culminated in the National Curricular Parameters for Secondary Education (*Parâmetros Curriculares Nacionais*, PCN), and the institution of the ENEM.

The New Curricular Guidelines

The first step in the reform was the inclusion of secondary-level schooling in basic education; in other words, the education available to all citizens had to be the educational foundation necessary to exercise citizenship. For this to work, professional education had to become a complement to basic education so that education for work did not become confused with professional education. In basic education, the contextual development of competences, abilities and contents had to constitute a basic preparation for work although it was not, strictly speaking, professional.

Two key ideas began to orient the policies of the government: improving the quality of basic education for everyone and diversifying post-basic education. As the final stage of basic education, secondary-level schooling had to prepare young people to enter the job market as well as to engage in further study, but its main aim was to educate people for citizenship.

In order to fulfil this aim, the reform emphasised the contextualisation of learning and the pertinence of contents and competences to be developed by schools. A pluralistic and diversified group of consultants, made up of specialists from various universities, state university professors, school directors, education secretaries and technical teams from the states, undertook to identify good practice, articulate the vision of the new curriculum, discuss the obstacles to financing the expansion of the system, and elaborate a strategic plan to better equip the education networks under the aegis of the states of the federation that is Brazil.

The involvement of the media in the process leading up to the reform was very relevant. There were constant interviews in the press, on the radio and television, an agenda of regional meetings throughout the country was defined, and there was articulation with the unions in 1995-97. At the end of 1997, a proposal of National Curricular Guidelines for Secondary Education was submitted to the National Education Council (Conselho Nacional de Educaçâo, CNE), although the proposal went beyond what is normally understood as curricular reform, because it addressed organisational and school management issues. The debate and public meetings at the CNE occurred throughout 1998 and in 1999 the Ministry of Education finally approved the guidelines.

In 1998, the CNE legalised the National Curricular Guidelines for Secondary Education (Resolution CEB/CNE no. 03/98), on the basis of the CEB/CNE Report no. 15/98. The PCN, a base document on the basic content of school subjects, are based on the Guidelines. The PCN are a common point of reference for the whole country, but they can be adapted to suit the characteristics of each region.

The new parameters for secondary education elaborated by the group of specialists hired by the Ministry of Education are based essentially on an articulation between students' various life contexts and basic competences and abilities, rather than on the accumulation of information. Understood as a general education, the new secondary education articulates a strong scientific and technological component with humanism, making it possible for schools to create various different possible paths when building the curriculum. The new secondary education should not be confused with professional education, which can be undertaken in specialised schools or in businesses without replacing the basic education offered by secondary-level schooling. In light of the above, the reform is based on three elements:

- *flexibility*, to meet the needs of different people and situations of change that characterise the knowledge-based society;
- *diversity*, which ensures that attention is paid to the needs of different groups in different areas and in different age groups;
- *putting knowledge in context*, which, by guaranteeing a common base for the national curriculum, also allows for the diversification of paths of curricular grids and the constitution of meanings that make sense of the learning process.

What does this mean in practice? Until the late 1970s, professional secondary education had to prepare people to be able to use machinery and direct production processes. The policy of turning part of secondary education into professional education arose from this. In the late 1990s, because of the 'information technology revolution', learning content was always changing, demanding of students the 'acquisition of basic knowledge, scientific training, and a capacity to use different technologies related to the area of activity' (Ministério da Educação, 2002, p. 15).

The proposals in this initiative are based on the analysis of the growth of enrolment in secondary education, taking into consideration that this growth affects state and night schools in particular, and therefore reflects the entry of new actors, including workers, into secondary-level education. According to Guiomar Namo de Mello, the reporter of Report no. 15 of the CNE, in order to welcome this new contingent – the influx of which will tend to increase even more over the next few years – secondary education cannot be just a passage to higher education but must be considered as basic education, offering basic competencies and life skills for all citizens. It is important as preparation for life and all kinds of work. Because it is basic, the point of reference will be the changing demands of the job market, which explains the importance of the capacity for continued learning; it is not aimed at those who are already in the job market, or who will enter it soon (Mello, 1998, p. 15). It was necessary to go beyond the two historical alternatives – academic or professional – to create a model able to take into account the necessary cognitive competences to continue learning, socialising, producing, and defining an individual identity. As many professions may cease to exist in the coming years and many others may be created, it is necessary to develop flexibility, creativity, polyvalency, and the capacity for continued learning.

The introduction to the PCN highlights that a curriculum must define contents and strategies to prepare citizens to develop knowledge in the three basic areas of human activity: social life (political relations), productive activity (work relations) and subjective experience (generation of symbols). These are the four premises 'noted by UNESCO as structural elements for education in contemporary society: learning to know ... learning to do ... learning to live ... learning to be' (Ministério da Educação, 2002, p. 15). Based on these premises the parameters propose a secondary education curriculum that is responsible for the general education of the student, while attributing meaning to school knowledge, stimulating the development of affective and cognitive competences such as the capacity to research, think logically, argue, work in a team, and develop ethical values like tolerance, generosity and respect for others. It also aims to be creative and learn to learn continuously through a learning and teaching process that is contextualised rather than compartmentalised and which is not based on the quantity of knowledge imparted or a mere exercise in learning by rote.

To meet these demands, the PCN put forward basic criteria based on two pillars: the Common National Foundation and the Diversified Section. The Common National Foundation must prepare students to seek, generate and know how to use information to solve concrete problems in the production of goods and services, because 'any competence required to exercise a profession, be it psycho-motor, socio-affective or cognitive, is a refinement of basic competences. This general education permits the development of competences that will manifest themselves as basic, technical or management abilities' (pp. 30-31). It is divided into the following areas: language, codes and their categories, natural sciences, mathematics and its technologies, human sciences and its technologies. The diversified section of the curriculum must take into account the social, cultural and economic characteristics of regional and local environments and of its clientele. Finally, the PCN very strongly recommends that all education should have an interdisciplinary and integrated focus: thus, languages, philosophy, the natural and human sciences and technologies must be considered as a whole, in order to overcome the separate and compartmentalised treatment that characterises school education dominated by separate specialisations. The context in which students live should also be taken into account, not as a restriction but rather to 'generate the capacity to understand and intervene in real life' (p. 36).

To achieve these aims, secondary education must be understood as a unitary modality that contemplates diversity and flexibility, so that the adoption of the new curriculum is concomitantly:

- *diversified* in terms of content and selected contexts, with a focus on areas of knowledge that respond to the needs of the production of goods, services, and knowledge of community life and individuals;
- *unified* in terms of cognitive, affective and social abilities, which constitute the basis of diversified contents, in order to guarantee a general common education for all.

Thus, professional education is considered as a complement to secondary education, and a complement to all basic education, demanding differentiated levels of schooling for different levels of qualification. The proper linkage between basic preparation for work offered by secondary education, and professional education, which aims to prepare people to exercise specific tasks at work at the technical or higher level, must be obtained by further study or directly at work.

The Search for Quality

One of the major challenges for the reform of secondary education in Brazil is harmonising the need to expand supply and efforts to ensure improved quality. There is an accelerated process of massification of secondary education under way, and improved quality must accompany the process of inclusion of historically excluded social groups. The indicators show that the efficiency of the system has improved: enrolment increased by 71% in 1994-2001; the number of finalists increased by 102% over the same period; the net enrolment rate of people between 15 and 17 years of age has increased from 16% in 1994 to 33% in 2001. Thus, there has been a doubling of the enrolment of youths in the right age group in just eight years.

The countries that have recently witnessed improvements in the performance of their students, like South Korea, promoted the expansion of the system and mass inclusion in secondary schools in the 1970s and later invested heavily in improved quality. It is, therefore, an enormous challenge to expand and ensure quality, a process that occurred over a period of two decades in developed countries.

The big challenge is to improve the pedagogical process in schools, with government authorities acting to promote and offer technical assistance to schools. This requires improved pedagogical practice in the classroom, a strong emphasis on programmes for ongoing teacher training and improved school management so as to promote progressive school autonomy in pedagogical, administrative and financial terms.

Better management means innovative management of the classroom and school administration, and improved management of the systems' intermediary organs. The basis for innovative pedagogical action is ongoing teacher training to serve teachers, and the development of resources and methodologies that suit the new curricular vision. Innovative management of schools also depends on the continued training of directors and school administrators, with the development of a culture of school planning, institutional evaluation and student learning. In this sense, Brazilian public schools are still very far from attaining the aims of the proposed reform.

Because of this, the MEC produced, published and distributed the PCN together with legal texts and a series of reference materials to support teachers. A series of programmes for secondary schools was produced, which were transmitted daily by School-TV (TV-Escola), the Ministry of Education television channel, which sought to offer schools a toolbox to implement the reform. This programming sought to fulfil three main aims: support the work of the teacher in the classroom; make available up-to-date materials and information to support the training of teachers and school managers; and disseminate the ideas behind the reform emphasising interdisciplinary and integrated learning.

The evaluation of secondary education through the ENEM and the National Evaluation System for Basic Education (*Sistema Nacional de Avaliação da Educação Básica*, SAEB) is also a central aspect of the reform and policy to promote improved quality. The ENEM, the mechanism to assess individuals after 11 years of schooling, seeks to implement the principles and guidelines of the reform of secondary education through an essay and an objective test. The SAEB promotes and evaluates the education system and identifies the main obstacles to the implementation of the reform, so that subsidies for improved education quality policies can be determined. The ENEM produces a wide-ranging diagnosis of student profiles, and the SAEB a profound diagnosis of systems of education, the organisational matrix of schools and a detailed profile of the teachers and administrators in the system.

The National Secondary Education Examination (ENEM)

The ENEM has been a valuable instrument in the policy to implement the reform of secondary education, disseminating its aims intensively throughout Brazil. The ENEM emphasises the evaluation of the profile of finalists emerging from this education level. Its main objective is to offer an assessment of student performance at the end of basic schooling, according to a structure of competences associated with disciplinary contents that the student has hopefully absorbed to meet the growing challenges of modern life.

The importance of a more analytically rich education content that is based on the development of logical thinking and the capacity to learn to know is at the heart of the ENEM, which seeks to gradually eliminate the huge curriculum and allow secondary schools to concentrate on what is important to teach. Thus, the school must allow students to develop more general language structures, the sciences, arts and philosophy in a learning dynamic that allows young people to mobilise these traditional areas of knowledge to seek creative solutions for day-to-day problems. After all, the value of education does not lie in the storage of a lot of information or the memorisation of facts, but in the development of mental structures that allow people and adults to solve new problems using well-established scientific theories.

The ENEM, which thousands of young students use to assess themselves, also assesses how far schools respond to the challenges posed by society, both in terms of the full exercise of citizenship and of offering adequate training for higher education, guided by the idea of ongoing education. By determining a set of competences and abilities that served as a point of reference for evaluation, the ENEM established for the first time in Brazil a benchmark for basic education finalists, in much the same way that other international examinations, like the Scholastic Aptitude Test in the USA or the Baccalaureate in France, among others, do.

In this sense, the ENEM allows the government to pinpoint and understand the dimension of the gaps that weaken the process of educating young people and make more difficult their individual fulfilment and insertion into society's production process. On the other hand, as an instrument of public policy, it seeks direct assistance from its target public to assess the guidelines to be followed.

The conceptual structure of the ENEM assessment has been improving since its first application in 1998, based on the key point of articulating the concept of basic education with citizenship. It is a single, multidisciplinary test consisting of an essay and 63 objective questions, based on a matrix of five competences and 21 abilities. Thus, unlike most examinations, it is not divided into areas of study. The ENEM follows the guidelines of the reform of secondary education and takes into account the guidelines of the parameters of the secondary education curriculum, demonstrating that it is possible to work with different contents in a trans-disciplinary way, and emphasising learning through the resolution of problems, by using topics that are part of the personal lives of students, the social life of the school and its context. The five areas of competence evaluated by the ENEM consider:

- fluency in Portuguese, and in the mathematical, artistic and scientific languages;
- use of concepts to understand natural phenomena, historical–geographic processes, technological production and artistic manifestations;
- use of data and information to make decisions in problematic situations;
- the construction of consistent arguments;
- the capacity to elaborate proposals to intervene in reality, respecting human values and taking the sociocultural diversity of the country into account.

Between 1998 and the fifth ENEM in 2002, 3.3 million students had been evaluated. The ENEM, which is voluntary and free of charge for students leaving public schools, is covering an increasing number of municipalities where examinations are held, with a view of facilitating access for those who are ending secondary education throughout the country.

The ENEM has made it possible to gain a more palpable understanding of the pillars structuring secondary education reform: an interdisciplinary approach, putting learning into context and solving problems; it has allowed teachers and education specialists to visualise clearly, the desired performance of young people as is required by each of the issues. In that sense, it is a powerful instrument to induce change in so far as it expresses what should be taught through what it assesses.

One of the main results of this has been the acceptance of the voluntary examination by schools through teachers and students. The ENEM is now considered an important element to understand the competences of secondary school finalists and, as Table III shows, the number of universities and other higher education institutions that make use of its results as a criterion for the selection of the candidates for graduate study is increasing. This observation leads us to the problem of entering higher education.

> The explicit strategy of the Ministry of Education was to attempt to encourage higher education establishments to review their entry exam[ination] (vestibular), either by taking ENEM scores into account when selecting candidates, or by creating tests in the spirit of ENEM. In that sense, the exam[ination] aims to evolve in a critical area, which is the fact that the process of selection for higher education has an enormous influence over what actually

happens in secondary education. (Abramovay & Castro, 2003, p. 220)

The self-exclusion of these students (secondary education finalists) is notorious in the most competitive entrance exams (vestibulares). At Unicamp, for example, only about 30% of final year public secondary school students register, although these represent more than 80% of enrolments from that level of education in the state of São Paulo. The three universities of the state of São Paulo decided to adopt the ENEM from 1999 onwards as a part of entry policy in order to make it possible to diminish the self-exclusion of candidates who often are not aware of the competences developed during basic education to the vestibular; in order to contribute to improve self-esteem; in order to create incentives to take an exam that is nationwide and covers the very large universe of students finishing basic education; and finally, taking into consideration the possibility of contributing to improving the instrument of evaluation in terms of content and form. (Cortelazzo, 2001, p. 7)

Thus, although higher education institutions decide autonomously whether and how to use ENEM results, and although the ENEM is not a prerequisite to obtain a degree, this is an examination that is valued by the Ministry of Education and by students, particularly in so far as it has gained some weight in the process of entering higher education.

Year	Number of higher education institutions that use the ENEM*	Number of municipalities that host the examination	Number enrolled in the examination
1998	1	184	115,575
1999	93	162	315,960
2000	199	187	352,487
2001	296	277	1,200,883
2002	338	600	1,327,577
Total participants			3,312,482

*The higher education institutions that already use the results of the examination as a selection criterion for their graduate courses.

Table III. Use of the National Examination of Secondary Education – ENEM. Source: Ministry of Education/INEP.

With the coverage obtained in 2002, it was possible to gain a nationwide view of the perception of young secondary school finalists of their school experience, the nature of the schools they attended and their opinions about the relationships developed in the context of learning and school socialisation. The 2002 ENEM sought to widen its understanding of the limits on and possibilities open to young Brazilians by more deeply identifying their values, opinions and attitudes. In this sense, the aim was to draw a map of their interests and expectations, the context in which their personal relations occur and the ways in which they enter the public debate. A pedagogical project that hopes to raise the quality of citizenship must be based on permanent and updated knowledge of the views and demands of people and thus complement the virtuous cycle of the schoolteachers' and schools' work with students.

The Most Significant ENEM Results Observed

Performance in ENEM is measured according to five basic competences: language fluency, understanding of phenomena, confronting situations and problems, building arguments and elaborating proposals to deal with real-life issues.

Since it was first administered, the examination has highlighted comprehensive reading as a basic competence that affects all the others both through the essay and the objective section. A more sophisticated reading ability presupposes the use of various psycho-linguistic mechanisms. The main one is the understanding of language – fluency in the official written language, the absence of which is detrimental for all other subjects, although it does not ensure comprehensive reading of itself. After all, 'reading the world' means fluent abilities and strategies to process information, including mathematical, scientific languages, texts with diagrams, graphics, tables, charges; in sum, the various kinds of complex social codes that are increasingly a part of and manifest in language.

Textual knowledge complements linguistic knowledge. The essay and objective part of the examination is organised into discussion texts, the organisation and structure of which the reader must master. The central element of the discussion text is the topic, which is presented through logical relationships – premises and conclusions, cause and effect, and so on. The difficulty that participants may have with managing the text probably reflects difficulties in comprehensive reading.

'Knowledge of the world' is another aspect of comprehensive reading and links up with the reader's background and its use in constructing the read text's meaning. This background articulates personal, interpersonal and social knowledge that is built up over various moments in life, and in the case of ENEM, evidenced mainly in a classroom situation. For the essay, various stimulating texts for reflection are provided to provoke an understanding of the topic through a reading process that triggers this 'knowledge of the world'.

In 2002, the examination results showed the same tendencies observed in previous years, which is precisely the absence of fluency in reading comprehension that seems to have been the main reason for the participants' weak performance. Generally speaking, one observes that the participants understand the essay topic but for the most part are unable to transpose the key ideas abstracted from the stimulating texts into their own essays. One observes the mere transposition of the stimulating texts, without an individual interpretation of the topic according to each participant's background. This was probably the case because the topic called for knowledge of different areas and specific languages and a capacity to establish relationships between the latter and the main focus on the texts.

On the one hand, traditional division of the school curriculum into separate areas of study probably increased the difficulty of interdisciplinary comprehension of the ENEM essay, which shows that the aim of the curricular reform has yet to be achieved. On the other hand, the participants showed a lot of difficulty in reading and in interrelating different stimulating texts. Those who understood the proposed essay topic were unable to transcend the interpretative/reproductive level because when selecting the information to argue the topic, they simply collated facts, data, arguments or opinions that appeared in the stimulating texts. Only around 13% undertook the comprehensive process, both reading the proposal and transposing it into their essays.

The difficulty with reading in the objective part of the test was also largely the main factor responsible for low student performance. According to the Pedagogical Report of the ENEM in 2002:

> The absence of reading comprehension fluency was possibly the cause of the level of performance attained. Only a superficial and fragmented reading can explain a choice of answers that reveals the reading of graphics dissociated with the proposal, alternative choices dissociated from the context, a difficulty in establishing relationships between languages expressed in tables, formulas, graphics, the choice of contradictory and mutually exclusive statements and arguments. (INEP, 2002a, p. 192)

Reading comprehension calls for students to demonstrate various abilities: word recognition, an understanding of grammatical and semantic relationships between words, and linking words and concepts through inference. It is likely that the non-assimilation of the basic content that is typical of the curriculum that should be in place for basic education, linked with the absence of reading habits, led to a superficial and fragmented reading of the questions, which seems then to have led to the choice of erroneous answers in the objective part of the test. The same kind of difficulty led to the elaboration of essays that while adequate in terms of the proposed topics, presented structural problems.

It should be remembered that in 2002 more than 73% of ENEM participants underwent secondary education within the state system. In 2001, the percentage was 66%. This means that the profile of the students assessed is closer to the profile of secondary school finalists from the state system than of students preparing to enter higher education.

The ENEM 2002 Results

The global average for the essay in the 2002 examination was 54.31 points. Most of the participants (72%) scored between 40 and 70 points and were classified as *Regular* to *Good*. A further 16% scored between 0 and 40, which was considered *Insufficient* to *Regular*. The 12% of the students scoring the highest points between 70 and 100 were graded as *Good* to *Excellent*. In 2001 the average for the essay was 52.58.

The topic chosen for ENEM 2002 – *The Right to Vote: how to make this conquest a means to promote the social transformations that Brazil needs?* – proved to be very current and was well received by the participants. Because Brazil was in the middle of an election year, with all the dissemination and debate that this involves, a greater number of participants were able to perform more satisfactorily. For this topic, participants did not have to resort to specific contents in various scientific areas and discussed the proposed topic with greater ease.

Table IV and Figure 1 present data on participants' performance, indicating the global average for the essay and each area of competence.

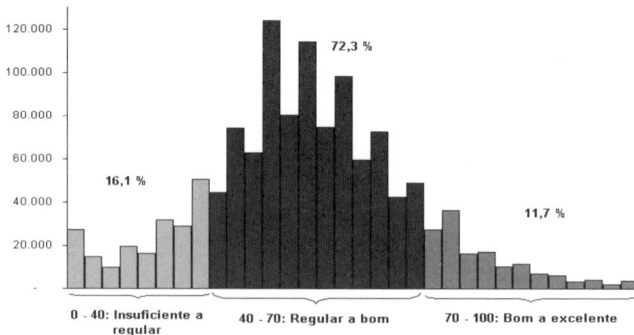

Key: 0-40: insufficient to regular; 40-70: regular to good; 70-100: good to excellent.

Figure 1. ENEM 2002: Distribution of global notes in the writing.

From among the five competences assessed (see Table IV) the participants did best in Competence I, which includes fluency in formal written language (relevance of the text, grammar and orthography), with an average 61.03 points. For this competence, 50% were *Regular* to *Good,* and 38.5% were graded *Good* to *Excellent*. The lowest average was for Competence III (selecting, relating, organising and interpreting facts, opinions, and arguments to defend a point of view) with 51.64 points; 60% of participants were classed as *Regular* to *Good* and 15.5% *Good* to *Excellent*. A pedagogical analysis of this competence reveals that most of the participants merely reproduced the arguments presented in the essay proposal.

	Mean score
Overall results	54.31
Competency I	61.03
Competency II	52.99
Competency II	51.64
Competency IV	54.14
Competency V	51.78

Table IV. Overall performance in the essay.

The objective part of the test is made up of 63 questions all worth the same number of points, graded on a scale from 0 to 100 points, which yields a total score corresponding to the sum of the points for each correct answer. Further, points are given to each of the five assessed competences according to the same scale.

For the objective part of the ENEM, which attained an average score of 34.13, 74% of the participants were graded *Insufficient* to *Regular*. A further 23.5% scoring between 40 and 70 were graded *Regular* to *Good*. The highest points were scored by 2.5% of the students, who were graded *Good* to *Excellent* (Figure 2). In 2001, the overall average for the objective part of the test was 40.56, a little above the result for 2002.

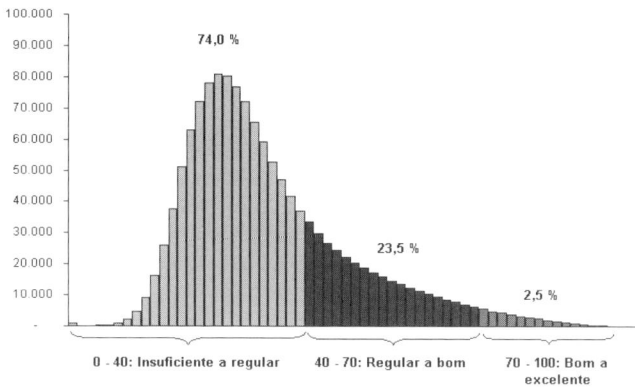

Key: 0-40: insufficient to regular; 40-70: regular to good; 70-100: good to excellent.

Figure 2. ENEM 2002: main results – overall performance in multiple choice.

107

The necessary knowledge for the participant to answer 63 multiple-choice questions is evaluated according to the five basic competences and 21 abilities. Competence II (understanding phenomena) attained the highest percentage score of 35.14%. Competency III (confronting problematic situations) scored a lower average, 32.26. The average in each of the five competences was mostly *Insufficient* to *Regular*, the same as the general average for the objective part of the test (see Figure 2). The essay and multiple-choice questions both took the same five components into account, making the student undergo two major tasks: one expressed through writing and another through reading; in other words, the participant had to discuss the proposed topic in the first part and read the questions and choose an answer from among five alternative responses in the second part. The practice of writing and reading is, like any other, based on the use of two cognitive systems: that which permits understanding and that which permits execution. The reading and writing competences assessed by the test are complementary and cannot be disassociated, and express the performance potential for the same five structural competences.

The kinds of school attended, the age of the participant, their income level and their parents' levels of education are factors that condition the performance of ENEM participants. These factors are interrelated and must be understood within a wider context. Students from higher income families normally have more educated parents and also have easier access to cultural goods such as books, computers, cinema and travel.

	Mean
Overall results	34.13
Competency I	33.72
Competency II	35.14
Competency III	32.26
Competency IV	34.55
Competency V	33.37

Table V. ENEM 2002: main results – overall multiple choice.

Generally speaking, the higher the income bracket and parents' education, the better the results. Young people from families with up to one minimum wage have an average performance of 26.01 for the objective part of the test, while participants with an income above 50 minimum wages get 52.67, as shown in Tables VI, VII and VIII. The association between low parental education levels and the performance of students was also highlighted by the 2000 International Programme for Student Evaluation (*Programa Internactional de Avaliação de Estudantes*, PISA) evaluation (OECD, 2001).

Family wealth	Multiple choice	Essay
Up to 1 minimum wage (*)	26.01	47.69
1 to 2 m.w.	28.28	50.54
2 to 5 m.w.	32.44	54.10
5 to 10 m.w.	38.15	57.57
10 to 30 m.w.	47.01	62.31
30 to 50 m.w.	51.80	64.54
More than 50 m.w.	52.67	64.34

Table VI. ENEM 2002: main results – performance x associated factors, average between multiple choice and essay.

Mother's education	Multiple choice	Essay
No schooling	26.36	47.28
First to fourth grade (primary education)	29.16	51.26
Fifth to eighth grade (primary education)	31.53	53.15
Incomplete upper secondary	34.29	55.21
Complete upper secondary	37.51	57.50
Incomplete tertiary education	42.78	60.35
Complete tertiary education	47.94	62.76
Post-graduation	48.60	63.58

Table VII. ENEM 2002: main results – performance x associated factors, mean scores for multiple choice and essay.

Mother's education	Multiple choice	Essay
No schooling	26.36	47.28
First to fourth grade (primary education)	29.16	51.26
Fifth to eighth grade (primary education)	31.53	53.15
Incomplete upper secondary	34.29	55.21
Complete upper secondary	37.51	57.50
Incomplete tertiary education	42.78	60.35
Complete tertiary education	47.94	62.76
Post-graduation	48.60	63.58

Table VIII. ENEM 2002: main results – performance x associated factors, mean scores for multiple choice and essay.

Some private schools do better than state schools, both in the essay and the objective part of the test. Students attending private schools obtained an average of 63.03 for the essay and 47.22 for the objective test. The averages for state school students were 52.10 and 30.39 for the essay and the objective test, respectively (Table IX).

Mother's education	Multiple choice	Essay
Public institutions only	30.39	52.10
Private and public institutions	36.77	56.42

Table IX. ENEM 2002: main results – performance x associated factors, mean scores for multiple choice and essay.

Another factor that deserves to be emphasised is the mismatch between the age of students and the number of years it takes to complete basic education (the so-called *série escolar*). Participants that undertook basic education in 11 years without repeating any years obtained the best averages in the objective test and the essay: 38.85 and 54.57, respectively. Some 51% of all participants have a mismatched record for basic education, secondary education, or both. Because this problem is so widespread, it has a negative impact on average performance levels, both among those who studied in state schools and those attending private schools, as the results of PISA and SAEB also show (INEP, 2002b).

School type	Years in school		Average	
	Basic education	Secondary education	Multiple choice	Essay
Public institution	8 years	3 years	33.58	55.82
	9 years	4 years	28.81	50.12
Private institution	8 years	3 years	50.39	64.93
	9 years	4 years	37.39	56.59

Table X. ENEM 2002: main results – performance x associated factors, average between multiple choice and essay.

The ENEM 2002 results match perfectly with the results of PISA, which is coordinated by the OECD in 32 countries and assesses education performance in a comparative perspective through a methodology that permits the evaluation of capacities and knowledge of 15 year-olds independently of the number of years spent in basic education. In Brazil, a representative sample of 4893 students between the ages of 15 and 16 of the country's public and private education systems were tested (Castro, 2003). Students were submitted to a test involving a wide range of tasks presented through different texts, ranging from the recovery of information to the demonstration of general comprehension, text interpretation and reflection on the content and characteristics of texts. The texts used included prose passages and documents such as lists, forms, graphics and diagrams.

The theoretical framework used for PISA is based on a wide-ranging concept of literacy that is also the foundation of the educational philosophy of the PCN and of the curricular proposals of Brazilian states and municipalities. This concept of literacy is defined as the capacity of an individual to master writing and its use in various circumstances of daily life.

110

According to the PCN, the proficient reading and production of texts –of various kinds and covering the most varied topics – is the most significant indicator of good linguistic performance and literacy.

The results of PISA in Brazil confirm the reading and text producing difficulties of Brazilian students, a fact already noted by other Brazilian tests, not only ENEM, as seen above, but also by the SAEB. These two national systems of evaluation have provided the state and municipal education secretaries with quite a detailed diagnosis of students' performance, making them valuable instruments in Brazilian educational policy.

There are some issues that should be highlighted, although none of them minimise the precarious situation in terms of reading and text production in Brazilian schools. First, the results of PISA should take the number of years spent in basic education (the *série cursada* variable) into account, as this appears to be a determining factor in performance in the Brazilian case. Only half of the population in the reference sample for Brazil was in secondary education, while practically all the 15 year-olds in other OECD countries were already in secondary education and had undergone an average of 10 years of schooling. Thus, overlong school careers can be characterised as a typically Brazilian variable. For this reason, Brazil recalculated performance averages without taking this variable into account. It was possible to observe that the level of proficiency of 15 year-olds in the correct school year is higher than the OECD ranking.

The impact of the sociocultural level of students on reading proficiency is also important, although this is not the only variable that explains the results. Among the countries participating in PISA, Brazil has the lowest GDP per capita and the highest income distribution inequality.

In the Brazilian case, the most important factor that explains the student performance is certainly the age–*série escolar* mismatch. In the three assessments mentioned – ENEM, SAEB and PISA – the longer the school career resulting from repeated years, the worse the performance of students, independently of the contents and series evaluated.

Conclusion: new challenges

All of the above shows that assessing both basic and higher education in Brazil plays a central role in education system reform strategy and in raising levels of quality. Ignoring the contribution of evaluation processes in the monitoring of policies would be a step backwards of incommensurable magnitude. Until the mid-1990s there was not even an awareness of the dimension of the problem. The progress made to date has been greatly assisted by the new culture of evaluation that began to gain ground in the country from the 1990s onwards, although there are various other challenges to be addressed. The production of reliable, competent information that is committed to the public interest is an indispensable requirement if Brazil is to continue paving the way for the much-desired aim of quality education for all.

Statistics and planning should give technical support to make that project viable. Today, there is an enormous amount of reliable information about education in Brazil. Evaluation mechanisms like ENEM and SAAB are essential to ensure increased efficiency and equity in the education system. The time has come to use them to shape school careers as a whole, so that basic education is viewed as a whole and not just as isolated phases or levels.

It is necessary to change the culture of the use of information on education so that public policy decisions do not just express the political will of the nucleus in power. The less that policy is fed by information, the more vulnerable it becomes to the pressure of political or corporate interests. It is also necessary to disseminate the Curricular Guidelines for Secondary Education geared to educate the individual, to guarantee basic preparation for the integration of the individual into the world of work.

Following progress with attaining universality, it is necessary to keep all students that are in basic education today in the educational system for at least a further three years, after they have concluded the eighth grade. It was only just before the start of 2000 that the country managed to make basic education universal. The minimum goal is now to avoid losing any students until they have completed the basic education provided for by the Constitution and the new LDB. We know that in contemporary societies it is also necessary to fix a minimum level of schooling for the population as a whole, independently of income or other potentially constraining factors.

Given the improvement in enrolment numbers in Brazil over the last eight years, it is necessary to find out how far this is accompanied by improvements in the quality of education. Over the last few years, Brazil has had to deal with the issues of quantity and quality practically simultaneously. Suffice it to remember that for the population between 18 and 24 years of age, the number of enrolments in higher education independently of age is only 15%, and the liquid rate of enrolment in secondary education is no more than 33%. In 1998, total public spending on education reached 5.2% of GDP, well above that of Argentina, Mexico or South Korea. We are talking about a situation of exponential multiplication of needs or having to provide for nearly 60 million students distributed throughout the school system. This is a population that is practically the size of the French population and almost double that of Argentina.

Addressing that challenge means promoting the capacity to read and understand texts. As the Pedagogical Report of the ENEM expressly recommends: 'the results of ENEM 2002 show that among the multiple challenges that Brazilian schools face, being able to learn how to read is the most socially valued and required' (INEP, 2002a, p. 192). Any coherent policy must take note of this fact.

It is a great challenge to make teachers in various disciplines aware of the idea that the development of reading abilities is an aim to be achieved by schools in various curricular areas and that the specificities of each curricular area offer singular opportunities to perfect different teaching abilities. In this sense, it is up to schools to bring their students into contact with a wider variety of texts in a creative way, so that students become fluent readers and producers of the widest range of texts possible.

From now on, in so far as secondary education increasingly contributes to share the professional destinies of young people, the reform of secondary education in Brazil marks the limits and possibilities of building students' future professional paths, and concomitantly, the future of the country.

Notes

[1] This chapter benefited from the valuable suggestions and contributions of Professor Simon Schwartzman and Professor Maria Inês Fini (coordinator of ENEM in 1998-2002). However, the analysis presented is entirely the responsibility of the authors.

[2] See the chapter by Claudio de Moura Castro in this volume.

References

Abramovay, M. & Castro, M.G. (2003) *Ensino médio: múltiplas vozes*. Brasilia: UNESCO, Ministério da Educação.

Castro, M.H.G.d. (2003) A participação do Brasil no PISA: uma ousadia construtiva. *X Seminario Nacional fo Pitagoras*.

Cortelazzo, Ângelo (2001) O ENEM e o ensino superior. *Revista do ENEM 1*, 7.

INEP (2002a) *Relatório pedagógico do ENEM 2002*. Ministério da Educação, Instituto Nacional de Estudos e Pesquisas Educacionais, Brasília.

INEP (2002b) *Relatório sínase de divulgação dos resultados – Saeb 2001*. Brasília: Ministério da Educacação, Instituto Nacional de Estudos e Pesquisas Educacionais.

Mello, G.N.d. (1998) Diretrizes curriculares nacionais para o ensino médio. *Parecer CEB/CBE*. Brasília: Conselho Nacional de Educação. Available at: http://www.mec.gov.br/cne/parecer.

Ministério da Educação (2002) *Parâmetros curriculares nacionais – ensino médio*. Brasília: Ministério da Educação.

Organisation for Economic Cooperation and Development (2001) *Knowledge and Skills for Life: first results from PISA 2000 – Education and Skills*. Paris: OECD Programme for International Student Assessment.

Brazilian Technical Education: the chronicle of a turbulent marriage

CLÁUDIO DE MOURA CASTRO

Technical schools combine a high school degree, technical information and hands-on vocational experience. This chapter narrates the turbulent cohabitation of the academic and the vocational curricula of technical schools in Brazil. In the final section, the balance between different levels and modalities of technical education is also discussed.

In Brazil, as in many other parts of the world – to wit, elsewhere in Latin America, the Arab world and Sub-Saharan Africa – technical schools are an unstable solution. They are supposed to be a combination of academic and practical training and, in most cases, the balance between the parts is lost, becoming something else that is less than satisfactory. While some European countries have managed to have moderate success with this formula, it tends not to work in most developing countries.

The formula survived in Brazil for many decades but was abandoned in the mid 1990s, creating some confusion. After the initial perplexities, a new system is beginning to take shape and show promising results. However, the new incumbents of the Ministry of Education, following the change of government in 2002, show interest in tampering with the delicate balance obtained.

The Catch-22: the more you improve,
the more dysfunctional it becomes

Around 1971 I was sitting in my IPEA [1] office when a visitor from the World Bank arrived. The man was very proud of the new Bank policies to invest in technical and comprehensive education in Brazil – as well as elsewhere in the world. As he explained, by combining an academic and a vocational curriculum, students would get, at the same time, a solid academic education and whatever it takes to prepare them for jobs.

As it happened, I had on my desk a number of tables from a survey of *Ginasios Orientados para o Trabalho* (GOTs), a network of junior high schools combining academic and vocational preparation.[2] The data showed the percentage of GOT students who wanted to take up the occupations offered by their schools. On average, only 2% of the students were interested in getting jobs related to the skills they were learning. Instead, almost all of them wanted to go to higher education. I showed him the tables and insisted that the same would happen with the World Bank schools. Needless to say, the World Bank officer was not persuaded by my tables. The Bank went on to invest heavily in technical and comprehensive high schools around the world.

In the late 1990s, John Middleton and Arvil Van Adams commissioned a vast number of surveys to find out what was happening with technical and vocational schools all over the globe. The results, used in the policy paper of the World Bank [3], showed that comprehensive high schools were an unmitigated failure and technical schools were almost as disappointing. The Bank shifted gears and stopped investing in these models.

In the early 1970s, when my research – mentioned above – showed that students were not interested in skills training, I asked a few of my graduate students to write term papers looking at what was happening in the federal technical schools of their home states. The numbers found anticipated what the World Bank found a decade later. Indeed, the schools were not producing the expected results, i.e. technicians who would work as technicians.

In a country with a very small enrolment in secondary education and a dismal quality in public schools, technical schools were offering a winning formula for students: free secondary education of high quality. Considering that the only other alternatives to quality education were the expensive private schools, it did not take long for students to realise that practically the only tuition-free schools offering a high quality academic education were the technical schools (most were federal, but a state such as São Paulo also had an extensive network of public technical schools). With the increasing demand for enrolment in the relatively few such schools (around one hundred in the federal system and another hundred in the São Paulo network), requests for admission expanded enormously and schools began to impose admission tests (known as *vestibulinhos*). Candidate to vacancy ratios soared to 10:1 and more. Cramming programmes to pass these tests also appeared.

Affluent students, particularly those from private primary schools, began to corner the market for technical schools. These institutions became, de facto, elite schools, preparing students for the most competitive entrance examinations for higher education. A survey conducted in the late 1980s indicated that among the 10 schools that produced the largest number of approved students to the most competitive São Paulo programmes (e.g. medicine, law and engineering at the University of São Paulo), one was an industrial arts federal technical school.

Lavish resources were dispensed to make them better, including a substantial loan from the Inter-American Development Bank (IDB).

116

However, the better these schools became, the less technicians they produced, because they were co-opted by the elites who were able to pass the *vestibulinho*. No matter how sophisticated the laboratories and workshops, the students were clearly higher education material and did not take very seriously the skills instruction. At best, they would take a technical job for a few years, to ease their personal finances, while attending elite universities. This was the catch-22. The better they became in everything, including their laboratory and vocational programmes, the less their students took interest in the technical dimension. This was because they also became equally good at academics. These were expensive schools, costing five to ten times more than the local public secondary schools.

To sum up, a set of close to one hundred federal schools were preparing technicians who hardly ever became technicians. They tended to come from upper-class backgrounds and have nothing in mind but the examinations for the best universities, be they in law or medicine. Hence, the schools lost the equity battle. The few students from a more modest origin who managed to enrol were quickly convinced that going to higher education was a better deal, having come so far up the education ladder in a country in which so few reached that level. Hence, industry was also on the losing end, since they were not getting the technical staff they needed.

Given the due differences, the situation was not too different from what was described by Philip Foster in his well-known 1971 paper on 'The Vocational School Fallacy in Development Planning'.[4] Technical schools in Africa did not prepare for technical jobs. In fact, in a field visit to a technical school in the Ivory Coast, I was told that when the students began to face a tougher job market, the solution was to prepare them better to enter university.

The situation persisted for decades in Brazil. In the mid 1980s, the Minister of Education appointed a task force to discuss technical schools and I became a member of this short-lived group. Most members were, one way or another, connected to the Ministry of Education. It is interesting to notice that this group was totally unconcerned with such a distortion vis-à-vis the original role of technical schools, namely, to prepare technical cadres for industry, services or agriculture. Instead, they reflected the general mood of the faculty of technical schools. They were proud of the academic excellence of their student body. Not becoming technicians was almost a mark of success. This was in line with what Ronald Dore (1997) called the 'academic drift'.[5]

At that time, I suggested that the schools be split into two separate tracks. One would offer the academic programme, attracting the upper classes. The other would only offer the skills training. Not being interested in practical skills, the upper-class students would not apply for the technical track, allowing those truly interested in skills to find vacancies. Perhaps the more modest students could not compete for the academic tracks in these schools, and would have to take their secondary education elsewhere, but at least, they would find vacancies in the technical tracks. It is instructive to notice that the members of the task force did not even take the time to understand my proposal. Their mindset was elsewhere.

There is nothing wrong with preparing engineers or medical doctors who have had to file, solder or hammer. Using one's hands is not a bad idea. However, in a country with over one hundred million inhabitants at that time, two hundred or so technical schools was a very scarce resource. These schools are much too expensive and scarce to impart a hobby or familiarise students with hand work. Industry needed skilled labour and had no other alternative solutions.

While Latin American education has a lot in common, both good and bad, this is an area where Brazil and her neighbours part company. Almost everywhere in the world, there is a close correlation between students' socio-economic status and the excellence of the schools they attend. It should be no surprise to state that the poor attend less expensive and worse schools. Technical schools in Latin America tend to be the poor cousins of the academic secondary. They offer lower quality education and cater to lower status students. As a result, there is much less interest in higher education. However, they have other problems. Their curricula are neither here nor there. They are not good enough at the academic level. They tend to be perfunctory and outdated at the technical level and the hands-on activities are not sufficient to prepare skilled workers: Jack-of-all-trades, master of none. By trying to offer too much, they end up offering a watered-down preparation on all three counts.

By contrast, Brazil invested very heavily in its relatively few technical schools. They are very good and very expensive. However, by boosting the quality of the academic side, they became a magnet to the elites. Hence, the catch-22: the better they became, the worse they performed their original task of preparing technical personnel.

World Trends in Technical Education

As mentioned, technical schools were having the same troubles in many other countries. Granted, Europe has had technical schools for many decades and they tend to work relatively well close up. But the conditions are quite different. Firstly, Europe has a much higher proportion of the corresponding age cohorts in secondary education or some other alternative at the same level, making the diploma less scarce. Secondly, Europe has very high quality academic public schools. There are no serious incentives for someone to attend a technical school in order to have access to the best higher education programmes. Thirdly, Europe has a clear segmentation of secondary-level technical schools. According to academic qualifications, students are tracked to programmes that are stronger or weaker in academic subjects and more or less geared to job preparation.

118

Even so, countries such as France, that have something similar to technical schools, still feel the weight of the academic bias in their technical programmes. Contacts with enterprises are not always easy. Inertia in changing occupational profiles is endemic. Therefore, a trend away from the conventional academic-technical schools can be discerned even in Europe. The French *baccalaureat* is divided into broad areas, such as commerce, biological or natural sciences, mathematics, and humanities. But they should not be confused with technical schools, despite the 'technical baccalaureat', because they give only the 'flavour' of occupations, along the corresponding lines, but are a far cry from job preparation. Argentina and Mexico seem to be going along this route of 'soft' career education.

The comprehensive high school of the United States is an interesting case. In theory, it offers the best of all possible worlds. Academic subjects, technology and shop, all under one roof. What could be better? But in practice, social cleavages are all under the roof of the same high school – while hidden in Europe by school segmentation. Tracking is rampant inside the schools and each track is typically attended by each social stratum. Working-class students, as well as low-performing students, go to shop classes. And both groups attend watered-down mathematics and science courses. Being dumped into one of them can be seen as a punishment. As a result, they have low status and can be demeaning. To sum up, comprehensive schools, on the whole, perform poorly at job preparation.

The more or less spontaneous response to the poor job preparation achieved by high schools has been the highly successful community colleges. In other words, job preparation is moved to the post-secondary level. But this trend to push occupational training up to the post-secondary level is not only American. It has become universal, with Lycées Techniques and Institutes Universitaires Technologiques in France, the Fachhochschulen in Germany and the technical colleges in the United Kingdom. This trend has reached Latin America where in Chile, Argentina and Venezuela, around one-third of higher education enrolment is in post-secondary short courses.

Another major trend is to offer job preparation in specialised training centres, unrelated to academic schools and not offering an academic degree. The Brazilian SENAI was the pioneer Latin American institution to create vocational schools outside the academic system and was cloned by practically all countries of the region. The rationale of this system is quite robust. It offers job preparation after one leaves regular academic school, whenever it might happen. Typically, it enrolled youth with four years of schooling, in the 1940s, when SENAI was created. As Brazilian mean school achievement increases, SENAI now receives students with as much as complete secondary education, in the most affluent states and in the more complex occupations (e.g. electronics). For the record, as much as SENAI (and SENAC, the corresponding institution for the service sector) perform quite well in their traditional skills training programmes, they also operated technical schools where they met the same predicament of the federal network. In most cases, students became infatuated by the academic track of the programmes and often went straight to higher education, largely frustrating the original intention of the course.

All in all, the standard formula of the technical school has not performed too well and is being progressively replaced by other initiatives. This is less the case in Europe where the highly segmented technical schools still resist. Of course, Germany never adopted this model, except for a few such schools in Bad Württemberg.

Finally, Divorce!

In the mid 1990s, after Paulo Renato de Souza became Minister of Education, the idea of a loan to beef up technical education was in the air. The Federal Technical Schools had lost their leading edge in technology and equipment and there was a chance to prepare a substantial loan, using FAT [6] money as counterpart funding. But the IDB was reticent about putting more money in an elitist institution that had failed to deliver a credible product.

At this time, I was an employee of the IDB and also advising the Minister on matters of education policies. To counter the reluctance of the IDB, the idea of splitting the academic and the technical segments of a technical programme was exhumed. Indeed, this was an obvious way to avoid the problem. If students could take the academic track by itself or the technical track by itself, or both, the reasons for university-bound students to enrol in the technical track would disappear. Why would a high status student want to spend time in shops or laboratories, learning an occupation that was not desired? For such students, it would be a much better idea to spend more time preparing for the academic degree, increasing the chance of passing a competitive *vestibulinho*. If that were the case, they would leave the technical track free for more modest students who could be interested in the occupations taught. These were the students unable to compete with the elites in the *vestibulinho*.

This was more than a hunch. In fact, the São Paulo SENAI had conducted a survey among students of three of its technical schools.[7] Two were regular technical schools, offering the standard fare of integrated technical and academic curricula. The third was called a *Curso Técnico Especial*, meaning that it was targeted to clienteles that already had a complete secondary degree. Therefore, they only took the technical courses, making the programme much shorter (one year, instead of three).

As it turns out, this natural experiment created the evidence that was needed to increase the confidence in the plan. In fact, the *Curso Técnico Especial* is a spontaneous version that anticipated the split technical programme. Comparing the socio-economic status of the three schools, it became obvious that the two conventional programmes had a clientele that was substantially different from the third, the *Especial*. The latter had students from a much more modest origin. In other words, by removing the academic track, the door was opened for more modest students to enrol, as they did not have to compete with the others.

The IDB agreed with the policy but wanted to ensure that enrolment at the academic tracks inside federal schools would be contained, to avoid distorting even more their original role of preparing technicians. This created a considerable tension between the Ministry of Education (MEC) and the IDB. Nancy Birdsall was the Executive Vice-President and had been previously involved in a research piece on Brazilian technical and secondary education. She was determined to ensure that the loan would not do more of the same that already existed. At one point, the whole project almost fell through. But finally, a working solution was found.

Implementation and Confrontation

For about a quarter of a century, technical education was stuck in the catch-22 predicament described above. The decisive factor to bring about change was the possibility of a 250 million dollar loan from the IDB. A loan can be a powerful weapon to break a deadlock.

Multilateral bank loans have what is called a conditionality; that is to say, the banks tell the countries that they are free not to take a loan. By the same token, the banks are entitled not to offer a loan, unless the country is willing to accept certain conditions. Conditionalities are powerful weapons. They can be used for positive or negative ends. They can be the catalyst of change or create horrendous crises and confrontations in the borrowing countries. And very often, the consequences of cancelling a loan because a conditionality was not satisfied are so dire that the banks pretend that they do not see its lack of enforcement. In other words, conditions imposed with a loan can be a good thing if well conceived and all goes according to plan. They can even be a blessing for a Minister who has to deal with recalcitrant actors and cannot afford to pay the political price of confronting them squarely. A positive conditionality reflects the wishes of the Minister – and hopefully the needs of the country – but enables the 'blame' to be diverted on the banks.

PROEP (Expansion Program for Professional Education) was a very benign case of conditionalities being used to boost reform. Before becoming Minister of Education, Paulo Renato de Souza was the Director of Operations of the IDB, being fully familiar with all the trappings of development banking. Breaking the catch-22 that preserved the elitism of technical schools was his goal, as much as that of the IDB staff involved in preparing the loan.

I was, at the time, an officer of the IDB and was as much involved in this loan as anybody else in the Bank. Therefore, the present chapter has all the advantages and disadvantages of being written by an insider in the reform that took place.

Once the split between the technical and the academic tracks of the technical schools had been decided, the rest was a matter of sorting out the details and finding a legal form to do it. The recently approved LDB (*Lei de Diretrizes e Bases da Educação*), the broad legal framework for education policy, made matters much simpler than initially thought. It was agreed, at the beginning, that students would take the technical track after completing secondary education. But it was subsequently decided that they could also do so while taking the last two years of secondary education. It was feared by the IDB that this latter alternative could create some loopholes to preserve the old system. But in hindsight, the fears were exaggerated. A more contentious matter was to decide what to do with the academic tracks to be offered inside the federal technical schools. Technical schools could respond to the new regulations by expanding them and shrinking the technical track, making them as removed from skills training as before. After much debate, it was agreed that enrolment in the academic track had to be reduced to half its present level. This was not a politically easy decision.

A major source of reaction when the new plans were first spelled out was an increase in the total workload of students who took both the academic and the technical tracks, compared with the previous load in the integrated programmes. Critics chastened the Minister for imposing on the poorer students – who wanted to get a technician's degree – a heavier workload than before. It is true that the workload increased. But the reason for the increase had absolutely nothing to do with the split imposed by the reform. It was the LDB that increased the workload of all secondary education, technical or otherwise. Had the LDB not been enforced, the workload of the split technical added to the workload of the academic would be exactly the same as before.

Once the broad outlines of the reform were agreed with the IDB, the Minister invited a number of leading principals of federal technical schools to present the new plans. I was at this meeting and was able to notice that the reactions from the principals were mild and more sympathetic than otherwise. The only complaint they expressed was the loss of contextualisation of subjects in the academic track. Some of the best technical schools had managed to bring the technical and the academic subjects closer together, using examples and illustrating the drier and abstract theories of the academic world with concrete examples from the technical end.

Soon, however, the tide turned against the Ministry. The same principals, who were so docile at the beginning, probably got much flak from their teachers and teachers' unions, particularly from those leaning to the left. As a result, they began to oppose the reform. Their arguments were less of substance than process. They claimed that they had not been consulted beforehand. This is only partly correct. It is a moot point, whether asking a representative group to participate in an open discussion on the proposed reform is a consultation or not. However, we all know that the alternative of calling in a broad consultation, with students, teachers and unions, leads to stalemate, due to the long tradition of obstruction from the organised left.

The leitmotif of the reform, namely, to make technical schools less elitist and more able to fulfil their mandate to supply technicians to industry, was never directly challenged. Principals claimed, unconvincingly, that the schools were not so elitist and that not all graduates went to higher education, though the data to support this never materialised. In other words, decade after decade, technical schools never went to the trouble of finding out how elitist their students actually were and how few graduates became technicians. Deep inside, they ultimately liked being an elitist institution, catering for the ablest students who had the most success in the most exclusive universities and who mostly came from upper-class families.

Ultimately, what convinced them not to take their objections to the reform too far was the 250 million dollars they could tap into. A well-prepared request to the Ministry could bring to the school a handsome amount of money, allowing reforms, expansions, even new laboratories and workshops.

It is interesting to ponder on the fact that the real losers in the battle to implement the reform never participated in the confrontations that ensued. If schools were to split the two tracks and the academic track had to cut to half its enrolment, the losers were clearly the elites who were getting a free ride on the best academic education offered by the public sector. Why did they not organise and obstruct the reform? Curiously, the opposition came from the left, which subscribes to an ideology where privilege is the enemy.

The hard core opposition to the reform came from a group of left-wing education researchers and professors. They ignored the elitist nature of the technical education being offered by almost all the technical schools. Why would the left choose to ignore the fact that a school designed to cater to modest youth trying to become technicians had become so elitist? Their arguments focused on two issues. The first was the alleged imposition of a reform agenda by a multilateral bank. Acacia Kuenzer, a well-known author in such matters, dedicated several chapters of her book on technical education to the so-called 'evil' influence of the World Bank on Brazilian technical education affairs. She discusses at length how the Bank dumped its cookie-cutter formulae on Brazil. Unfortunately for the credibility of her arguments, she got the name of the Bank wrong. The World Bank never considered lending money to technical education in Brazil. It was the Inter-American Development Bank that made all the negotiations and the loan.[8] As previously mentioned, it is true that the IDB wanted to see the reform approved, as a precondition to make the loan. But the reform was designed by Brazilians, inside and outside the IDB. And it had roots in past attempts to move along equivalent lines. But, ultimately, the argument hinges on the moral and political justifications for the conditionalities that are part of multilateral bank loans. This involves value judgements. It cannot be proven right or wrong.

The second argument is far more abstract and goes back to this group's conception of education. At least a decade before, much attention was paid to something called *politecnia*. Maybe the roots are in Proudhon, but the real father of *politecnia* was Gramsci, in the late 1920s, while in an Italian jail. *Politecnia* is a school conception in which the academic and the vocational, the study and the work, are all combined in a seamless process. To those espousing the principles of this school of thought, splitting the academic and the technical tracks was seen as straight on rejection of this principle, and, therefore, it was flawed.

There are many problems with the defence of *politecnia*. First of all, it was conceived in the 1920s, before the significant modern technological revolutions took place. In addition, practically all the vocational and technical education systems of the world took shape after that and all made honest attempts to bring the world of work closer to the world of schools. But more importantly, *politecnia* is a utopia, since there are no schools anywhere in the world that adopted this model in its pure form. Comparing any existing system with a utopia does not yield a fruitful discussion, because we are comparing something that bears the imperfections of the real world with the purity of something that only exists in the imagination.

If we want to look at the closest real-life materialisation of *politecnia*, the American comprehensive high school comes to mind, or the polytechnical schools of the former USSR, with vacations spent working in factories. But on both counts, the existing research does not show very flattering results. American high schools disappoint in their attempts to impart an occupation to students and the experience of Russian students in factories is even worse.[9]

To the present author – who is far from neutral in this discussion – the opposition from the *politecnia* group makes no sense. The quest for intellectual integration of academic and technical subjects is real and important. However, it was neither achieved automatically by the previous Brazilian system nor is it impeded by the reform that split the two. In fact, in some of the technical schools where the students take the academic and the technical tracks at the same time, administrators claim that they have achieved a good degree of integration. Furthermore, good academic education is a combination of theory and its applications. Students should practise the application of theory as part of the learning process. Good education does not need a parallel goal of job preparation to be credible and useful. Using one's hands is a good way of learning about the world – which includes all sorts of theories. In fact, it has been said that theory comes through the hands. But this only requires simple laboratories and workshops to do practical projects. It is very different from job preparation.

Finally, Business as Usual and Growth

The reform process commenced in 1995, and after several years this is a good time to take stock of what has transpired so far. There are two main issues in front of us. One has to do with the numbers. What happened with enrolment figures? The second has to do with the clientele of the technical schools. Have they become less elitist?

Despite the remarkable improvements in school statistics that took place during the tenure of Paulo Renato de Souza, the statistics that could give us a picture of technical education are difficult to interpret. The first complication results from the fact that secondary-level teacher preparation was counted as technical education. So also was the old bookkeeping programme, an obsolete track in traditional high schools. Worse, there was no census of technical and vocational education. The first one took place in the year 1999. But with the reform, the students from technical education migrated from the regular school census to the census of vocational and technical education. Bookkeeping courses disappeared – not a great loss. Teacher training programmes also shrank, for reasons unrelated to the reform. As a result, it became very hard to disentangle what was happening. Comparisons are very difficult because the 'before' is in a database that is not comparable with that of the 'after' situation. In the last months of the tenure of Paulo Renato de Souza, both INEP (the statistics and evaluation branch of the Ministry of Education) and the Cabinet of the Minister tried to disentangle the figures. But the results are less satisfactory than one would have expected, considering how much statistics have improved.

Years	Technical high schools	Teacher training (secondary level)		Bookkeeping	
1996	2,503,644	851,551	34.0%	743,866	29.7%
1997	2,381,701	828,017	34.8%	647,533	27.2%
1998	1,896,521	742,105	39.1%	446,070	23.5%
1999	1,379,359	615,670	44.6%	246,938	17.9%
2000	907,479	519,095	57.2%	91,181	10.0%
2001	444,018	260,975	58.8%	29,445	6.6%
2002 *	202,000	109,000	53.9%	8,900	4.4%
Growth rate. 1996-2002	-92%	-87%		-99%	

Table I. Enrolment in technical high schools (old model).
Source: MEC/INEP: (2002) preliminary data.

It would seem that the reform played havoc with enrolment immediately after it was implemented. Of course, it caused the integrated programmes to be pared down, as prescribed in the law. It also provoked an immediate crisis in private technical education after it was implemented. This was confirmed by the administration of one of the largest private technical schools in the

125

country. In fact, this school had to open very quickly the four-year undergraduate programmes in order to survive the crisis. In the public technical schools, the results are less clear. But on the whole, there seems to have been a sharp fall in enrolment, again immediately after it was implemented.

However, as the dust settled, growth resumed. Present numbers seem to show a very steep increase in enrolment. In other words, from a purely quantitative point of view, the reform has succeeded, even if belatedly.

Enrolment in technical education between 2000 and 2001 grew at 68% and 63% at federal and private institutions, respectively. Municipal and state schools did not grow at all. In fact, state secretaries of education were never keen on technical education and saw in the reform a good excuse to escape from it. The 2002 census shows 560,000 students in 2,800 technical schools.

Technological and *seqüenciais* are also growing fast. *Seqüenciais* went from 421 to 660 programmes, between 2000 and 2001 (see below for definitions of these other post-secondary programmes). Table II shows the enrolment in technological programmes, reaching 18,000 students.

Admin. status	Technician	Superior[a]		Total	Share of enrolment[b]
		Technologist	Sequencial		
Brazil	462,258	63,046	18,242	543,546	17%
Federal	56,579	6,618	450	63,647	12%
State	159,745	12,720	2,812	175,277	35%
Municipal	15,412	812	206	16,430	19%
Private	230,522	42,896	14,774	288,192	14%

[a]Year 2000 Census of Higher Education.
[b]Share of category divided into the total enrolment regular and short post-secondary education.

Table II. Enrolment in post-secondary education, Brazil 2001.
Source: MEC/INEP/SEEC.

On the elitism issue, federal technical schools were never keen on collecting such data. However, conversations with staff and principals of several such schools suggest that the students from the technical tracks have indeed become much less affluent. By contrast to federal technical schools, the public system of technical schools from the state of São Paulo has always been much more forthcoming with such studies. It has recently released some very instructive statistics. Table III shows a very sharp decrease in the participation of students from the higher income brackets and an equally sharp increase in the share of low-income students. If making the clientele of these schools more in line with the occupations taught was the goal of the reform, the table is an unmistakable proof of success. That is to say, the appropriation of technical schools by the social elite was terminated.

Family income	1995	2002
	%	%
0-5 times the minimum wage	32	57
11-20 MW	21	8
21-30 MW	5	1

Table III. Enrolment and source context in Sao Paolo: 1995-2002.

The other face of the reform is the large number of schools that benefited from the PROEP loan. Indeed, up to 2002, 331 schools signed agreements to receive funds to be expanded, repaired or built. Initially, the federal schools were the first to take advantage of the funds. They are closer to the Brasilia administration and understand better what it takes to get the funds. Then, state schools started presenting their requests. The so-called community schools took much longer to understand what it was all about. These are non-government, non-profit institutions, scattered around the country. But once they found out how they could bid for the PROEP funds, they took it in earnest and came forth very aggressively.

A new government is now in place, already for six months at the time of writing. What can we say about its encounter with technical education, inside the walls of the Ministry? It is very difficult to piece the situation together. The Minister has been silent on the subject. The person in charge of technical education has not said much, except to propose an extra year of secondary education, only in the public institutions, and devoted to vocational subjects. In other words, it has proposed exactly the formula that around the world has shown the most disappointing results. This proposal, however, does not seem to be going very far. If nothing else, this is enormously expensive for the state systems of education that operate and fund secondary education, and the federal government would not have the requisite funds to transfer to the states. At the same time PROEP disbursements were interrupted, even though no administrative irregularities have been found. Millions of dollars stopped flowing to half-finished schools and laboratories. No good reasons had been given for this freeze. A few names associated with the *politecnia* movement have been consulting with the Ministry. It is being said that their goal is to reverse the main thrust of the reform, i.e. to integrate the technical and the academic tracks once again. Whether they will succeed is anybody's guess.

The Elusive Balance: the staircase theory

In very traditional systems of education, it is as if God had determined that occupations either require a complete secondary education or a higher education programme lasting at least four years. Nothing in between exists.

In all mature societies, education systems respond to the obvious facts that the intrinsic difficulties of occupations widely differ and the time it takes to prepare a serious professional to discharge them can be less than four years. Therefore, the systems adjust by creating shorter courses. Countries usually come up with more than one alternative that lasts less the than the classical four years. Indeed, there are no good reasons to suppose that all in-between occupations take exactly two or three years.

In France, there are the *Lycées Techniques* but there are also the *Institutes Universitaires de Technologie*, with different durations. In the United States, there are one-year technical courses and also the two-year associate degrees. These are interesting variants on the response to complex situations. However, the presence of several post-secondary alternatives in any one country brings obvious difficulties of establishing for each of them the rules, requirements and privileges for the diplomas and certificates.

For want of a better description, I am calling the balancing act necessary to address such complexities the staircase theory. The crux of this notion is that we need stairs composed of different programmes, each step taking a little longer than the previous, with no huge gaps in the middle. More complex occupations are taught in higher steps in the staircase, requiring longer courses of study. But since education markets are seldom unregulated – even in the most unregulated country, the United States – there are rules and regulations, pertaining to each of the steps of the staircase. In most cases, these regulations set a minimum number of credit hours, sometimes curricula and syllabi and the rights and privileges that go with each modality.

The balancing act has to do with how the regulations of each step compare with those of the others. If a step taking fewer years grants too many privileges, compared to that immediately higher, the incentives to enrol in the higher step are reduced. For instance, if the law were to allow the same privileges to two-year courses that are given to four-year degrees, the reasons to spend four years in school would be sharply reduced. If the lower step has too few benefits, in terms of what one can do with the diploma, it will languish and enrolments will dwindle, reducing the range of effective alternatives.

The reform that created the new generation technical schools – disentangled from secondary education – was implemented at the same time that two additional categories of post-secondary education took shape and began to grow. Brazil has presently three categories of post-secondary courses, lasting less than the conventional four-year programmes:

Technical Education

This is the category focused on in this chapter. It can last from one to two years (or even more), depending on the complexity of the occupation. Business degrees can be completed in one year, automation and robotics in two. The certificates are not officially considered as higher education. In addition to the loss in status, graduates cannot use the credits if they move on to higher education.

Sequential Education

This is a possibility opened by the LDB (Education Law) approved in 1995. Institutions accredited to offer four-year degrees can offer two-year courses in any subject for which they are accredited. They do not need to request permission to open such courses and there are no official curricula to be followed. It is a very flexible alternative. However, the law was too cryptic in defining such programmes, leading to much discussion and disagreements. In a recent and controversial decision, the National Council of Education decided that this is not true higher education. Or perhaps we could say that it is higher education but not quite on a par with other alternatives, since the graduates are not allowed to go on to postgraduate schools (be it the standard Master's or doctorates, or what is in Brazil called *especialização*, i.e. an abbreviated version of postgraduate programmes).

Technological Education

This post-secondary alternative has existed for many years. But it has had a bumpy ride, from its early start in the 1960s. The first course on *Engenharia de Operações* (operations engineering) was created emulating the American community colleges. In recent years, the effort by the Ministry of Education to regulate, develop curricula and streamline this modality has resulted in its explosive growth, from the late 1990s. One of the legal provisions that boosted its growth was the higher education status, allowing graduates to move on to post-secondary programmes of any variety. On the downside are the strict requirements to open such programmes, such as the case with four-year programmes sponsored by institutions that do not have the status of universities or *Centros Universitários*. To get permission, institutions have to submit complex projects to the Ministry of Education and the delays in processing them are one of the most critical determinants of expansion of different levels of education and the different status of institutions.

Therefore, the balancing act that the educational authorities have to manage involves these three modalities. Students can leave secondary school and go to the market, they can take the one-year technical courses, they can take the two-year *Sequenciais*, they can take the two to three year *Tecnológicos* or they can enrol in regular four-year schools. The privileges and limitations of each level have to be managed, so that the staircase is preserved and one step does not endanger or destabilise the others that lie above or below.

From the perspective of the students there are considerations of status, transferability to higher levels, duration and labour markets. A diploma after one year is in itself attractive. But its status cannot be the same. The possibility of transfer is always desirable, but at what price? For older students, is investing four years to get a degree worthwhile? *Sequenciais* are more focused and specialised, a boost to those who have a clear market niche in mind. But they do not allow for enrolling in graduate schools and may end up having less status.

For those who operate the schools, the difficulties of each alternative also have to grow stepwise, lest mutually negative effects arise. This is true not only for the modalities of education considered above but even more so for the types of institutions. The privileges of universities – that can open courses freely – and the unbelievable amount of red tape to shepherd through a request for a new programme for those that do not have this status have been a source of profound distortions in the higher education scene. Private universities grew by 356% between 1985 and 1998. In the same period, stand-alone programmes hardly grew at all. Such rules may distort the stepwise pattern in any of the three technical modalities.

In the present Brazilian scene, expansion of public schools of any of these steps or varieties is severely constrained. There is the financial stalemate of education budgets and the high costs per student of public education, bound by inflexible personnel rules, privileges and many other political restrictions. Therefore, the growth is practically dominated by private schools (be they for profit or of the not-for-profit variety, the latter including many disguised for-profit operations).

To a very large extent, the growth of each modality will be determined by legislation that constrains or makes it easy to open schools or operate them. Therefore, the National Council of Education has been the stage of fierce – if somewhat disguised – battles to shape legislation pertaining to each.

Universities are free to create four-year programmes and *Sequenciais*, without asking permission from the government. The decision of the National Council of Education to consider that *Sequenciais* are not pure-blood higher education (no access to postgraduation courses) was a boost to the *Tecnólogos*, which *are* higher education. But the law requires permission to open up a *Tecnólogo* from all institutions, including universities. This has hurt the universities, because it lowered the market value of *Sequenciais*, which can be opened by universities without previous permission.

University lobbies tried to force the National Council of Education to increase the minimum workload of *Tecnólogos*. This would increase the duration of the courses to three years, making a new and still unknown modality of education too close to the traditional four-year degrees. It would be a strong disincentive to its growth.

There is also a new proposal to lower the minimum duration of regular higher education programmes to three years. Combined with the increased duration of the *Technólogo*, it would be fatal to the latter. But the latest twist is that the Council now wants to keep the *Tecnólogo* shorter and also reduce to three years the regular Bachelor's degree. With that scenario, the *Tecnólogo* may still prosper.

While the present chapter is essentially about technical schools, now that technical schools are, de facto, post-secondary institutions, their situation cannot be properly understood unless we consider the entire set of post-secondary institutions with which they compete. Any imbalance in the restrictions or privileges granted to each technological degree may endanger or even kill them. This is more so due to the relatively fluid and unpredictable nature of legislation concerning such matters. The staircase theory suggests that the manipulation of incentives and legal restrictions to each modality of technical education is one of the most critical factors in determining their future. Unless there is a stepwise progression in difficulties, prizes and privileges, the balance between each modality may be destabilised, resulting in the crippling of one step or another. And in a highly regulated school environment, labour markets are not necessarily the decisive factors in determining the balance between them.

The Myth of the Transfer Function

In an ideal system, after a certain age, students should be able to continue their studies or pause anytime, having already received a sound preparation for jobs. Therefore, systems made up of modules are always on the wish list of school planners. In the parlance of the United States, transfers to higher steps in the education staircase are desirable.

However, there are real and there are administrative barriers to this smooth and seamless progression. Taking engineering as an example, advanced degrees may require calculus, high-level physics and other complex and difficult subjects. If a shorter course is to be designed in such way as to allow for transfers to a higher level, the students of these courses must also take them. In the United States, the tendency is to offer undergraduate programmes that do not require so many prerequisites (theory is moved up to the Master's level). In addition, the first two years are very open-ended, with many general studies subjects. Therefore, those with an associate degree may be able to move to Bachelor's programmes in engineering – even if taking some additional course may be necessary.

But when we look at the engineering curricula of Latin American colleges, there are too many such theory requirements. A two- or three-year course that wants its students to move up to a regular Bachelor's programme must offer a curriculum that ends up being almost a clone of the first two years of the long course. The price is obvious. There is no time to take the practical courses that prepare for the job market.

The first operational engineering courses were victims of this problem. They made a serious effort to allow students to transfer to regular four-year programmes, but given the curriculum rigidities of such courses, in order to permit transfers, they had to sacrifice severely the job-oriented training. As a result, since the graduates were not prepared for real jobs, almost all of them migrated to regular engineering courses, defeating the purpose of a shorter programme.

The problem today is no different from what has been described above. To allow for transfers, there are only two paths. Either the job preparation is curtailed or the curricula of the four-year courses need to be seriously modified. The first alternative will never lead anywhere. Why would anybody want to take a short course that does not prepare for jobs? The second alternative is possible but politically unfeasible in most cases. Four-year programmes have higher status and their graduates monopolise the cadres of ministries of education. In Latin America, the only cases of transfers take place in private institutions where the owner of the four-year programme is the same as the owner of the shorter programme.

The situation with technical courses, vis-à-vis technological degrees, is no different. It is possible to make provision for the transfer. But thus far, this remains no more than a promise.

Therefore, the transfer function, the pride of the community colleges of the United States, remains a far-away dream. In most cases, it is far more productive to give up such hopes for the time being, and focus on giving the best job preparation that is possible within the time constraints that currently apply.

The Rough Ride of Technical Education

This chapter has reviewed the trajectory of technical schools in Brazil. It is somewhat different from that of other countries but, in the end, equally plagued with chronic problems, of which the main ones are summarised below.

- Planners, parents and egalitarians are all seduced by the all-in-one formula proposed by technical schools. A secondary diploma, together with technical culture and job preparation, seemed like a winning proposition. However, this formula is increasingly being perceived as a hopeless solution – except in a few advanced countries. The balance between the three ingredients is difficult if not impossible to achieve. Often, it is overambitious, trying to do too much and achieving too little.

- In most developing countries, technical schools tend to be poorer than their regular academic counterparts and end up being weak in academic subjects, obsolete in technology and insufficient as a preparation for skilled jobs.

- Brazil is an exception, having expensive and tuition-free technical schools, offering high-quality education. This has generated a catch-22 type of situation in which the better the school becomes, the more it attracts elite students and, therefore, the less interest the graduates have in the technical jobs for which they are prepared. Instead, they go to the best university programmes. Both equity and efficiency suffer.

- With the political thrust offered by an IDB loan, a reform was undertaken to split technical education into two tracks. In other words, technical schools were to offer a stand-alone technical programme for students who already had a secondary diploma or were attending another school where they could earn it. The purely academic track could continue to exist and could continue to attract the elites. However, the elites would not want to enrol in the purely technical track, because they are not interested in jobs. Therefore, less affluent students could find vacancies.

- The reform was initially resisted but was firmly implemented. At first, there was much confusion and enrolments went down. Progressively, as the dust settled, growth has resumed. Just as important, the social class level of the technical track has gone down substantially, meaning that the new students have a social profile that is more in line with the status of the occupations offered. In other words, the reform has succeeded in increasing equity and in graduating youth interested in the jobs for which training is offered.

- At the same time that these changes were taking place, two other post-secondary modalities were officially created and their legal status defined: Technology programmes and *Sequenciais*. Since these three courses of studies and their diplomas are heavily regulated, the pacific co-existence of the three modalities, plus the traditional Bachelor's programme, depends on the balance between the time it takes and the privileges granted to each course. In other words, the future of the new technical education is contingent on all the factors that regulate their operation, vis-à-vis the other modes.

Now that this difficult and sensitive reform has been undertaken there is the opportunity for Brazil, as the leading economy in Latin America, to operate a technical education sector that is beneficial to both the demands of industry for increasing skilled labour, and the national population in terms of access, opportunity for skills development and regular income.

Notes

[1] Instituto de Planejamento Econômico e Social, the policy and research branch of the Planning Ministry.

[2] Claudio de Moura Castro, Milton Pereira de Assis, & Sandra Furtado de Oliveira (1978) *Enseñanza técnica: Rendimientos y costos*. Montevideo: CINTERFOR.

[3] The World Bank (1991) *Vocational and Technical Education and Training*. Washington, DC: The World Bank.

[4] Philip Foster (1971) in *Readings in Economics of Education*, pp. 614-630. Paris: UNESCO.

[5] Ronald Dore (1997) *The Diploma Disease*. London: Institute of Education, University of London.

[6] Fundo de Auxílio ao Trabalhador, a fund that accumulates a tax imposed on the payroll of workers.

[7] SENAI SP.

[8] A. Kuenzer (2001) *Ensino Médio e Profissional*, pp. 46-47. São Paulo: Cortez Editora.

[9] Claudio M. Castro, co-authored with Marina Feonova & Anna Litman. (1997) *Education and Production in the Russian Federation: what are the lessons?* Paris: UNESCO, International Institute for Educational Planning.

Models of Teacher Education and Shifts in Politics: a note on Brazil

MARIA C.M. FIGUEIREDO & ROBERT COWEN

The narrative aim of this chapter is to sketch the evolution of the models of teacher education in Brazil at different times – which were characterised by different politics. Thus, the analytical aim of the chapter is to illustrate the relations between patterns of Brazilian teacher education and external and internal politics. There is nothing particularly subtle about the analysis, or the realities: the changes in politics were large and the impact on teacher education provision was typically dramatic, sometimes at the level of intentions but often in practice, also. The story in other contexts, such as the former USSR or Nazi Germany or in the United Kingdom recently, is familiar and equally dramatic but in these countries the developments were peculiarly idiosyncratic and autarchic. Brazil is an interesting case in that the international (as well as the domestic) shifts in politics can be made visible in their relation to reforms of teacher training.

The Early Model of Training Teachers

The early model was remarkably colonialist, in that it drew very directly on the experience of Portugal. Initially, in the eighteenth century, teachers in Portugal and in all its colonies were offered no formal training. Teachers were selected through examinations. The Portuguese Regulation of 6 November 1772 was crisp and definitive:

> I declare that the exams for teachers which will take place in
> Lisbon are to be attended by the president; in his absence a
> member of parliament must be present, together with two
> examiners appointed by the president ... In the overseas domains
> such exams will follow the same principles. (Moacyr, 1936, p. 24)

This was not then merely a centralised model – it was a confident, monopolistic, metropolitan definition of a universal solution for problems of teacher training in an entire empire. The solution in one sense highlights the colonising confidence of Europe in this period and, in another sense, the relative unimportance attached to teacher training. Certainly, a solution, of a sort, was found.

However a subsequent shift in the external politics of Brazil produced another remarkable compression of political power into educational formations: the choice of the metropolitan model of a good educational system shifted from Portugal to France. The scenario began to develop at the beginning of the nineteenth century, with the transfer of the Portuguese Royal Family to Brazil. Paradoxically, France – the country which had produced disturbance in Europe and a shift in colonial relations across the globe – was taken as the example of good educational practice. Institutions of higher education were established on the Napoleonic model of the French *Grandes Écoles*. Under French influence, radical new principles started to frame discussions of education. It will be recalled that in France after the 1789 Revolution, arguments for a national system of education and the provision of normal schools under the responsibility of the state were put forward. In Brazil, following these principles, it was argued that primary education ought to be provided to all and ought to be secular (a policy which Napoleon, given his willingness to work with the Catholic Church in the provision of elementary education, had not adopted).

As in France, these principles for the expansion of education led to the need to provide institutions for the training of teachers. Thus, around the 1830s, efforts were made to create normal schools in the different provinces. The model reflected the cultural and political agenda of elites who were themselves influenced by European, particularly French, culture (Villela, 1992; Tanuri, 2000). Centralisation – as in the French model – was a powerful motif. Each province in the colony was given the power to legislate about public education but at the primary and secondary levels only. The central government was to be in charge of education at all levels in the capital and higher education in the whole country. This motif of centralisation, which reflected initial Portuguese assumptions and the subsequent example of France, continued to characterise a fairly permanent definition of the distribution of power in the educational system in Brazil. The system remained heavily centralised until a few years ago.

However, even heavy centralisation is not enough to invalidate some of the principles of good comparative education as these were beginning to be defined in the late nineteenth century, and in particular in Sir Michael Sadler's later and famous view, in 1900, that the world is not a garden from which educational snippets may be taken for easy and successful transplantation: in Brazil the implementation of normal schools was not successful. It had become apparent how fragile the schools were. About 25 years before Sir Michael Sadler came up with his metaphor, the President of the Province of Paraná had pointed out in 1876 that Normal Schools are 'exotic plants: they are born and they die almost at the same day' (Moacyr, 1940, p. 239).

Nevertheless, what was emerging was a clear social location for teacher training which reflected the political principles of class formation in Brazil. Curriculum content was very simple: it was of primary school level, with only one subject devoted to teacher training. Teachers were badly paid and there were few of them. Preference was given to men (only at the end of the nineteenth century were women very gradually accepted into teacher education) and teaching was accorded little social prestige even in the late nineteenth century.

It took a new internal political agenda to revitalise teacher training – a process which overlapped with the end of the Imperial period and the beginning of the Republican period. The ideological, cultural and political debates and struggles, which led to this political shift, had produced new aspirations for nation building, in which education was increasingly seen as a fundamental instrument for social and economic change. This affected the institutionalisation of teacher education. Curriculum content was reformulated. Though there were regional variations, a typical curriculum structure for teacher education in a normal school at the end of Empire is shown in Table I.

Year	Subjects
1	Grammar and national language
	Arithmetic
	French grammar and language
	Christian principles
2	Grammar and national language
	Geometry
	French grammar and language
3	Geography and history
	Chemistry
	Didactics and methodology

Table I. Teacher education curriculum structure.
Source: Tanuri, 2000, p. 67.

With the foundation of the Republic, and during the next 30 years, different Brazilian states reformulated their normal schools following mainly the model implemented in São Paulo. No major changes took place, except for two innovations. First, under the influence of the philosophy of positivism, the teaching of sciences was introduced into the curriculum for teacher education. Second, although there was normally only one subject, called Pedagogy and Headship, which was directly addressed to the pedagogical training of the teacher, other subject areas specifically aimed at those going into teaching took an increasing emphasis: for example, methods of observation, and learning methods.

The next major policy intent was signified by the (educational) Reform Law of 1892. In teacher education, two innovations were particularly relevant. The first was the institutionalisation of a dual-track system for the preparation of teachers: some normal schools, located at the lower secondary level, aimed at the training of primary school teachers; and other normal schools, located at the upper secondary level, were devoted to the training of teachers for secondary schools and even for the preparation of teachers for normal schools themselves. The second signifier of the intent to innovate was the creation of a normal school at higher education level – again following the example of the French *École Normale Supérieure* (Tanuri, 2000). This model was a vision of a particular future, but the class base of the educational system was already clear and the systems for preparation for the other professions were already powerful. The proposal was never implemented.

The Interwar Period

However, the next layer of exposure to international ideas was indeed important in its effects. Brazil participated in the flurries of new optimism about the necessity for, and potentials of, good education that marked this period. Also, Brazil was urbanising and as it did so its class base was changing – paradoxically highlighting the need to do something about rural education. There was clearly a political and social need for more attention to the provision of education and its expansion, preferably by using fresh ideas about teaching and learning.

After World War I, during the late 1920s and early 1930s, a series of reforms of teacher education took place in a number of states. Some state governments (Minas Gerais, for example) took the initiative to bring in missions of European educators and to send Brazilian teachers for study visits to the USA (mainly to Teachers College, Columbia University, New York). A series of seminars, publications, and national debates on education were part of the so-called New School Movement. Academics who had been in close contact with John Dewey and were inspired by this philosophy discussed issues such as the kind of knowledge teachers should have, the role of the state in education, the universalisation of education, and the expansion of the public schools system (Cury, 1978; Lima, 1978; Mendes, 1986).

Part of this discussion included proposals for shifts in the role of teachers and new ways of educating them. There were claims for the revision of traditional patterns of teaching which were considered inflexible and divorced from children's developmental needs. Teaching methods were criticised for excessive verbalism and more active teaching methods were advocated. The debate included a concern for details, such as a practical approach to the teaching of sciences and mathematics.

Not surprisingly, this active and stimulating debate produced new models for teacher education which emerged in different states, especially in those which had distinguished comparative educationists and sociologists of education as Secretaries of Education or as advisers to the government: persons such as Anisio Teixeira in Bahia, Mário Casassanta in Minas Gerais,

Lourenço Filho in Ceará, and Fernando de Azevedo in the Federal District and in São Paulo. The interesting singularity was the creation of rural normal schools, aimed at reinforcing rural values and at keeping rural workers in rural areas. Clearly, this in one sense was part of a democratising movement. But of course the sociological implication in the short term was that the class base of Brazilian education was not going to change quickly.

Although the new institutional structures of teacher education remained basically the same, there were innovations, with regional variations. Curriculum content, for example, was widened to include a range of new pedagogical and professional subjects: in addition to didactics, pedagogy, psychology, history, philosophy and sociology of education, there were biology, hygiene, drawing, crafts, and teaching practice for the different school subjects. However, a typical normal school curriculum (for primary school teachers as in Rio and in São Paulo) was still centred on the so-called pedagogical subjects, emphasising the 'sciences of education' (Villela, 1992; Tanuri, 2000). There were also two institutional innovations, one of which was parallel to the existing normal schools: the Institutes of Education. Curriculum content remained the same, i.e. centred on the pedagogical subjects. The other innovation was the creation of INEP (*Instituto Nacional de Estudos Pedagógicos* – National Institute of Educational Research). INEP was originally intended to provide training courses for school administrators, head teachers and school inspectors. It gradually developed into a famous centre for educational research in the country and recently INEP became the main institution for the evaluation of education in Brazil.

As a reflection of the development of the urban school system and its expansion there now developed courses of Pedagogy in the Faculties of Philosophy, Sciences and Languages in the University of São Paulo (USP) in 1938, and in the University of Brazil in 1939. These courses initially trained, at undergraduate level, the so-called specialists in education, i.e. school inspectors, administrators, pedagogical counsellors, and supervisors. The courses also trained teachers for normal schools (in didactics and the foundations of education: psychology of education, philosophy of education, sociology of education). The faculties also trained lower and upper secondary school teachers who were to teach specific subject areas such as the arts, biology, chemistry, physics, geography, history, languages, mathematics, music and sciences.

These educational innovations and new projects in teacher education were, however, framed within authoritarian educational laws especially under the Getúlio Vargas government. Educational legislation emphasised the power of the central, federal, government in the formulation of general guidelines for education which were to be implemented in individual states. Governmental policies reinforced the existing socio-economic power structure and had a direct impact on the social control of education (and on higher education particularly). In such a context, educational institutions had little autonomy. All state services were highly centralised, and all educational institutions were subject to legal control, including teaching certification (Tollini, 2002).

The Post-war Conservative Model

This political control was accompanied by a de facto and subtle institutional confirmation of the class base of the educational system. In the early 1960s, after Law 4,024 of 1961, the dual-track system for normal schools was gradually replaced by a single one: primary school teachers were trained in normal schools, at the secondary level. But an emergent and different dual-track system was already being magnified: the Faculties of Philosophy, Sciences and Languages, founded in the 1930s, expanded considerably in the 1960s and in the 1970s. These Faculties of Philosophy, Sciences and Languages became very popular because they permitted the expansion of higher education at low cost. They were also considered a good and reliable instrument for social and professional mobility of existing or potential members of the politically conservative middle classes (Figueiredo, 1987).

Within the non-university sector of teacher education there was confirmation of the domestic politics of class and teacher education stratification in 1971, with Law 5,692. Secondary education was divided up in different vocational streams which would train young people for the world of work. Thus, secretaries, laboratory technicians, and primary school teachers, for example, were trained in secondary schools. Through Law 5,692 teacher education became another vocational stream in secondary education; consequently it lost prestige and professional status. Even the Institutes of Education were abolished; as a result, teachers for normal schools and educational specialists were to be trained only in the courses of Pedagogy, located mainly in the Faculties of Education or in the Faculties of Philosophy, Sciences and Languages.

The stratification was clear: teachers for grades 1-4 were to be trained in secondary education (three years minimum), although little change occurred in curriculum. The common core curriculum included Portuguese, social sciences and sciences, teacher training centred on the so-called foundations of education (biology, psychology, sociology, history, and philosophy), school administration, and organisation and teaching practice. Teachers for grades 5-8 and for secondary education were to be trained at higher education level. Curriculum content remained the same.

Criticisms of the consequences of the new legislation for teacher education emerged. It was argued, for example, that normal schools lost their particular specificity and became merely another branch of the secondary school. Also central to the debate was the question of the kind of knowledge teachers were supposed to have (Santos, 2002).

This critical movement was part of a political struggle. The domestic stratification of teacher education was linked to the particular sources and politics of educational advice which the Brazilian government had sought overseas. As had happened with the University Reform of 1968, the criticisms of the 5,692 Law of 1971 originated in reactions against the economic and political ideology of the military government under the influence of American technical assistance.

After 1963, close relations between Latin American governments and the USA had developed, based mainly on geopolitics. The American Department of State through the United States International Development Agency (USAID) reformulated its policy in Latin America, particularly in education. Various agreements were signed and technical assistance from the USA increased. The human capital theory, favoured and disseminated by international organisations, replaced the concepts of citizenship and equality, developed by previous liberal and populist political movements. Governmental policies and strategies were heavily based on planning, notably of higher education for the labour market (Figueiredo, 1987).

The criticisms of Law 5,692 and other major educational reforms in Brazil, and elsewhere in Latin America, emphasised the strong influence of USAID experts who favoured a specific model for economic and social development. Within this ideological frame, education was conceptualised as a tool for development and the schools were supposed to train the workforce. The Brazilian military government had shifted to techno-bureaucratic solutions in all public policies.

Consequently, teachers were expected, in vocabulary familiar in English educational discourse right now, to be 'competent', that most chilling and limiting of visions. They were supposed to use a range of new techniques and new technologies in teaching, especially audiovisual technologies. The reorganisation of the Pedagogy courses, initiated in the 1960s, broke any potential emancipatory versions of the 'good' knowledge of educators as this had been defined by the New School reformers. The reorganisation of the Pedagogy courses emphasised training in the different specialised areas, i.e. school supervision, administration, inspection, and counselling (Silva, 1999; Santos, 2002). The educational profession became very fragmented and teacher training became deprofessionalised. There was a loss of quality especially in the training of primary school teachers: teacher education was like any other stream in secondary education and with the expansion of courses, mainly on an evening shift model, teacher education was affected by a diffuse and unevenly educated intake of new students, who were seeking to change their existing jobs (as domestic helpers or factory workers) for white-collar work.

The Contemporary Debate

These new patterns of teacher education soon became the centre of national debates in the 1980s and 1990s. These debates, coordinated nationally by the National Movement for the Reformulation of Teacher Training, were very important. They represented a social as well as a professional struggle.

With the new kinds of recruits to the cohort of working teachers and with the new opportunities in a freshly democratised Brazil, there were new possibilities for effective protest and change. Overall, the context in which the new Brazilian Constitution was promulgated and Law 9,394 was passed was very favourable for educational reforms. In the early 1990s, education gained a new momentum. Diversified social movements tried to build and redefine social and political spaces. In addition to various professional associations (teachers, academics, scientists, workers), other organisations emerged: shanty town movements, (urban and rural) land occupation movements, and consumer movements. Gradually these movements and professional associations gained political significance (Figueiredo, 2002).

Classic problems, however, remained. There was concern with the gradual loss of social prestige by teachers, and loss of professional identity. Very worrying were falling numbers of applicants, mainly for primary school teaching, and the ways in which intellectual training was becoming dissociated from some of the practical and craft knowledge needed in school contexts. The research base of educational studies was weak.

But this time, in a new domestic political context, the debate was different. Everywhere there were arguments for reforms to be preceded by discussions about the redefinition of the role of teachers (Mello, 1984). Thus, the national debate about teacher training at major conferences and in the organisations discussing graduate education was informed by a strategic and political concern: to ask what teachers were doing in a socio-economic and political sense. The major principle that emerged emphasised the relationship of education with the less privileged social classes and the need to take this principle into reforms of teacher training. Since the 1980s, courses of Pedagogy, throughout the country, have been changing in structure and content.

Paralleling these discussions about the new 'culture' of teacher education, since 1995 the educational system as a whole has gone through a series of changes. A new Law of Directives and Basis for National Education was approved in 1996, and Law 9,394 produced a major change in teacher education. By 2007 all normal schools ought to have been abolished. The present aspiration for teacher education is an all-graduate profession to be achieved by 2006, with the creation of Higher Education Institutes for Teacher Training (Aguiar, 1997).

What exists now in Brazil is a proliferation of new initiatives in teacher education courses provided by universities in partnership with the State Secretariats of Education or by the universities themselves. There are a variety of initiatives. For example, in the state of Paraná there is a huge programme to train a considerable number of teachers electronically and through video conferencing.

In such innovations, course design and curriculum content must follow guidelines from the National Council of Education and individual State Councils of Education. Thus, although new partners such as the Secretariats of Education and the higher education institutions (single colleges or universities) are responsible for curriculum design, the curricula are subject to central surveillance and approval by the National Council of Education. Similarly, the National Council of Education approves the pedagogical subjects offered by the Faculties of Education or similar higher education institutions. Within in-service training courses, pedagogical subjects and teaching practice for elementary school subjects are compulsory. The study of school subjects (Portuguese, history, geography, mathematics and sciences) is not legally compulsory but most programmes have made them compulsory in a practical sense.

Thus, since the 1980s, there has been a new alertness to the politics of teacher education and an increasing interest in the sociological analysis of teacher training, within the frame of critical theory and theories of conflict. Central to the debates about teacher education is an awareness of the political nature of teachers' practices and the commitment of teachers to the poorer classes. In education, especially in universities with very strong programmes of graduate education, post-structuralism and postmodern theories (Foucault, Perrenoud, Derrida, Althusser, and Lacan) have been framing the academic production of books and articles and the theoretical approach of dissertations and theses. Educational research has emphasised issues such as gender (the feminisation of the teaching profession), class, race, how teachers' knowledge is created, the role of teachers as reflective practitioners, the power relationship between the state and education, and the role of international agencies in educational projects (such as the large-scale educational projects in Brazil, in partnership with State Secretariats of Education). The World Bank concepts of equal rights have been an object of critical analysis, as has the priority given to in-service training if it is based on cost–benefit analysis. Anxieties have been expressed about ideas which suggest that the objective of teacher education is merely to produce technically competent teachers; that is to say, in classroom management. Emphasis is now also given to strengthening teachers' subject knowledge and not merely to the provision of pedagogical knowledge and classroom control. However, a partnership between educational research and school practices is yet to be established. Similarly, the extent of these critical analyses of education (which cmphasise the political, sociological and cultural aspects of schooling) on educational policies is not very clear.

Conclusion

Following Law 9,394, also known as the Darcy Ribeiro Law, 768,000 primary and secondary teachers working in both municipal and state systems must, by 2006, have a higher education qualification. By 2007 all normal schools ought to have been abolished. The massive training programme for primary school teachers will certainly reach the targets. This in one sense is good news. It is also good news that the need to improve teacher education is at the centre of debates in education. However, Santos points out that:

> There is a series of problems arising from this situation that will influence the prospects for improving teacher education system for the future in Brazil. These problems include linking improved performance to better salaries, reducing educational inequalities between rural and urban regions (by implementing experimental projects that combine work and study) and also making use of distance learning. Changing the structure of university courses for teacher training, even if this requires changing the structure of the university itself, is another problem. Establishing educational policies that are oriented more towards practical necessities, without losing sight of political, social, and cultural problems, is yet another issue. Finally, establishing a more productive partnership between educational theories, university research and the practical realities of teaching is also a key problem that needs solving. These are some of the challenges and prospects faced in teacher education in Brazil, which, despite the fact that they occur with great intensity and frequency here, are also part of educational reality in most parts of the world. (Santos, 2002, p. 88)

What is not transparent are the procedures for quality control. This might impair the quality of education in the long term. We might be talking here of a neo-diploma disease, particularly if we think of the kinds of postgraduate training being offered in some universities. A number of institutions offering teacher training programmes are of a lesser status, with very little experience in research or of graduate education. This issue ought to be considered seriously by policy makers and by academics. Overall then, Brazilian teacher education is at an interesting turning point. Its history is not necessarily a guide to its future.

Certainly, Brazilian teacher education has some distinctive patterns and some new dangers:

- It has been affected by international influence (Portuguese, French, American). Currently a danger is that international influences stressing efficiency (such as international agency interventions or an excessive admiration for foreign models of 'quality control') will disturb its indigenous trajectory of reform.
- Teacher education in Brazil has been framed by some extreme domestic politics, notably in the period of the generals. Currently a danger is that the marked politicisation of educational studies will produce politically correct criticism – and an inability to act.

Nevertheless, discursive space now exists in Brazil for a continuing debate about the future of teacher education, not least in relation to the socio-economic stratifications of Brazil and its emergent domestic politics. Brazil, with all its difficulties, is a country of open educational vision. This is probably preferable to the overconfident technocratic certainties about how to manage teacher quality (and university quality) which are so corrosive in countries such as England – which now needs a Freire of its own, a counter-vision. As Freire puts it:

> When our task begins to become clear, we have to take charge of our praxis in a much clearer way. Then we discover the need to become more and more competent in order to do what we would like to do, to make what we would like to make. Along these lines, there is a Letter in which I discuss the qualities or the virtues of the progressive teacher. It is important to say that when I speak about qualities or virtues, I am not speaking about qualities we are born with. I am speaking about something which we make, we build by doing, by acting. I am sure that no one was born as she or he is; one becomes ... Thus virtue means that I have to create quality by putting into practice the quality I would like to have. (Freire, 1995, p. 19)

At least the Brazilians are trying to formulate the questions. Unfortunately, policy makers for teacher education in England know the answers.

References

Aguiar, M.A. (1997) Institutos Superiores de Educação na Nova Lei de Diretrizes e Bases da Educação Nacional, in I. Brzezinski, (Ed.) *LBD interpretada: diversos olhares se entrecruzam.* São Paulo: Cortez.

Cury, C.R.J. (1978) *Ideologia e Educação Brasileira.* São Paulo: Cortez.

Figueiredo, M. (1987) Politics and Higher Education in Brazil: 1964-1986, *International Journal of Educational Development,* 7(3), pp. 173-181.

Freire, P. (1995) The Progressive Teacher, in M. Figueiredo & D. Gastaldo (Eds) *Paulo Freire at the Institute,* pp. 17-24. London: Institute of Education, University of London.

Lima, H. (1978) *Anisio Teixeira, estadista da educação.* Rio de Janeiro: Civilização Brasileira.

Mello, G. (1984) *Magistério de 1°grau : da competência técnicia ao compromisso.* São Paulo: Cortez.

Mendes, D.T. (1986) Anotações sobre o pensamento educacional no Brasil, *Revista Brasileira de Estudos Pedagógicos,* 68 (160), pp. 493-505.

Moacyr, P. (1936) *A instrução e o império: subsídios para a história da educação no Brasil (1823-1853),* São Paulo: Editora Nacional, vol. 1., cited by L.M. Tanuri (2000) História da formação de professores, *Revista Brasileira de Educação,* Mai-Agos, 14, pp. 61-88.

Santos, L. (2002) Contemporary Problems in Teacher Education in Brazil, in E. Thomas (Ed.) *Teacher Education Dilemmas and Prospects – World Yearbook of Education*, pp. 81-89. London: Kogan Page.

Silva, C.S.B. (1999) *Curso de pedagogia no Brasil: história e identidade.* Campinas: Autores Associados.

Tanuri, L.M. (2000) História da formação de professores, *Revista Brasileira de Educação*, Mai-Agos, 14, pp. 61-88.

Tollini, I.M. (2002) *Estado e Educação Fundamental.* Brasília: Editora Plano.

Villela, H. de O.S. (1992) A primeira escola normal do Brasil, in C. Nunes (Ed.) *O passado sempre presente.* São Paulo: Cortez.

Higher Education in Brazil: public and private

EUNICE R. DURHAM

Introduction

Two characteristics mark the development of higher education in Brazil. The first is the fact that it developed late, with the first higher education institutions established only in 1808, and the first universities even more recently in the 1930s. The second, which is of particular relevance for this study, is the precocious development of a powerful private education system alongside the public. From the 1960s onwards this sector changed: it was no longer a case of parallel public and private systems with similar missions and aims, but rather of a new system that subverted the dominant idea of higher education based on a link between teaching and research, academic freedom and the public interest.

The growth of this new kind of private higher education is a relatively recent phenomenon that has had a particularly strong impact on developing countries. It is a phenomenon that has generated little research, perhaps because, until relatively recently, the expansion of this type of private higher education had not affected the countries where most research about higher education is done. It is only in the last few years that researchers have become more concerned with the meaning and impact of this kind of higher education.

The peculiarities of the Brazilian case, where this tendency became apparent early on, are evident when one compares it with other Latin American countries. In Latin America as a whole, as in Europe, until the end of the 1980s the higher education system consisted primarily of two kinds of universities: public secular, state-funded universities, and Catholic universities, at least some of which depended totally or partially on public funding. Other, smaller, less important institutions existed on the fringes of these university-dominated systems.

Such is not the case in Brazil. First, until recently, universities have been only a small part of the higher education system. Second, in addition to church-related institutions and non-profit private higher education schools created by local elites, there was a proliferation of another type of institution from the 1970s onwards: schools run like businesses that are neither universities nor linked with the Church, and which are explicitly or indirectly profit-oriented: in short, just businesses.

In Brazil, what has become clear and has permeated the higher education debate since then is the worrying expansion of this kind of private establishment. The literature on higher education in Brazil to date consists largely of a battle by intellectuals and students against private schools and in defence of state universities.

The analysis of this problem is crucial for an understanding of the peculiarity of higher education in Brazil. It is therefore important to provide a historical introduction on the development of Brazilian higher education in order to permit an understanding of the creation of the system in a complex and heterogeneous context.

The history can be divided into periods that largely correspond with the main political transformations that occurred in the country. The first, which coincides with the monarchic period, takes place between 1808 and the beginning of the Republic in 1889. It is characterised by the establishment of a model of autonomous schools for the training of liberal professionals by exclusive Crown initiative. During the second period, which covers the whole period of the First Republic between 1889 and 1930, the system became decentralised and other, both public (state or municipal) and private schools, emerged alongside the federal establishments. Until the end of this period, there were no universities in Brazil, only autonomous higher education schools focused on a single field of study. The following phase begins in the 1920s, is consolidated in 1930, and coincides with the end of the First Republic and the establishment of the New State; the authoritarian government of Getúlio Vargas. It was during this period that the first universities in the country were created. This period ends in 1945, with the fall of Vargas and redemocratisation, and gives rise to a new phase that ends in 1964. It was characterised by an increase in the number of state universities. The following period begins in 1964 when a new authoritarian era was inaugurated, during which time the university model was reformed and the private system underwent accelerated development, leading to the development of what Geiger calls a 'mass private sector' (Geiger, 1986). The current period began with the process of gradual redemocratisation in 1985. It has been shaped by the 1988 Constitution, the new 1986 Law of Guidelines and Foundations for National Education (*Lei de Diretrizes e Bases da Educação Nacional*, LDB), and by profound change at the political-economic levels as well as in education. Within this period, it is possible to distinguish the phase between 1995 and 2002, which coincided with the two mandates of President Fernando Henrique Cardoso. This period ended in 2003, and there is now profound uncertainty as to the future direction of higher education.

The Beginnings

Brazil had no universities or higher education establishments during the colonial period, unlike Spanish America where Catholic universities were created as early as the sixteenth century when colonisation began. The Portuguese Crown policy was to prevent the formation of a colonial intellectual class, and to concentrate higher learning in the metropolis. Even the Jesuit attempt to establish a seminary that might create a Brazilian clergy, along with a good part of the little organised education that existed in the colony were destroyed, when the Marquis of Pombal ordered the expulsion of the Company of Jesus at the end of the eighteenth century. It was only in the beginning of the following century in 1808, when the Portuguese Crown and the whole of the court moved to Brazil under the threat of the Napoleonic invasions, that higher education took off in Brazil. Three schools were founded in the year that the Portuguese king (then regent of the throne) arrived in Brazil.[1]

At the time there was no concern with or interest in creating a university. The aim was to train some professionals, such as lawyers, engineers and doctors, to satisfy the needs of the state apparatus and the local elite. The possibility of placing higher education in the hands of the Catholic Church, as in the Spanish American colonies, was not even contemplated. With the inauguration of republican governments in the newly independent countries the other Latin American countries experienced a new tendency to replace or create alongside old counter-reformation Catholic universities a new secular, state university system. In Brazil, history took a different turn. Given the presence of the Portuguese court in Brazil, not only was independence delayed, but occurred with the preservation of the monarchy and the Bragança dynasty, which ruled the country until the end of the century. This characterised a markedly different historical development from that of the other countries of the continent, in which independence gave rise to republican regimes and ideals. The process was also different where education was concerned, as the model established in 1808 was maintained in Brazil. A state system under the influence but not directly administered by the Catholic Church was established in accordance with the Portuguese tradition from the previous century, but it consisted of the creation of autonomous schools, rather than universities, to train liberal professionals. The creation of such schools was an exclusive prerogative of the Crown. This Napoleonic-inspired model was based on the pragmatism that guided the Portuguese modernisation project at the end of the eighteenth century, whose most notable legacy in the field of education was the reform of Coimbra University (Teixeira, 1969).

Throughout the nineteenth century, the Crown maintained the Portuguese tradition of retaining a monopoly on higher education, resisting pressure from the Church to create Catholic establishments. The system expanded very slowly and at the end of the period, which culminated with the Proclamation of the Republic in 1889, there were only 24 professional

149

training schools of this kind (Teixeira, 1969), all of them created by Crown initiative and independent of the Church. It was the dissemination of positivist ideas among republican leaders at the end of the century that contributed to opening up the system to initiatives other than those led by the central government, although these still followed the model of isolated schools to train professionals.

After the proclamation of the Republic, the new Constitution decentralised higher education and permitted the creation of new establishments, both by other state institutions (state-level and municipal) and by private groups. Between 1889 and 1918, 56 new, mostly private, higher education schools were established. On the one hand, there were Catholic establishments committed to providing a church-sponsored alternative to public education institutions and, on the other, there were schools created by local elites who hoped to provide their states with higher education facilities. Of the latter, some were backed by state-level governments or were promoted by them, while others remained essentially private.

Thus, the diversification of the system dates back to this period and is still a characteristic of Brazilian higher education today: it created state-funded secular, federal or state-level institutions alongside church-sponsored or secular private ones. Throughout the whole of the First Republic (1889-1930) the model of autonomous schools to train liberal professionals was prevalent. The attempts to create universities were rare, and none succeeded.[2]

The Movement to Modernise Education

The 1920s witnessed a strong modernising movement in the country. Urbanisation and the economic transformations brought about by industrialisation were accompanied by a genuine cultural renovation. The modernisation movement also affected education and various members of the education establishment proposed and partly achieved deep reforms at all education levels. The banner of the movement was free and universal primary school education. Together with a small group of scientists, the modernising group also proposed that higher education be modernised, calling for the creation of universities that would be, in the language of the period, 'centres for impartial learning' rather than mere 'teaching establishments'. The proposal meant far more than the mere creation of universities; it was about an all-encompassing reform of the higher education system as a whole, about the replacement of autonomous schools by large universities with a capacity to develop the basic sciences and research as well as professional training. The system had to be public, not linked with the Church. The model was similar to the German, but adapted to innovations inspired by the North American model.

The banner of educational reform was appropriated and reformulated by the Vargas government, which took power in 1930, and marked the end of the First Republic and the beginning of the fascist-inspired so-called New State (*Estado Novo*).

The elaboration of the reform was marked by an intense struggle for hegemony over education, and higher education in particular, between conservative Catholic elites and liberal intellectuals of the period (Schwartzman et al, 2000). Indeed, the Church had always attempted to gain hegemony over higher education, as it had done successfully in many other Catholic countries. In exchange for political support for the new regime, it asked the federal government to give the Church the task of organising the first publicly funded Brazilian university. In fact, the Church obtained various concessions, particularly the introduction of religious education in public schools, albeit optional. However, despite the strong influence it exerted over the organisation of the University of Rio de Janeiro, it did not get what it wanted: the public financing of church-sponsored institutions. The opposition of liberal intellectuals was very powerful, and the monarchic and republican tradition in Brazil was different, marked by the predominance of a secular state education system inspired by the French model. The church-sponsored schools that had multiplied during the republican period remained a private education sector. Thus, one can see that the public/private education divide was strongly permeated from the outset by the state/church-sponsored education divide.

The private sector as a whole, and the church-sponsored one in particular, were already quite strong at the start of the period. The data for 1933, when the first education statistics were formulated, shows that private institutions accounted for around 44% of enrolment and for 60% of higher education establishments. However, the whole system was still of very modest proportions. The whole of the student population numbered only 33,723 students.

The reform negotiated by the Vargas government was a compromise between conservative and innovative forces. The universities were established, as was the legal framework for all such institutions to be created in Brazil. Although the university was established as the preferred means for higher education, the reform did not abolish the autonomous schools. The freedom for private initiatives to create educational establishments was also maintained by the legislation, albeit under government supervision.[3] In fact, the reform provided for the regulation of both public and private higher education by the central government. Indeed, the legislation was extremely detailed and even ruled on issues like the appointment of professors, curricula, the duration of courses, the disciplinary system, the payment of taxes and the monthly payment of fees by students. Thus, there was a return to the centralising tendency of the monarchic period, not in terms of a monopoly on the creation and maintenance of education establishments as before, but in terms of a bureaucratic control over norms and supervision of the whole system.

When examining the structure of the new universities, which was similar to the Italian system, the conservative nature of the higher education reform is apparent. The proposed university model largely consisted of a confederation of schools that maintained much of their previous autonomy. Indeed, many universities were simply created by bringing together pre-existing institutions. The courses were strictly separated and organised according to different careers, each under a specific faculty that even determined the number of students that could embark on each career. For this reason, then as now all courses, whether university or non-university, were similar and all degrees were equally valued. As is still the case today, there was no general pre-professional education in the Anglo-Saxon tradition. The whole academic structure centred on the figure of the life-appointed professor. The congregation of professors in each unit exercised academic power, and even had the autonomy to nominate and dismiss assistants.

The innovation in the system was the creation of a Faculty of Philosophy, Sciences and Letters, which offered Bachelor's degrees in the different fields of the physical and exact sciences, biological sciences, humanities and human sciences. Although originally conceived as an American-style college offering a basic grounding prior to professional training, it was never able to fulfil this role. The inclusion of an Education sector meant that graduates of Bachelor's degrees could also acquire a professional teaching qualification, so that the Faculty of Philosophy, Sciences and Letters became yet another school for the preparation of professionals rather than becoming the intellectual centre of the university. Nonetheless, it was this faculty that provided an umbrella for the institutionalisation of basic research in Brazil in a few universities, although most of them became mere teaching institutions.

The first three universities created in this period are representative of the conflicts that marked the reform. The National University of Rio de Janeiro created by the federal government wholly represented the conservative nature of the Vargas government reform, which insisted that it was obligatory for all other universities to adopt the model. The University of the Federal District, also in Rio de Janeiro but older than the Federal University, followed an innovating model created by Anízio Teixeira, the most innovative of Brazil's 'Education Pioneers' and the then Secretary for Education of the Federal District. This university was short lived. It was ferociously attacked by the Catholic Church, which saw it as a centre of liberal anti-clericalism, and was closed down by the New State in 1935 as part of the repression against the Communist uprising. Finally, the University of São Paulo, created by a state-level government that opposed the Vargas regime, managed to maintain its innovative character despite the stiffening of higher education legislation in 1937, not least because of the importance of the Philosophy Faculty, created with French, German and Italian professors.

It was this university that somewhat precociously institutionalised research as one of the basic functions of a university.

All these innovations did not lead to a large increase of the system. During the Vargas period, which ended in 1945, the system expanded very slowly. In that year, it had about 42,000 students, of which 48% were with the private sector. In 15 years the system created only three universities, all of them public (See Table I).

Year	State		Private		Total
	n	%	n	%	n
1933	18,986	56.3	14,737	43.7	33,723
1945	21,307	52.0	19,968	48.0	40,975
1960	59,624	56.0	42,067	44.0	95,691
1965	182,696	56.2	142,386	43.8	352,096
1970	210,613	49.5	214,865	50.5	425,478
1980	492,232	35.7	885,054	64.3	1,377,286
1990	578,625	37.6	961,455	62.4	1,540,080
1995	700,540	39.8	1,059,163	60.2	1,759,703
2000	887,026	32.9	1,807,219	67.1	2,694,245
2001	939,225	31.0	2,091,529	69.0	3,039,754

Table I. Evolution of enrolment in state and private higher education establishments in Brazil, 1933-2001.
Source: Censo e Sinopse Estatísticas do Ensino Superior, MEC.

The Second Republic

In the post-war period, between 1945 until the establishment of the military regime in 1964, the higher education system continued to grow steadily until 1960. In this 15-year period, the number of students rose from 41,000 to 95,000, in response to increasing demand by a middle class growing as a result of the process of urban-industrial development. It was in this period that the network of federal universities, and the Catholic University of Rio de Janeiro (the first in a series of Catholic universities) were formed, that the São Paulo state university system expanded, and that new, smaller, both state and municipal institutions were established in all regions of the country. Between 1946 and 1960 18 state universities and 10 private ones were established.[4] Most of the latter were church-sponsored.

Throughout the period, the states, through their deputies, constantly demanded the creation of federally funded universities. The process occurred with the creation of campuses with the fusion of mostly private institutions that already existed. The usual procedure was for local elites to create some schools and later call on the Federal government to federalise them and create a new university. The universities set up in this way did not correspond at all with the demands of liberal intellectuals of the 1920s and 1930s. The teaching body was improvised and made up of local liberal

153

professionals who had no experience with or interest in research and were uninformed about universities in other countries. It is not surprising, therefore, that these new universities were simply federations of schools tied to a traditional and routine form of teaching based, at best, on a bookish provincial erudition. Nonetheless, it was these institutions that allowed for the effective widening and diversification of the courses on offer, encompassing new fields of knowledge, particularly given the legal obligation of including a Faculty of Philosophy, Sciences and Letters in any university structure.

If one ignored the years that experienced sharp and atypical variations, which seem to result from statistical accidents and may be the result of federalisation, there is great stability in the relative participation of the private sector throughout the period, which represented between 47% and 45% of enrolment.

Although a cursory analysis of the numbers creates the impression of continual and smooth development of the higher education system, this was not in fact the case. The growth of the system as a whole, while not small in percentage terms, was insufficient to absorb the explosive increase in demand for higher education at the end of this period, which fed pressures for reform not only in Brazil but also in other countries.

In Brazil, the constant demand for more vacancies targeted the non-fee paying state universities. Indeed, with increased demand, there was an accumulation of excess candidates made up of students who passed their school examinations and could not be admitted due the lack of places. The admission of these excess students became an important demand of the increasingly active student movement. This pressure began to show results in the beginning of the 1960s, when the rate of enrolment accelerated.

Although what we call the first modern period (1931-45) was marked by the struggle between Catholic and secular elites, the period was also marked by other struggles, whose main protagonist was not the intellectual elite but the student movement. Student mobilisation in favour of a reform to democratise access and university government is a global phenomenon, like increased demand for university education. To a greater or lesser degree, none of these student movements limited themselves to education issues, also contesting established governments.

In Brazil the movement was not just about university issues either. This period, particularly from the 1950s onwards, was marked by intense social conflicts and the growing involvement of university students in the politics of the period, among which various parties and militants of Marxist orientation were a strong presence. In fact, modernisation and capitalist expansion in the period aggravated the situation of the rural population in the regions with more traditional economies and made apparent the depth of economic, social, political and educational inequalities, which generated a general climate of social agitation. The issues that sensitised and mobilised students were not just those pertaining to higher education, but also included the fight against imperialism, capitalism and the latifundia, and in favour of nationalism, development, combating illiteracy, agrarian reform and anything popular: popular democracy, popular education and popular culture. Marxism became the dominant ideology of the movement (Durham, 1994).

The student movement was very important in this period, and more precocious than its European and North American counterparts. As in the rest of Latin America, the strength of the Brazilian student movement was largely a product of centralised organisation through the National Union of Students (*União Nacional the Estudantes*, UNE). In Brazil, this organisation was not created in opposition to the state, but was an initiative of the Vargas regime, which sought to reproduce the corporative organisations of Italian fascism in Brazil. This guaranteed students financial resources and the power of direct contact with the state. This strange relationship with the state, however, did not lead to the taming of the movement. On the contrary, its combative nature is part of the Latin American student tradition, and Brazilian students, like their counterparts in other parts of the continent, tended to see themselves as a sort of national political, social and cultural vanguard and representative of popular interests. In Brazil, from the nineteenth century and even before the creation of the universities the student movement was a school for political leaders.

During the second half of the 1950s, the movement focused on a congressional debate on the Law of Guidelines and Foundations for National Education (*Lei de Directrizes e Bases da Educação Nacional*, LDB) incorporated into the 1946 Constitution that had reorganised the political system after the toppling of the New State. Along with other liberal and left-wing intellectual circles, the students wanted a deep reform of the whole education system to the existing structure and a break with a model that had arisen from the political compromises of the New State. For higher education, the aim was to expand the free state universities, associate teaching with research as a motor for national development, in alliance with the popular classes in the struggle against social inequality. Students even demanded the replacement of all private education by public institutions. This demand directly challenged the interests of the private sector dominated by traditional autonomous higher education schools, which feared limits on its freedom to expand and opposed a project of state university domination. This new clcavage created between the private and state sectors continued through the following decades, and was no longer the old struggle between the religious and the secular.

The private sector was in fact marked by the absence of educational progressiveness and an attachment to traditional bookish learning, which was uninterested in issues like the qualification of teachers and curricular innovation that agitated the state sector. There were exceptions, but only very few. The most important among them were the Catholic universities of Rio de Janeiro and São Paulo, which even supported the student movement. In fact, the position of the Church had changed considerably by this period, and because of the influence of the Second Vatican Council and Liberation Theology, a left-wing Catholic sector had emerged, which believed that the salvation of souls had to be accompanied or preceded by the liberation of the poor and oppressed from their conditions of misery and political marginality. Literacy was considered to be one of the fundamental instruments for this liberation, and it was to be accompanied by political awareness. Catholic university youth became an important and radical segment of the student movement and gave rise in the period that followed to one of the clandestine segments of the armed struggle against the military government.

The LDB, which finally gained power in 1991, constituted a victory for conservative private sectors, in practice ensuring the preservation of the existing system. The law and its complementary parts essentially preserved the status quo and focused on establishing mechanisms to control the expansion of higher education and the content of teaching. The Federal Education Council (*Conselho Federal de Educação*, CFE) was reformulated, acting with the Ministry of Education and representatives of the state and private sector as the new key control mechanism. Its responsibilities were, among others, to fix higher education studies curricula for all institutions and authorise the creation of new courses and federal or private sector institutions. Given its new powers the Council quickly became the main focus of pressure from the private sector in defence of its interests.[5]

Defeated by the vote, the students adopted more radical positions and made the issue a banner of opposition waved on the streets against the government. They added to their demands proposals that were widely consensual among the Latin American student movements of the time: the idea of democratic university government exercised autonomously by teachers and students in conditions of equality.[6]

The Military Regime and the Reform (1964-80)

The military coup of 1964 radically altered the political scenario. The student movement reorganised itself as part of the resistance against the regime and the state university became its stronghold. Thus began a direct confrontation between students and the government.

Initially, the government intervened in the state universities to remove teachers that were seen to be Marxist and linked to the students. Later, a Decree Law issued by then President Castelo Branco in 1967 prohibited the 'organs of student representation to engage in any action, demonstration or propaganda of a party-political, racial and religious nature, and the incitement, promotion or support of collective absences from school work'.[7] This did nothing to cool off the movement but actually radicalised it. Great marches rejecting the regime set off from the universities. There were field battles between state university students and students from parts of the private sector that supported the government. The fight between the student movement and the military government peaked in 1968, in the wake of the great student demonstrations of the period. The May movement in France had reinforced the position of Brazilian students. Students occupied the state universities and established egalitarian student–professor committees as new academic decision-making organs in defiance of the law. The military government hardened its position and the period ended in 1968 with the destruction of the student movement by military repression, the imprisonment of its leaders and a new ban on teachers. For more than a decade, the universities were considered centres of subversion and kept under severe vigilance.

It is difficult to understand the ongoing debate in Brazil about higher education without taking the importance, power and enthusiasm generated by this movement into account. The struggle against the military regime involved great sacrifice on the part of the political leaders who suffered imprisonment, torture and persecution. Thus, the ideal image of the university and higher education of the period became the only fair and politically correct one, connected as it was with the mantle of student heroism in the struggle against the dictatorship. The model of higher education articulated in this climate of revolutionary exaltation has served as the measure of all political struggles waged since then over this issue: the dominant idea was that education should be ministered by free, state universities that associated teaching and research and were autonomously governed by representatives directly elected by teachers, students and non-academic university workers. All courses should lead to full graduation, with a right to a Bachelor's degree or a professional degree that ensured access to a regulated profession. All other institutional or curricular structures were considered a distortion of the model and should be abolished. It became almost impossible to undertake a realistic critical analysis of the changes taking place in higher education.

After the defeat of the student movement and in a context of intense political repression, the military government promoted a profound reform of higher education. The reform largely incorporated the demands of the student movement that corresponded with the consensus prevailing within academic circles and even among Ministry of Education technicians, who were then influenced by the American model. Even the government generally recognised the need for a profound reformulation and modernisation of higher education in Brazil. The figure of the professorial chair (*cátedra*) was abolished and replaced by departments. The autonomy of the faculties ended: internal structures were divided into Basic Institutes divided by areas of knowledge, and Faculties or Schools, which offered professional training. The credit system was introduced and it was proposed that a basic course be attended prior to professional training to give students a more solid general education. The representation of students and different categories of teachers was made possible in internal decision-making organs. However, the logic of the new structure inspired by the American model was cut short because careers were still separated and degrees validated as a necessary and sufficient condition for exercising a profession. The basic course proposal failed because student enrolment was still organised by careers. The difference was that students, while divided by rigidly separated courses, acquired part of their education outside the professional schools, in the Basic Institutes. The reform also failed to make curricula more flexible, as they continued to be rigidly defined by the Ministry of Education through the CFE.

The wide-ranging curricular reform necessary to widen access to higher education did not occur. Neither the universities nor the Ministry were able to promote an effective education reform: this should have accompanied university reform because the opening up of higher education to wider layers of the population, a social demand, could not be accommodated simply by increasing enrolment in the same traditional courses while preserving the old conception of the professional degree and the same kind of teaching.

The reform clearly aimed to reorganise the whole system of federal university education and to promote research according to student demands and the modernising ideals evoked since the 1930s. However, it was incomplete and failed to become institutionalised. Small archipelagos where research flourished dotted the sea of public education. Widespread research activities were more of an ideal than a formal aim, and certainly not a reality.

It is worth noting the peculiarities of the case of São Paulo at this point, and the pioneering nature of the state in the implementation of modernising measures. While in the rest of the Brazilian states the system of state universities is almost entirely federal, in São Paulo the system was state-based. The first state university in São Paulo, the University of São Paulo founded in 1934, far preceded many others in institutionalising research, full-time research and in offering doctorates. The model was followed with the expansion of the *Paulista* system through the creation of other universities, and research was institutionalised in all of them. The state was also a pioneer in the creation of a modern agency for the support of research, the FAPESP, which was independent of the federal government and consolidated the state's leadership in academic research.

Federal research incentives for the system as a whole were instituted through coordinated policies that mainly affected state universities. Two key institutions that were created in the 1950s that both focused on the preparation of Brazilian researchers were reformulated and strengthened. One of the fundamental obstacles for the development of university research was the absence of a sufficient number of qualified researchers in the country. The National Campaign for the Improvement of Higher Education Personnel (*Campanha Nacional de Aperfeiçoamento do Pessoal do Ensino Superior*, CAPES) organised a grant programme that financed the creation and expansion of postgraduate study. The explicit aim was to prepare teachers with Master's and doctoral degrees for the university. The financing programme of the National Council of Scientific and Technological Research (*Conselho Nacional de Pesquisa Científica e Tecnológica*, CNPq) [8], which also offered grants for Master's and doctoral degrees to prepare researchers in

Brazil and abroad, was widened and reformed. The innovation introduced by these agencies was that their laws and regulations did not favour bureaucratic control but rather were based on peer evaluation of the financed programmes and projects. Thus was instituted in Brazil a model programme for support for postgraduate study and university research. In reality, the results were not immediate but, rather, felt over the long term. In the short term they were not very visible, not only because of the long maturation period of the project, but also because the accelerated expansion of the education sector prevented it from having a stronger impact on research incentives within the university ethos. The number of qualified personnel to sustain the increase in enrolment was insufficient; alongside the few new Doctor's and Masters' graduates, a great number of teachers with no degrees or preparation for research were hired. Nonetheless, the general orientation was institutionalised, and the instruments to guide it created. A long-term policy was institutionalised that is still in place today.

Another important initiative was the introduction and widening of a new working regime in federal universities of Full Time Dedication (*Tempo Integral*), which paid teachers according to the time spent on research, thus doubling salaries. In effect, the programme was less efficient an incentive for the development of research because it was not rapidly accompanied by a system of evaluation, and thus ended up being merely a policy to complement salaries. Nonetheless, it created favourable work conditions for the development of research by graduating or recently graduated Master's students. For the same reason, however, the state university tended to become an increasingly expensive institution, and thus failed to expand to meet demand. It was restricted to an elite group of students with stronger basic schooling or, in other words, the new middle classes.

When evaluating this period, it is necessary to take into account the fact that the military regime promoted the strong economic development of the so-called 'Brazilian Miracle' of the 1970s. This economic prosperity directly benefited the middle classes, which became more numerous and well off, feeding the demand for higher education. Federal resources and the education budget increased. Thus, federal institutions in this period experienced a prosperity that they had never known before and never experienced thereafter.

Economic prosperity, and the links between the regime and these new middle classes that supported it, perhaps help to explain why in Brazil, in contrast to other Latin American countries like Argentina and Chile where authoritarian regimes led to a huge decline in enrolment and concomitantly to a contraction of the university system, political repression did not limit the growth of state or private higher education, but rather promoted it. University and non-university higher education expanded in an extraordinary way, from the inauguration of the regime in 1965 to the end of the 1970s. In about 15 years the number of students enrolling in higher education increased from 95,691 in 1960 to 1,345,000 in 1980, with 1968, 1970 and 1971 showing the highest growth rates.[9]

Studies undertaken in Brazil during this period transmit a strong conviction that the military government was promoting the privatisation of education. In fact, this is not quite what happened. In absolute numbers there was a substantial growth of the state and not just the private sector. Enrolment in the state sector increased in this period from 182,700 to 492,000, which means it increased by about 260%. There was no privatisation of education, but rather a rapid expansion of the private sector, which grew in this period by 512%, from 142,386 to 885,054 students.

There was in fact a shift in relative weight. The private sector, which had about 45% rate of participation until 1965, reached 50% in 1970 and thereafter reached and maintained a 60% participation rate. At the end of the decade of the 1970s, the higher education system had changed significantly and the development of the state and private sectors diverged.

The increase in demand for higher education is associated with the growth of the middle classes and new job opportunities created by the more modern sectors of the economy and by the state technical bureaucracy. In order to respond to this generation of mass demand the public sector had to create new kinds of courses as well as new institutions. When demand for higher education in the USA increased in the twentieth century, democratisation of access was ensured through the creation of community colleges, which proved to be very effective in responding to this kind of demand. This did not happen in Brazil so it was not possible for the state sector to absorb demand. The private sector also was unable to absorb the demand because it concentrated on offering low-cost courses. For this sector, research, which was neither lucrative nor sustainable through the payment of fees, was neither an aim nor an interest. New private universities were added to the 20 that existed in 1975 but expansion occurred largely through the proliferation of isolated schools, which focused on offering low-cost courses with lower academic demands: courses in administration, economics and to train teachers (see Table II).

In fact, private higher education institutions had become a big business. Some new education establishments emerged from the transformation of secondary schools. However, the profitability of these undertakings attracted new kinds of entrepreneurs without a prior commitment to education. The private sector became market-oriented as it focused on increasing profits by captivating available demand. Thus was formed what Geiger calls a 'mass private sector', which developed alongside the state sector that focused on responding to more qualified demand (Geiger, 1986).

What can be called the entrepreneurial private sector grew to satisfy the most immediate social demand to obtain degrees. This tendency was reinforced by the long-standing notarial tradition in Brazil, which associates a higher education degree with access to a specific regulated profession and ensures degree-carriers of privileged access to the job market. Thus, education establishments where the quality of education is secondary are still profitable. The private system divided itself into a non-profit community or church-sponsored sector, akin to the state sector, and an entrepreneurial sector.[10]

	Universities		Faculties integrated		Establishments isolated		Centres university		Total
	St.	Pte	St.	Pte	St.	Pte	St.	Pte	
1970	32	15	–	–	139	463	–	–	639
1975	37	20	–	–	178	625	–	–	860
1980	45	20	1	10	154	643	–	–	882
1986	48	20	1	58	184	548	–	–	859
1990	55	49	–	74	167	582	–	–	918
1996	68	59	3	84	147	490	–	–	850
2000	71	85	2	88	132	782	1	49	901

St. = State; Pte = Private.

Table II. Evolution in the number of state and private institutions, 1970-2000.
(The statistical inclusion of integrated faculties began in 1980.)
Source: Censo e Sinopse Estatísticas do Ensino Superior, MEC.

Another important change that shaped the system as a whole was the concentration of new private sector enrolment in the South-east region. This was a result of the close link between the expansion of the private sector and the market, and therefore the concentration of growth in the more economically developed regions. In the poorer regions like the North or the North-east, private investment was limited and the absorption of demand depended on the public sector, particularly the federal universities. Indeed, the state sector responded more closely to social interests and was more equitably distributed in the country as a whole.

At the end of the 1970s, the Brazilian higher education system had changed profoundly, with increased enrolment, new stimuli for degree study, public sector research, and the creation of a new entrepreneurial profit-oriented private sector without a commitment to research or quality teaching, which coexisted with a non-profit private sector that more closely followed the model of the state system.

The 1980s

The 1980s was a decade of crisis and transition. Politically, it was marked by the long and gradual process of redemocratisation that began with a decline in political repression, continued with the election of a civilian president in 1985, and culminated in a new constitution in 1988 followed by the first direct presidential election the next year. Economically, it was a decade of economic crisis and growing inflation. For higher education, it was a period of stagnation.

It is rather surprising the system should stop growing abruptly after a period of accelerated growth. Stagnation affected both the state and private sectors, although the latter more than the former. The percentage of private education enrolment declined in the period. This phenomenon is probably linked with the economic crisis, although other factors help to explain stagnation and another problem affecting Brazilian higher education: its anomalously small size compared with that of comparably developed countries in Latin America. Even at the peak of growth, the gross rate of enrolment in higher education relative to the 20-24 year-old population was never greater than 12%. In the 1980s and most of the 1990s the rate fell to 11 and 10%. It was only in 2000 that it repeated the highest levels of the past, which suggests that a new phase of accelerated growth may be in the offing. The explanation lies in previously attained levels of education.

As Simon Schwartzman's chapter in this book shows, if higher education is a relatively recent phenomenon in Brazil, the establishment of a state system of basic education is even more recent. In 1960, in the midst of student mobilisation, almost 40% of the population was illiterate and less than 50% of children between the ages of 7 and 14 were enrolled in school.[11] These rates improved consistently, but it was only in 2000 that a net rate of 97% of school attendance for this age group was reached.

The problem was compounded by very high rates of failure to pass from one year to the next (repetition) and of truancy in basic education. Thus, a very small proportion of the population actually attained a medium level of education and an even smaller percentage completed basic education. As a result, although the rate of enrolment in higher education is very small, there is a very strong relation between the number of places in higher education and the number of people leaving secondary education. In 1980, the proportion was 1:3 school leavers per place, which is much more than the system could absorb. In 2001, the proportion was 1:5. Thus, what one can see is that there have always been structural obstacles to widening higher education, which are related to the social inequalities that characterise the country.

These figures lead one to conclude that the growth of the 1970s was only possible because there was repressed demand from old secondary school leavers and from people who had completed supplementary courses and had been unable to enter higher education at the customary age: an older population already inserted in the job market.

This view is confirmed when one analyses another phenomenon that marked Brazilian higher education, and the private sector in particular, from this period onwards: the high percentage of night courses. Night courses generated a new demand in so far as they made it possible for a large contingent of older secondary school leavers already inserted in the job market for whom higher education levels held the promise of job promotion to gain access to higher education. The fact that private sector night courses make few demands in terms of school qualifications facilitated access for this population group.

Unfortunately, it was only in 1986 that statistics began to differentiate between enrolment in day and night courses. In that year, already in the middle of the period of stagnation, 76.5% of private sector enrolment was for night courses. In the federal universities, on the other hand, the percentage was only 16%. It is interesting to note that it is exactly in the universities where there is a discourse exalting democracy and commitment to the lower classes that resistance to the creation of night courses was greatest. The exception among the state universities is the University of São Paulo, which introduced night courses in 1952, well before the great movements in favour of the democratisation of access to higher education. The increase in night course in federal establishments was very slow, and in 1999 it covered only 21.4% of students.

Given the importance of the very slow growth in the number of recent secondary school leavers, once repressed demand was absorbed there was no longer a sufficient number of candidates to fill existing places in the private system.

It is only more recently that the situation has changed, with an accelerated increase in secondary students resulting from the expansion and improvement of basic education in previous decades. Even so, the relationship between school leavers and available places fell again to 1:5 in 2001, after reaching 1:8 in 1997.

The scarcity of candidates in the 1980s and 1990s promoted an intensification of competition among private sector establishments. The universities were in an advantageous competitive position because they had the autonomy to create and extinguish courses and available places and thus to respond more agilely to the preferences of their clientele. The larger establishments that offered a lot of courses were also in a better position to face sharp changes in demand in one or another area of study.

It is thus easy to understand why the private sector focused on increasing the size of establishments through fusions and by incorporating small institutions, creating federations of schools and then seeking to transform them into universities, in order to acquire autonomy and escape the control of the CFE. The CFE was inundated with this kind of request and lobbying of the Council intensified. From 1975 to 1985 the number of private universities was stable, with a total of 20. However, the Federations of Faculties or Integrated Faculties grew substantially. This new kind of structure was recognised officially only in the 1980 statistics, which indicate that there were 10 establishments of this kind. Five years later, there were 58, and in 1990 they numbered 74. The increase in the number of universities, on the other hand, is a phenomenon of the second half of the 1990s. Between 1985 and 1990 there was a 100% increase, from 20 to 40.

Thus, at the end of the 1980s there was a new inflection of the private sector. Until then the private universities were predominantly confessional or community based non-profit institutions, which tended to follow the state university model. The expansion of private universities after 1985 resulted from the pressure exerted by the profit-oriented sector focused on mass education and with no interest in developing research activities and qualifying teaching staff.[12]

In order to understand how this happened, one must analyse the university recognition mechanism administered by the CFE. Although all the legislation stated that universities, unlike other education establishments, had to associate teaching and research, CFE criteria made no such demands. The main criteria were the range of areas of knowledge covered by the courses and the existence of minimal infrastructural conditions. For the private sector, the constitution of Federations of Schools was the first step towards obtaining the desirable status of 'university' and the autonomy that went with it. The application of these criteria led to the multiplication of private universities but did not entail improved quality of education, teaching staff, or the development of research. Nor did it entail the creation of a university ethos of academic freedom and of prizing competence in these establishments.

An analysis of the period is incomplete without an examination of the struggles waged within the higher education sector upon the emergence of a new political actor: the movement of higher education teaching staff led by the National Association of University Teachers (*Associação Nacional dos Docentes Universitários*, ANDES), which in a way replaced the student movement and adopted many of its demands of past decades. This movement was practically limited to the state sector.

To understand the nature and power of this movement, it is necessary to analyse the negative effects that military repression had had on the state universities in the preceding period. The gravity of the confrontations that occurred prior to the 1968 reform, and the force of repression that accompanied it, left profound marks on the state universities. For students and teachers, they delegitimated not only the regime but also the reform itself.

As noted above, the reform included measures for effective internal democratisation of universities and a substantial increase in the participation of students and teachers in their management. It also included measures to promote stronger academic values (structuring careers and valuing research). However, the new university structure made it difficult for the authoritarian regime to exert ideological and political control over them. For this reason, parallel non-academic mechanisms for political-ideological control were set up, corrupting and disturbing the whole system. These mechanisms included direct police repression, on the one hand, the banning of academic leaders that were considered left wing, and ideological triage. These controls were implemented by representatives of state intelligence and information agencies, who operated without a legal or institutional framework, with the newly hired elements in the rectories linked to the university power structure.

On the other hand, there was intense manipulation of the leadership election mechanism, exerted through direct and indirect pressures, to ensure that regime sympathisers would remain in the university administration.

The implementation of these control mechanisms facilitated all kinds of illegitimate interference and permitted the removal of a good part of the universities' intellectual leadership in favour of teachers protected by the central government or by local oligarchies allied to the regime. The reinvigoration of a merit-based system through the structuring of careers was thus weakened; autonomy was destroyed and systems of co-optation and clientelism were strengthened. In this context, students and teachers took refuge in intransigence, attributing all the evils of the university to the dictatorship and thus failing to engage in a deeper reflection on the problems facing the universities. At the same time, they symbolically expressed their resistance to the regime by defending a radical egalitarianism that contributed in other ways to delegitimate the academic values of merit and competence.

The devaluation of academic values was compounded by the expansion of public federal universities that, as noted above, increased teaching staff without demanding academic qualifications. Further, because new contracts were made outside the traditional teaching staff selection mechanisms, opportunities for clientelistic manipulation to obtain jobs at federal universities increased. Parallel hiring systems were established, giving rise to a great heterogeneity in salary levels, which contributed to a general climate of dissatisfaction among teachers, particularly among teachers that were new, least qualified and did not benefit from job stability.

On the other hand, research activities developed through the programmes of the development agencies (CAPES, CNPq, FINEP, FAPESP) ended up becoming a parallel system, which created a direct relationship between researchers and development agencies and thus operated above and beyond the universities' power structures. It did strengthen academic values in so far as it was legitimated by the quality of scientific research and the competence of researchers, but it did so by dissociating the recognition of those values from the university as a whole. The system therefore operated by creating and maintaining 'islands of competence' that were like enclaves in the fabric of general mediocrity of university institutions.[13]

The teachers' associations were organised by academic leaders who had been marginalised from the administrative organs of the state universities. The movement denounced as illegitimate the political instruments that guaranteed the perpetuation of power of a small incompetent administrative minority allied to the regime. The main banners of the movement were autonomy and democratisation, or the widening of teacher and student participation through representation mechanisms. The movement was legitimated by the defence of academic values and was backed by the scientific competence of its leaders. In sum, it was a movement through which the politically excluded groups that had intellectual prestige within the universities sought to regain a place in institutional management. Initially, the movement was marked by a predominantly 'academic' orientation, within which the need for reform was amply debated. Because the existing situation against which these teachers protested was supported by the authoritarian regime, the movement acquired a wider anti-regime political connotation from the outset. For the movement, democratising the university was a metonymy for social democratisation.

As its oppositional nature became increasingly explicit, the movement attracted all left-wing university sectors and its political nature became more pronounced, in accordance with the mobilisation of civil society at the end of the 1970s. In this context, and given the presence of the most radical sectors of the left, the issue of democratisation was also radicalised, becoming the almost exclusive topic of relevance and the rhetorical link with other civil society movements: the strong attack on authoritarian structures within and without the university relegated to a secondary position a reflection about the more specific problems of the higher education system and of more academic issues.

Unlike the student movement, which was intensely linked to the social struggles of the period, the teachers constituted an internal university movement without wider social bases. For this reason, they sought to increase their power in the struggle against the authoritarian structure by seeking allies within the university institution, establishing an alliance with students and non-academic workers. The idea of democratisation was reinterpreted to mean egalitarian participation for the entire 'university community'. In fact, this brand of egalitarianism was a common characteristic of the more radical left wing groups of the period and permeated the whole range of social movements that proliferated at the time.[14]

Given that the constitution of the movement of teachers' associations was concomitant with the progressive reduction of public funds for higher education and a consequent downward pressure on salaries, it very quickly took on a new, unionising, dimension. By becoming a union and organising salary demands, the movement became stronger and more all-embracing, but it also changed its composition and reinforced its alliance with non-academic workers, encouraging them to build up a parallel trade union organisation.

In this context, the academic aspect became marginal. Although concerns with the competence of professors, the quality of teaching and the development of research were frequently a part of the discourse of the movement, its role was primarily to legitimate salary demands, and mobilisation to defend academic values was rare. Indeed, it is easy to understand that the more union oriented the movement became, the more it incorporated the least qualified professors and those uninterested in academic issues. Thus, the greater the emphasis on egalitarianism, the less important were professional qualifications as a criterion for the selection of university leaders.

The strength of the union or corporative aspect of the teachers' associations movement was largely a product of the hegemonic position then and still occupied by the federal universities. This is because the federal universities constitute a numerous and powerful bloc unified by common interest, and because they possess the same interlocutor and administrator in the Ministry of Education (MEC). It is therefore impossible to understand the nature of the movement's demands and resistance, if one does not recognise that they emerged from the problems, needs and demands specific to the network of federal universities.

In the federal universities, the selection of leaders was always directly subordinated to the MEC and therefore much more subject to political interferences and the interests of local oligarchies, for which the federal universities constituted an important source of resources and patronage. In some states, like Alagoas, the federal university budget was larger than the state budget itself. Indeed, political pressure to influence the composition of lists sent to the central government for the selection of rectors was an established practice that undermined the administrative and academic autonomy of the universities. In this context, the struggle for direct elections by leaders became of fundamental importance, as it was the only way to break with traditional mechanisms of domination and to establish minimum levels of university autonomy. Because the Ministry was a very powerful opponent, the alliance with workers and students became crucial. Thus, the formula for direct tripartite elections became an indisputable principle. It is easy to see that the more authoritarian the historical behaviour of rectors and the greater the support that political forces gained from the government, the more exacerbated became the struggle for tripartite direct elections – with the vote of teachers, students and non-academic workers. On the other hand, because previous selection mechanisms had never accentuated academic criteria of qualification and competence, it was easier for the teachers' movement to abandon those values in favour of a position of radical egalitarianism that met with widespread support among students and non-academic workers for whom, obviously, issues of career and graduate degrees were subtleties of secondary importance.

The teachers' movement attained some expressive victories with the formation of this monolithic bloc and through its direct confrontation with the MEC [15], and came to dominate the debate about university reform. The basic confrontation mechanism was the successive and prolonged strike action that systematically left the whole teaching structure in disarray, with very negative consequences on the preservation of academic values. This process continues to have an important negative impact on the ability to deal with the issue of a new university reform. The strength of the teachers' movement and the power of its union dimension often contributed to obscuring or relegating to a secondary position the discussion of university reform, or the more serious problems of the higher education system in general. This happened because the debate focused on internal problems of the state universities and concentrated excessively on issues linked with the increase in public funds, career structures, salaries, and the best way to administratively represent the corporative interests of teachers, non-academic workers and students.

At the end of this period, a new group began to organise itself that opposed the orientation and positions adopted by ANDES. It was made up of university researchers who concentrated on analysing the Brazilian higher education system, qualified MEC technicians who knew the complexities and the problems of the system well, and rectors from the federal universities of São Paulo. They had in common a familiarity with research on university issues undertaken in Europe and the USA and with the reforms being undertaken there. The big underlying question that was being addressed in the international debate and that influenced this group was the changing role of the state from executor to regulator and evaluator of policy.

The issues introduced by this group were autonomy and evaluation. Although autonomy was also a banner of the ANDES, it meant direct elections to executive positions and no academic demands on teachers and non-academic workers holding those positions. In the new debate, autonomy meant decentralisation of administrative responsibility and a necessary association with state control through evaluation mechanisms; the idea was that university resource allocation should be performance-linked with the institution's engagement in teaching and research tasks. The first time that this issue entered the public debate was in 1985, with the constitution of a high-level commission proposed by president-elect Tancredo Neves. With his death on the eve of his taking office, the proposal was adopted by his successor, President Sarney, and implemented by the then Minister of Education, Marco Maciel. After the commission ended its work, Maciel created a special group, the GERES, to elaborate and detail legislation to implement the recommendations. Given the negative reaction of teaching staff, Maciel backed down and shelved the work of the Commission and GERES. Despite this initial setback, the issue had been raised and remained in the public debate and inspired new reform proposals.

Another attempt to implement these ideas occurred in 1991, when José Goldemberg, a former rector of the University of São Paulo who defended evaluations, became Minister of Education. There was no time for implementation, however, as the minister resigned less than a year later because of the conflicts with the then president of the republic, Fernando Collor de Mello. Following the impeachment of the president and the inauguration of a new government representing traditional Brazilian political sectors, the project was abandoned. The following government took up the issue again in 1995, as described below.

The Recent Past: 1995-98

The recent period coincides with the two mandates of President Fernando Henrique Cardoso, during which there were very substantial changes in economic and social policies and important reforms in education, particularly in primary education: there was a change in the system of funding of basic education that promoted access to, permanence in and successful completion of basic education, which became practically universal in this period; a primary and secondary education curricular reform was implemented; the whole system of education statistics was modernised and became more efficient; the system of evaluation of school performance was improved, and programmes for teacher training were widened. Eight years of administrative continuity permitted consistent change in the whole system. As a result, there was an explosive increase in enrolment in secondary education at the end of the period, as a result of those who had initiated basic education in the previous decade coming out of the system.

These results are linked to the resumption of growth of higher education in the last five years. In fact, growth in this period was surprising: it represented 82% of total enrolment. As in the 1970s, however, growth was concentrated primarily in the private sector. The participation of this sector, which was around 60% between 1980 and 1998, reached 69% in 2001, accounting for 115% of the increase in enrolment as a whole. As in the 1970s, the public sector grew at a slower rate, by less than 36%. Its participation in the system as a whole declined from 41.6% in 1994 to 31% in 2001. This expansion took place in all the regions of the country except the North-east.

It is possible to link this worrying decline in the relative weight of the state sector with the fact that higher education policy did not incorporate the proposals formulated by the ministry, or the Education Policy secretary. These focused on the creation of a mass state system of education based on quality that might counterbalance the elitism inherent in the exclusive concentration on research universities. Nonetheless, there was progress where evaluation was concerned, with the creation of a system for education quality control with enormous potential.

This system was incorporated into the new LDB voted in December 1996. The new law introduced important innovations into the system as a whole. First, it clearly defined the role of universities in the higher education system, requiring an association between teaching and research, with the production of scientific knowledge as a necessary condition for gaining or renewing credentials. It is true that the link between teaching and research had been made by all other prior legislation but there had never been a mechanism to ensure its implementation by the private sector. This is clear in the analysis of the process of approving the creation of new universities by the CFE. The law also demanded that the universities should require a minimum level of qualification of teachers and instituted a work regime without which research would not have been possible: at least a third of teachers had to have

Master's or doctoral degrees and a third had to be exclusively dedicated to that job. The approval of these provisions was particularly difficult, as it was strongly opposed by the private sector lobby. Because of this, the demands of the original proposal were reduced from half to a third. Although apparently bureaucratic, these legal provisions established very objective criteria that therefore substantively altered the process of university creation.

Another very important innovation was the requirement for a periodical renewal of credentials of higher education institutions after an evaluation process. This made it possible to correct the distortions and deficiencies of the existing system, threatening the position of universities that were nothing more than great teaching units, which ceased to be immune to a periodic process of government control. The universities were given a period of eight years to comply with the new legal requirements.

The law also provided for the periodic renewal of recognition of higher education degrees. State recognition of both federal and state-level courses has always been a requirement to legalise degrees in Brazil, including university degrees. When properly applied, the procedure guaranteed minimal standards for new courses, but it could not ensure that conditions would not deteriorate. The requirement for periodic renewal of recognition made it possible to exert a permanent pressure on institutions to ensure the maintenance of minimum levels of quality.

By creating a special niche for universities, the law recognised the heterogeneity of a system in which research universities and other kinds of teaching-focused institutions co-existed. However, the LDB maintained a rigid bureaucratic control over the latter institutions. It would have been desirable to grant autonomy to other kinds of teaching establishments in order to limit bureaucratic centralism, had such a measure been accompanied by a system of periodic evaluation and renovation of credentials to limit abuse. A presidential decree of the following year created a new category of establishment, the university centre. These were not required to undertake research but only to provide excellent teaching standards. These institutions were granted academic autonomy to create courses and increase places, and submitted to the periodic evaluation system.

The system became much more flexible but subject to mechanisms of quality control. This flexibility applied to courses as well, with the abolition of the minimum curriculum that made all education, both public and private, stick to curricula that were rigidly defined by the CFE. In its place General Curricular Guidelines were adopted. Further, the law also provided for short sequential courses for basic or complementary education.

The new legislation did not affect the public federal and state-level universities much: for better or worse, these had developed their own research activities as a result of prior policies, and had increased the full-time dedication requirement and given their teachers degrees. For the private universities, however, the legislation threatened a loss of status and autonomy. The reactions of the private sector to the new legislation are assessed below. What follows is an analysis of the policies and initiatives of the Ministry.

The efficacy of the new legislation as a whole depended on creating an evaluation system and this was the main concern of the Ministry even before the law was approved. The key measure adopted in this regard did not focus on evaluating teaching institutions but rather, the quality of the courses. This was done through the creation of a National Course Examination, commonly known as the *Provão* (Super Test), which consists of objective tests applied to all graduates of a course or university career. The examination is obligatory for students and a condition for obtaining a degree, although it is not an instrument for passing or failing individuals. The aim is to evaluate the courses offered by different institutions, classifying them according to the average grades obtained by their students.

The *Provão* was strongly resisted by the administrators of private teaching institutions and by the students and teachers of the state sector. Although opposition by the former was predictable, the resistance of the latter was surprising, particularly as the first applications of the *Provão* proved that the quality of courses in public institutions was higher than that of the private sector. The explanation for this phenomenon lies in the corporative nature of the public sector, which is led by the teachers' union with the support of students. The latter always tenaciously opposed any evaluation that might permit comparisons between public institutions, as this was seen as a threat to the principle of isonomy, or the egalitarian distribution of benefits and rewards within the sector as a whole. Indeed, defending isonomy is a precondition for the monolithic unity of the members of the union. The only form of evaluation that is acceptable is a self-evaluation that is not based on a comparison between different institutions and is not associated with a differential distribution of resources and benefits. The implementation of the new system was only possible because it had strong support from the media and society. The publication of results by the press awakened great public interest and legitimated the *Provão*, making the examination the most powerful instrument ever created in Brazil to establish incentives to improve the quality of teaching, particularly as it even has an effect on the education market. The private institutions that have better classified courses have used that classification as publicity to attract students. Indeed, demand has in fact been shaped by the results of the evaluation.

The *Provão* was first applied to three courses (Administration, Law and Engineering). New courses were added every year and by 2001 the *Provão* was already evaluating 20 courses, including the most sought after ones, and covering 1,293,170 students. It thus covers the vast majority of graduating students. At the same time, a qualitative evaluation mechanism was introduced, constituted by commissions of peers, the Commissions for the Evaluation of Teaching Supply Conditions (*Comissões de Avaliação das Condições de Oferta de Ensino*), which complemented and corrected the *Provão* evaluation. Although the Ministry managed to implement evaluation instruments for graduate courses, it practically ignored institutional evaluations, which are essential for the implementation of the LDB. This task is relatively easy to institutionalise, however, using existing systems, which include those that have an impact on graduate studies that work alongside the new *Provão* and the Evaluation Commissions, and those that have an impact on postgraduate studies and research, like the long-established evaluation by the CAPES and CNPq.

All these initiatives had important repercussions on the system, although they are still not consolidated. The impact on the private sector was greater, particularly in the case of the universities, as these were threatened with the loss of autonomy or with being issued lower credentials and thus being demoted. They therefore undertook a series of internal measures to comply with the legal requirements at the lowest cost possible.

It became apparent that one of the biggest obstacles was the easiest to overcome: increasing the number of staff with postgraduate qualifications. In this regard the private sector had an absurd corporative advantage, which had been inserted in the text of the 1988 Constitution itself: the right to retirement with a full salary for teachers at all levels of education with a minimum of 25 years of work for women and 30 years for men.

This unjustifiable privilege led to an authentic exodus of more qualified and experienced staff from the public universities, who began to complement retirement benefits with new jobs in the private sector. This measure had another deleterious effect on the public sector: because retirement benefits are paid out of the education budget, an increasing percentage of the resources for education is taken up by the growing number of retirees. This scandalous corporative privilege has become nothing less than a public subsidy to the private sector, which has been spared much of the onus of ensuring that its staff is properly qualified.

The private sector did made some effort in this regard as postgraduate qualifications for teaching staff did become an increasingly important criterion for all forms of evaluation. Thus, enormous pressure was generated to approve new postgraduate courses in the private institutions themselves. Indeed, there were significant increases in the number of teachers with Master's or doctoral degrees, an essential condition for the recognition of a postgraduate course. But given the absence of a research tradition and the lack of any real understanding of the meaning and contribution of research, the private universities found it very difficult to recognise the proposed courses and mobilised to limit the rigid demands that CAPES had managed to institutionalise for this level of education. In the interim, and given the growing market for postgraduate and continuing education, the whole sector of specialist courses was expanded, over which there is little quality control.

Other subterfuges were used. As scientific output is one of the main ways to prove scientific activity, the private universities created their own reviews (non-indexed), exerting pressure on their teachers to produce articles. Another subterfuge consisted in opening up to the global higher education market. Unable to create their own postgraduate courses, the private sector reached agreements with foreign universities interested in exploring the graduate course market through long distance or semi-attended courses. In such instances degrees are obtained from abroad, which therefore escape the rigid quality control of the CAPES.[16]

It is true that there were initiatives that were more in keeping with the spirit of the law. Various institutions, including for-profit education establishments, established small, effectively serious, research groups with retired public sector staff. These were in a position to obtain funding from public agencies and thus satisfy legal requirements. For the most part, however, these are small enclaves in huge institutions that are basically focused on mass education and have no capacity to influence graduate courses. The fate of these groups is rather problematic, because their survival depends entirely on the financial strategies of private university administrators.

There is a basic problem in profit-oriented institutions that underlies all these initiatives: the already mentioned complete absence of academic freedom and the appropriation of university autonomy by the administrators or owners of establishments. In fact, the teachers in these institutions constitute the proletariat of the education system, as they are submitted not only to the decisions but even the caprices of the owners. Directors are generally appointed by the owners and are often relatives, and qualified personnel are rarely appointed. In this way, the profit-oriented private universities are frequently a falsification of the university model that inspired the legislation and movements for higher education reform.

However, one should highlight the role of the non-profit, community or confessional institutions, which have sought to implement the university model that associates teaching and research, invests in serious pedagogical projects, and exercises some degree of academic freedom. This segment has contributed in a very positive way to develop Brazilian higher education.

Despite all the innovations, there were important omissions in recent education policy that have had a particular impact on the state higher education system, leaving unresolved the structural problems that stifle their operation and expansion. In fact, there was no initiative by public institutions to meet with increasing demand for post-secondary level education by a population with a previous basic education that is insufficient to permit success in research or in institutions focused on postgraduate studies. Federal and state-level governments continue to concentrate resources on providing free university education and on increasing stimuli for research and postgraduate studies. There was no diversification of types of establishments or of teaching programmes to meet the needs of an increasingly heterogeneous demand. There was also no effort to create an open university with public funds that might offer high-quality long distance or semi-attended courses. This job was delegated to the public and private universities that minister attended courses, and which do not have the necessary competence in this new area or the resources to create the necessary new competences. Public university initiatives have been very limited and private university initiatives lack the necessary quality. Indeed, long distance learning has promoted pressure to open the system to the aggressive foreign institutions with an interest in exporting courses, particularly at the postgraduate level. Thus, the democratisation of education with the absorption of a more popular kind of demand is increasingly dependent on the private mass education sector, for which this continues to be a very lucrative activity. The short-term vision of this sector, on the other hand, has not promoted a renovation of education that can correct the deficiencies of the prior schooling of this kind of public or to offer training that adequately responds to the growing demands of the job market.

During this period there was also no administrative reform of public education, and of the relationship between these institutions and the state so as to break rigid bureaucratic centralism and promote the necessary rationalisation of available resources. The problem resides in the absence of administrative and financial autonomy of the state universities, with the single exception of the São Paulo state universities. Without this autonomy, it is impossible to change the nature of management and establish a funding system that associates funding with performance quality criteria. The 1988 Constitution, which is extremely detailed, actually granted teaching, scientific, administrative and financial autonomy for the universities. But while academic freedom was established, legally granted autonomy did not flourish given the continued submission of the universities to the rigid rules of the public bureaucracy on admissions, firing and staff salaries, and the complex budgetary controls of the government. The control over new contracts was still exercised directly by centralised government organs, as was control over regulations governing careers. Salaries, which consume about 90% of resources, are directly administered and paid out by the Ministry. The freedom to determine what to do with the remaining 10% is limited by the rigid separation between the financing and capital budget and the itemisation of expenditures by the National Congress. Although research does in fact depend on the quality of projects and the competence of researchers, research depends on funding agencies and is extra-budgetary. There is still no system of institutional evaluation that integrates teaching and research.

The situation is further aggravated by the fact that, in the wake of the democratic exaltation that accompanied the creation of the constitution, the corporative teachers' and workers' movement obtained important victories that, in addition to the retirement benefits already mentioned, ensured total job stability, impregnable salaries and the permanent incorporation of any temporary benefit that might be conceded as a result of the exercise of a post, scientific production or pedagogical innovation. The composition of teaching staff has become extremely rigid and practically immune to any merit-based evaluation. As a result of this, any innovation in the system depends entirely on increased resources. J. Joaquim Brunner analysed the impossibility of modernising and rationalising public universities in a system like this, which was established in practically all the countries of Latin America (Brunner, 1991). Without far-reaching reform, public education cannot increase its capacity to attend the demand of the population.

One can only regret and lament that the opportunity to implement such a reform was lost when it could have been implemented in the very favourable eight years of Fernando Henrique Cardoso's stable government.

Perspectives

On 1 January 2003 there was a massive political change with the victory of the Workers Party in the presidential elections and the coming to power of President Luiz Inácio Lula da Silva. A party that was part of the opposition to the previous government and one of whose slogans was 'put an end to everything that's there' (*acabar com tudo que está aí*) took power.

Indeed, there has been a strong tendency to dismantle the administrative machine that unfortunately has also affected technical sectors. In the Ministry of Education, the change has consisted of the replacement of previous civil servants with members of the Teachers' Union, which always violently opposed evaluation procedures and intransigently fought a university reform that might differentiate institutions according to merit and performance and that could threaten the stability of teachers and existing corporative benefits. On the other hand, there is as yet no consistent and integrated proposal for a new higher education and evaluation policy. In the first months of government there were only isolated and casuistic initiatives.

In the absence of a system to evaluate the quality of teaching, it is difficult to implement a policy to limit abuse in the private mass education sector, particularly as teachers' union activities have been limited to the state sector (where job stability and the difficulty of suspending the payment of salaries means that strikes imply no risks or costs). In this context, the issue of qualifications and working conditions for teachers in private mass education institutions has hardly been touched. Without better working conditions, the quality of education cannot be improved. Although there has been a significant improvement in salaries in many private institutions, salaries depend on the number of classes taught and there are no incentives for ongoing teacher training and to improve qualifications. Teachers give up to 40 or even more classes a week in overcrowded classes without the support of pedagogical planning. They are, therefore, unable to offer appropriate teaching for a public that suffers from serious prior schooling deficiencies.

It is too early to tell, but I see few prospects for deeper reform and I fear that the reforms undertaken in the previous period may be destroyed, and that the leap will not be made to consolidate a system to renew credentials based on institutional evaluations.

Notes

[1] That year were created the School of Surgery and Anatomy of Bahia (today the Faculty of Medicine of the Federal University of Bahia), and the School of Anatomy and Surgery of Rio de Janeiro (now the Faculty of Medicine of the Federal University of Rio de Janeiro), and the Marine Guard Academy, also in Rio. Two years later in 1810, the Royal Military Academy was founded, which became the Central School, and thereafter the Polytechnic School (today the National School of Engineering of the UFRJ [see Schwartzman, 1991]).

[2] The near absence of demands for the creation of universities during the First Republic stands in contrast with the colonial and imperial periods, when dozens of projects indicated the advantages of creating a university in Brazil. Anísio Teixeira refers to the existence of 24 such projects between 1808 and 1872. Souza Campos lists 30, including the Jesuit (1592) and Inconfidents (1789) proposals made before King João VI, and six after the Empire. There is some dispute over which might have been the first Brazilian university. However, the first federal university was clearly the University of Rio de Janeiro, established in the 1920s as a federation of isolated establishments with the single purpose, as the legend goes, of giving King Albert of Belgium the title of an *Honoris Causa* degree during his official visit to Brazil (see Teixeira, 1969; e Cunha, 1980).

[3] Decrees 42/83, 2.076/40 and 3.617/31 of the reform established that the creation and maintenance of higher degree courses was 'free and the public powers, legal or natural entity, and private law can minister them, as long as they are authorised by the federal government' (Mendes & Castro, 1984, p. 33).

[4] Until 1971, official statistics do not discriminate between universities and other institutions. However, Helena Sampaio's research shows that although only three universities were created during the Vargas period (two state and one Catholic university, the Rio de Janeiro University established in 1944), in the period that followed, between 1946 and 1960 (just before the large expansion) another 18 state and 10 private universities were established (Sampaio, 2000, p. 70).

[5] In 1984 the CFE was extinguished because of strong suspicions of corruption and constant attrition with the Ministry of Education. Two years later, a new Council was created, the National Education Council (*Conselho Nacional de Educação*, CNE).

[6] This position goes back to the movement for the Reform of the University of Córdoba in Argentina in 1918, which became a kind of myth of the Latin American student movement.

[7] Article 11 of Decree Law no. 228 of 18 February 1967 (Instituto Nacional de Estudos Pedagógicos [INEP], 1969).

[8] Actually, an admiral founded the CNPq with the support of the military. It must be remembered that there were technocratic-modernising sectors within

the military, which considered essential the country's scientific capacity for economic and military development.

[9] Although growth in the 1960s was higher in relative terms, in this case one has to take into account the low starting point and the absolute number of new students absorbed: 329,787 students in 1960-70, and 951,802 in the following decade.

[10] It is impossible to document statistically the importance of this sector because until 1996, all establishments were formally non-profit based. The affirmation is based on a qualitative analysis and the author's familiarity with the system, given her participation in governmental decision-making bodies.

[11] It is important to clarify, however, that until 1970 there were only four years of mandatory schooling, between the ages of 7 and 11. In 1971 it increased to eight years, between the ages of 7 and 15.

[12] Until 1997 the law did not permit the establishment of institutions for profit. Profits were made through subterfuges like the nomination of owners to management positions with very high salaries, the diversion of funds for other projects or for the private use of owners (such as the acquisition and maintenance of executive jets, luxury cars, the use of huge representation budgets). It was never possible to establish effective control over these expenditures.

[13] The expression 'islands of competence' is Oliveira's (1984).

[14] It is important to note the affinities of the teachers' movement with other social movements of the period, with which it shared 'communitarian egalitarianism'. For an analysis of these social movements and the peculiar position adopted with regard to the state, see Durham (1984).

[15] It consisted largely of the approval of a Single Juridical Regime for the federal higher education system as a whole, which abolished different hiring and salary systems and ensured the general job stability of teachers and administrative staff.

[16] The legislation establishes that these degrees should be re-evaluated by Brazilian universities that have Master's and doctoral programmes that have already been recognised by the CAPES. This norm, however, has been difficult to apply.

References

Brunner, J.J. (1991) *Educación superior en América Latina cambios y desafíos*. Mexico: Fondo de Cultura Económica.

Cunha, L.A.C.R.d. (1980) *A universidade temporã: o ensino superior da colônia à era de Vargas, Coleção Educação e transformação*. Rio de Janeiro: Editora Civilizacão Brasileira, Edições UFC.

Durham, E.R. (1994) Introdução, in R.S. Kent (Ed.) *Los temas críticos de la educación superior en América Latina*. México: Fondo de Cultura Economica.

Geiger, R.L. (1986) Private Sectors in Higher Education: structure, function, and change in eight countries. Ann Arbor: University of Michigan Press.

Eunice R. Durham

Instituto Nacional de Estudos Pedagógicos (INEP) (1969) Ensino superior, coletânea de legislação básica: Ministério da Educação e Cultura, Instituto Nacional de Estudos Pedagógicos.

Mendes, C.A.M.d. & Castro, C.d.M. (1984) Qualidade, expansão e financiamento do ensino superior privado. Rio de Janeiro: Associação Brasileira de Mantenedoras de Ensino Superior.

Oliveira, J.B.A. (1984) Ilhas de competência: carreiras científicas no Brasil. São Paulo: Editora Melhoramentos.

Sampaio, H. (2000) Ensino superior no Brasil – o setor privado. São Paulo: FAPESP/Hucitec.

Schwartzman, S. (1991) A Space for Science: the Development of the Scientific Community in Brazil. University Park: Pennsylvania State University Press. Available at: http://www.schwartzman.org.br/simon/space/summary.htm

Schwartzman, S., Bomeny, H.M.B. & Costa, V.M.R. (2000) Tempos de Capanema, 2nd edn. São Paulo, Rio de Janeiro: Paz e Terra; Editora da Fundação Getúlio Vargas. Available at: http://www.schwartzman.org.br/simon/capanema/introduc.htm

Teixeira, A. (1969) O ensino superior no Brasil – análise e interpretação de sua evolução até 1969. Rio de Janeiro: Fundação Getúlio Vargas.

178

The State and the Market in the Regulation of Higher Education in Brazil

MARIA HELENA DE MAGALHÃES CASTRO

Introduction

Eunice Durham shows in this volume that Brazilian private higher education changed its role from an acceptable non-profit supplementary sector modelled on the 'public good' paradigm to that of a business that counterfeits the higher education model adopted in the legislation. So far, the government's attempts to deal with this situation have not succeeded. The most vocal representatives of the public sector charge the government of wrecking the public system and 'privatising' higher education, allowing for the proliferation of low quality, profit-oriented private education. Representatives of both the non-profit and for profit private institutions complain about unreasonable demands and controls on their activity by profuse government regulations. Today, this sector absorbs about 70% of enrolments and comprises 88.1% of all kinds of institutions, university and non-university, large and small.

This chapter presents a somewhat different perspective for looking at the issues involved in state regulation of private higher education. It will be argued that market forces have become an unavoidable feature of higher education around the world, including in the well-established formerly state-controlled higher education systems of western Europe. Further, it is assumed that private institutions can excel, as they can also crowd the bottom end of the academic quality continuum. It all depends on contextual factors and on the policy environments in which they operate. There are all kinds of private institutions, among them many of the leading universities in the world, not only within the American Ivy League, but institutions such as the International Management School in Paris (INSEAD), the Monterrey University in Mexico, the Catholic Universities and the Getúlio Vargas Foundation in Brazil, the Wasedo or Keio universities in Japan; the *Ateneo de Manila* in the Philippines, the Universidad Javieriana in Colombia, INCAE in Nicarágua, among others (Altbach, 1999, pp. 1-2).

The old institutional framework for the management of higher education did not resist the pressures of the last few decades for universalisation of access and lifelong education. Higher education became too expensive by the early 1980s even in countries like Britain, the Netherlands and Scandinavia. As Michael Shattock stresses:

> No government has been able to pay fully for the transition from elite to mass and from mass to near universal higher education, so that for quality not to fall institutions have been forced to generate an increasing amount of resources either from students or from other private sources. (Shattock, 1999, pp. 24-26)

It is not only a question of money: The state alone does not have the competence to keep up with events in the increasingly dynamic, diverse and internationalised higher education sector, nor to devise and implement the policies and incentives that are needed to induce desired behaviours in a timely fashion.

In Europe, where 85% of enrolment is still in public institutions, the public sector is full of entrepreneurial universities involved in increasing their earnings and competitiveness in their countries and abroad (Trow, 1993; Clark, 1998; Shattock, 1999). This is also due to new challenges posed by technology, the entrance of new parties into tertiary education, and other realities of the current international environment. Throughout the 1990s, new compelling reasons emerged to reinforce the need to break with the old model of direct state regulation:

> technology, globalization, and competition have caused the ground to shift under higher education, defying national borders and calling into question long-lasting honored traditions and long-held assumptions, creating a brave new world for higher education. Many believe that [we are] in the midst of the early stages of a revolution. ... Globalization has underscored the imperative for institutions to internationalize. ... New players, such as Microsoft and Novell, have ridden the technology wave into tertiary education ... (Green et al, 2002, pp. 3-4)

The question is not whether countries should or should not accept higher education institutions that work according to market rules, but how and what to do to make sure that market competition produces institutions providing quality education and other relevant services. Brazil has experienced periods of strong and weak regulation, and neither has led the market to compete for quality.

This analysis is based on the Brazilian experience with external evaluation committees instituted by the Ministry of Education and the Brazilian Council of Rectors; and on recent European literature. In the next section, we shall see that there are two main trends in the management of the expansion and internationalisation of higher education: one through the development of self-regulated systems, the other through privatisation. In both cases, there are markets and competition, which have to be regulated in new ways.

The overview of these international trends sets the framework for the second part, which discusses the tensions between state and market in higher education in Brazil over the last eight years from the standpoint of three important market failures, namely: (1) social inequity, (2) asymmetry of information, and (3) biased and incomplete coverage of higher education's functions. We conclude by suggesting how a better institutional framework could be devised.

The Self-regulation Mode

A significant number of western European and Commonwealth countries dealt with the expansion and the new higher education environment through the transfer of authority from the state to the universities. As Marianne Bauer explained in 1994:

> A growing awareness of the uncertainty of conditions, goals and the meaning of progress has led to questioning the power of the State, further reinforced by the darting development in electronic communications. Because of the changing context and ideas, governments are moving away from the State Control model towards the State Supervising model (Neave & Vught, 1994; Vught, 1989), giving up their attempts to regulate all aspects of the higher education system and transferring basic decisions and responsibilities to the institutions themselves. ... The universities, in turn, have to ... move away from an organization of loosely coupled units of professional, disciplinary clans ... towards an organization of self-regulation with its demands on leadership, co-operation and information feedback. (Bauer, 1994, pp. 135-136)

The institutions were thus freed from bureaucratic controls and encouraged to grow and find ways to respond to the new challenges. This was possible due to a series of favourable conditions. Expansion took place earlier than elsewhere and took off from a platform of well-established multipurpose university-based systems that comprised more than 35% of enrolment by the mid 1990s (Task Force on Higher Education and Society, 2000). Further, reforms were undertaken by rich countries with the cooperation of their higher education communities (with the notable exception of the UK). In other words, these higher education systems have been able to respond to the new challenges within their own institutional framework. They did not have to allow expansion to be taken up by a new private sector.

In the reformed arrangement, the higher education communities, including the scientific societies, began to share several functions with the government, beyond their traditional roles of teaching and research. They have seats now in all kinds of forums, councils, boards and committees dealing with policy making, implementation and review. They participate in many kinds of assessments, auditing and evaluation procedures, and are asked to write commissioned studies and reports. They help in the definition of data collection instruments, and take part in the analysis of the results; they negotiate the criteria for the allocation of public funds among different institutions. Simultaneously, the European Union was promoting the participation of the academic community in projects to assess and integrate higher education for the Union. The new programmes, studies and debates enhanced the academic's role in shaping not only a supranational post-secondary policy framework for the EU, but national ones, as well (Altbach, 1999; de Wit, 2001).

One effect of this new political-institutional engineering has been the growing intensity of interactions of institutional leaders among themselves, with governments and other stakeholders. A 1994 survey of 11 large European universities showed the deep changes taking place in the job description of leaders and participants of the surveyed universities (Holtta & Nuotio, 1995).[1] Coordinators and heads of department took the role of implementing the budget and hiring academic and administrative personnel; the higher administration started to use internal and external information more effectively, to devise institutional policies, and spend more time in external interactions and participation in representative bodies and buffer institutions linking the universities, the government and other sectors. Within universities, institutional questions became part of the job description of everybody, including professors and researchers, while national issues and those related with the higher education system as a whole became part of the job description of university rectors and other senior managers.

Thus, expansion is being absorbed by a reformed higher education system. Free and well aware of the challenges facing today's higher education, the universities accepted the responsibility to find additional resources to supplement the subsidies they continued to receive from governments.[2] They began to charge tuition fees and to act according to the principles of managerial and financial efficiency, in market-like environments. The reform strengthened institutional coherence and management, tipping the balance of institutional authority to mid and high management levels. The state, in turn, stepped back from direct control to a remote administration role carried out through oversight and the administration of incentives and constraints, in tune with the higher education community.

Self-regulated higher education systems encompass many other components, beyond a less interventionist state, a market-like environment, and higher levels of responsibility, participation, and negotiation roles on the part of the higher education community in the policy dilemmas. Along with the new 'social contract', these systems possess much better information, new and more comprehensive evaluation systems, and consistent efforts to keep up with international quality standards (Thune, 1994). In the same vein, Burton Clark shows how modern European entrepreneurial universities look remarkably unlike the classical institutions of the past (Clark, 1998). They combine a self-image of innovative, troubleshooting and entrepreneurial organisations with the ability to develop profitable 'developmental peripheries', from science parks to teachers' colleges, and the selling of research and teaching services in global niches. From these peripheries they draw discretionary funds that enable them to finance and experiment with new ideas, and to not miss new opportunities for lack of funding. Shattock corroborates:

> Across Europe the loosening of centralized financial regulation has led to new centres of innovation and initiative in universities being opened up. The dialogues between colleagues at European conferences are now all about universities relating to industry, region, and to new clienteles. Increasingly, European universities seem relaxed about following a modern university agenda while not jettisoning their respect for the essential characteristics of university life. (pp. 24-26)

The new profile of higher education is not without its problems, as witnessed by an ongoing debate carried in the Newsletter of the Boston College's Center for International Higher Education. One issue is the very concept and adequate entitlement of institutions to use the term 'university' (Altbach, 2001). Levy, for example, argues that many of the traditional universities are not, any more, bound by the classic parameters. Not only has market-driven behaviour became a survival tool for the old reformed universities, but, in addition, a real market sector is growing, particularly in fields like business administration, computer sciences and other new professions. And this is not all for the bad, since the new 'pseudo-universities' in many instances offer more student-centred curricula and relevant services than the traditional faculty-centred institutions (La Belle, 2002).

The main difference between the self-regulated and the privatised system is not the presence or absence of market logic, but the fact that, in the self-regulated systems, the institutions are well established, created in the tradition of academic values and public responsibility, which few of the new, private institutions ever had. Another important difference is the presence and participation of the academic community and their representatives in the higher education policy making, implementation and review, so remarkable in the European context. The self-regulation response to the expansion problem and the other current challenges is especially relevant to a discussion of Brazil because the western European old public higher education framework forms the tradition still adopted here. We shall return to this point later.

Privatisation

The boom of private higher education is typical of (although not exclusive to) middle and lower income countries, in which both the coverage of higher education and the public budgets are much more limited, turning the market into a very important resource for expanding and updating the higher education sector. In comparative terms, private higher education is most powerful in Asia. In a number of Asian nations, including Japan, South Korea, the Philippines and Indonesia, upwards of 80% of students attend private institutions. The private sector has substantial shares in Thailand and Taiwan, and is the fastest growing segment in Malaysia, China and Vietnam, the same being the case in many countries in central and eastern Europe and in the countries of the former Soviet Union. In Latin America, the private sector is numerically dominant in Brazil, Colombia, Peru and Mexico. In the majority of the other countries it is also the fastest growing segment (Altbach, 1999, pp. 1-5).

Private higher education systems are very heterogeneous, for at least three reasons. They embody a large diversity of institutions and services: take place in very different countries, and are very difficult to regulate. However, the literature converges in pointing out some regularities: private institutions (1) with very few exceptions, have not been directly funded by the governments; (2) have been relatively free from regulations (since they were assimilated to the non-profit sector); (3) have clustered at the lower end of the higher education quality and reputation continuum [3]; (4) have concentrated their activities in the supply of courses in the applied social sciences and other low cost and high demand vocational studies; and, finally, and differently from the other group, (5) have responded more readily to multinationalisation, in part because external control is less stringent and in part because there is more entrepreneurialism (Altbach, 1999).

A good part of these meagre results can be attributed to the difficulties governments face in regulating private higher education. As Altbach notes, 'its resources do not come from government; ownership is not in government hands, and accountability is spread to many institutions and groups. Coordination or control by government have proved to be difficult and costly' (Altbach, 2001, p. 64). In Latin America, the current procedures for control and oversight of private higher education institutions by governments tend to be both excessive and ineffectual and, so far, they have made little difference in the end state of the private higher education sector (Castro & Navarro, 1999). The fact is that countries which cannot afford to expand their higher education systems without the help of a private sector have not yet fully understood what 'living with the market' means. Unlike western Europe, where decision-making concerning higher education reforms has been participative and closely accompanied by intense scholarship and research, the literature on the private sector is still very limited (Balán & García de Fanelli, 1993).

State and Market in Brazil (1995-2002)

Brazilian private higher education shares some of the general characteristics highlighted in the international literature, reviewed above: it receives very little or no public resources; most institutions are non-university teaching places, clustered at the lower end of the academic quality continuum; they face harsh competition; and receive the least educated students. Typically, these are older than average, are the first generation in their families to get to higher education, and attend evening courses because they are already in the workforce.

There are, however, some peculiarities. Since 1997, there is a legal distinction between non-profit and for-profit institutions; there are several assessment procedures in place, including peer review visits and an innovative National Graduation Examination for students obtaining their BA degrees, which is used to rank the course programmes according to their students' achievements. The government controls the awarding of university status to private institutions, and only those accredited with this status have the freedom to decide which courses to offer, and how many students to admit. But, even they undergo government limitations on the tuition fees they can charge, and on how they deal with the students who fail to pay their fees.

During Cardoso's administration (1995-2002), the policy environment went through other important developments, as well. The government's institutional framework went through two relevant changes, mentioned by Durham – the extinction of the old Federal Council of Education (CFE) and replacement by the National Council of Education (CNE); and the transformation of the National Institute for Education Research, known as INEP, into an important agency for data gathering and education assessment at all levels. Both measures, though, remained incomplete. The new Council still lacks the conditions (authority, budget and cadres) to fulfil its intended functions and INEP also lacks personnel and institutional autonomy to ensure continuity to its activities. Several other measures are worth noting for they were driven to improve flexibility and to stimulate the expansion of the private sector with quality.

- Permanent licenses were replaced by periodical renewal of accreditation through evaluation of courses and institutions.
- The legislation about philanthropy was changed, allowing for the legal existence of for-profit institutions. Two-thirds of the private institutions are now defined as for profit, and not eligible for tax relief.
- An unambiguous definition of 'university' was introduced, based on the combination of undergraduate with graduate education and research, with a significant proportion of the teaching staff with full-time contracts and advanced degrees. A previous requirement of 'universal coverage' of academic disciplines was abandoned.

- A new type of institution, 'University Centre', was created, to provide university-like autonomy to private institutions committed to good quality teaching but without a significant research and graduate education component.
- All institutions were given more flexibility to determine the curricula of their courses.
- Two new types of shorter undergraduate programmes and of a new professional, non-academic Master's programme were introduced.
- Important improvement in the production of information about courses and institutions was made.
- There were new instances (advisory boards and committees of different kinds) for participation of the academic community in policy making and implementation, in assessments, studies, and data analyses.

These measures have not been sufficient to deal with the problems of quantity and quality in Brazilian higher education. Coverage is still only 10% of the age cohort – one of the smallest in Latin America.[4] On the other hand, the remarkable expansion in enrolment and in the number and size of the new private universities has been thwarted by the extremely small completion rates (see section 'Inequity'). In terms of quality, the course assessments have regularly placed private institutions at the bottom, with few exceptions.

Regardless of the pace the expansion of private sector will attain from now on – and even in the case, not improbable, of suffering a crisis of adjustment – it is already much more troublesome than it needs to be. If the three market failures in education are well addressed, private higher education could make a much better contribution, as it has made in several other countries.

Market Failures

The market failures in education are serious and need to be addressed. The remedies, though, are quite commonsensical. First, there is a strong *asymmetry of information* between buyers and sellers of education. Second, the system is *socially inequitable,* since access to education depends on the ability to pay for it, in the absence of appropriate student loans and fellowships. Third, the system is *geared to the least expensive and most profitable careers*, and does very little in terms of research, graduate education and extension work.

Asymmetry of Information

The first asymmetry is that students, from candidates to graduates, know much less about the course programme, the institution and the career than the school owner and its academic and administrative staff. The students cannot discern what is good or poor almost by definition – they are buying education, that is to say, criteria, information, and skills they do not have.

The right choice in this circumstance depends on the available information. Secondly, higher education is expensive both financially and in terms of opportunity costs. It is a medium-term service delivered throughout a span of years, and it takes even longer, after graduation, to find out its worth (Trow, 1993). In terms of the principal–agent theory, educational contracts do not allow the buyers (principals) to see how the institutions and their teachers (agents) make their choices to better (or worse) fulfil their contract. This happens not only because education activities are carried out behind closed doors, but also because of the multiplicity of principals the agents respond to. The principals can be the students and their families, and the agents, the providers of education, which includes the government, the educational institutions and their teachers. It is also possible to think of the Ministry of Education and other education authorities as the principal, regarding the institutions. A third possibility would be to consider rectors and school owners as principals, regarding the teachers and employees they hire (Vargas, 2002). Besides these main actors, there are other stakeholders and influential parties, including the teachers' unions, federal and local bureaucracies, politicians, providers of educational services, the mass media, and privileged users. Some of these actors may cooperate, but their goals are not necessarily coincident. Therefore, each principal has to be concerned with the influence of other principals in the agent's behaviour.

The agents that deliver the service, the school and the teacher, have to respond to different principals and this gives them a large manoeuvring space, which is further strengthened by the opacity of a service that takes years to complete, and many more years to show its results.

This situation leads to two consequences, post-contract opportunism and adverse choice. An example of post-contract opportunism is when institutions seduce the candidates to participate in free and easy entrance examinations and pay their initial fees, when it is clear that they do not have the financial and academic conditions to continue their studies and get their degrees. Adverse choice happens when the agent has some relevant information that is not passed on to the principal – for instance, when the agent knows that the university library is out of date, or that the teachers are not very good, or that there are not enough students to complete a class in the course programme chosen, meaning that the freshmen will be incorporated to a class of another course programme, etc.

The standard solution for the asymmetry of information in the principal–agent model is to include in the contract clauses that require the agent to reveal all its information (Vargas, 2002). But, both in the USA and in Europe, contracts (or regulations) are not deemed to be enough. Financial incentives are needed too. The two requirements imposed on the institutions to become eligible to integrate the US official student financial aid system are to be accredited by their respective regional agency and to participate in the Integrated Postsecondary Education Data System annual data collection system (INEP, 2001). A strong financial incentive (student aid) has, thus, been effectively used to produce information of two kinds: detailed institutional records and quality assessment. Also, it is no coincidence that in the USA, the government funds the huge ERIC (Educational Resources Information Center) free information service.

Information asymmetry can only be reduced where there is plenty of good information at very low or no costs. In a scenario of opaqueness, the market is bound not to serve society well, but under abundant information, students make better-informed choices and the market is bound to respond with better services. Private institutions will invest in quality when and where it translates into reputation, visibility and, consequently, money. Reputation and visibility, and thus quality and transparency, depend on information. One of the main responsibilities of the state is to stimulate, produce and disseminate information, so as to allow consumers to choose what is best for them, preventing inefficiencies (drop-outs, disenchantment, default, etc.) and unfair trade.

But there is another aspect relating the redressing of asymmetry to quality: the less qualified institutions resist or are less able to provide information about themselves. This calls for other measures oriented to quality improvement. This has been successfully attained through qualitative and interactive evaluation processes, involving on-site peer review committees. This kind of assessment makes possible the provision of tailored assistance and negotiated monitoring of flawed institutions. Besides, such assessments also produce first-hand information on difficulties that might be relevant for policy making.

Good information means accurate, updated, comprehensive and comparative information. It also means information that has been processed and formatted to be helpful for different users (policy makers, rectors, media, scholars, etc.), including the public at large.

The information on higher education that is already available in Brazil is significant, but very little of it reaches the general public in a simple and manageable way. The main sources are as follows.

- The yearly higher education census provides information on all higher education institutions. However, a system to validate the information provided by the institutions is still to be established, thus only a small subset of the information gathered is published and placed on the Internet by the Ministry of Education. Differently from other countries, like Chile, this is still not an instrument that students can use to choose their courses and institutions.
- Each year, higher education institutions are required to send their institutional catalogues to the Ministry of Education, with information on their academic programmes, installations, and financial resources. So far, however, these materials are piling up in Brasilia, with no use.
- Peer groups in assessment missions write detailed reports about the institutions they visit. More recently, this information was drastically reduced with the adoption of standardised forms that were supposed to

facilitate data processing and comparisons. However, the Ministry has only used this information to run the bureaucratic routines and feed its archives, without any other treatment.

- The National Courses Examination (*Provão*), applied to students graduating from most careers, provides not only comparative information on the students' performances, but also a host of socioeconomic information on the students, the students' assessments of their courses and institutions, and questionnaires applied to course coordinators. So far, very little of this material has been analysed and published within academia.

- There was a large effort to link the several databases on higher education owned by the federal government into an integrated system, SIEd-Sup, which was supposed to feed an Internet-based information system of higher education for students and candidates. So far, however, this system has not been made public.

- Finally, the Ministry put all the higher education legislation on the Internet (*Prolei*), together with an online system (*Sapiens*), which allows higher education institutions to follow the whereabouts of their administrative requests and procedures within the government offices. The formatting of Sapiens to accept 31 kinds of requests only neutralised the gains attained by online tracking, for the institutions lost the right to officially place a demand for the Ministry's attention to new, not anticipated issues.

On balance, policy makers and, to a lesser degree, some higher education academics and practitioners, have much better information now than before. But the waste of (untreated) information is many times greater than the improvements achieved. This is partly due to the Ministry's sheer lack of people and time to process, analyse, format, and publish it. Even within this selected circle of authorities and experts there are serious limitations. Problems of reliability and lack of consistency abound in the official data and in the institutions, including the federal universities. The information collected by the Ministry of Education is neither validated, nor even used by the institutions who originated it, to feed their internal decision-making. There are also problems of timing stemming from the instability of private institutions and the many entrance opportunities they create within one academic year. It is difficult to keep up with the constant changes in the provision of course programmes. Students, thus, cannot rely on the published information to make their decisions.

As for the students and the public opinion, they are left with the information provided by the Ministry of Education, particularly, the scores of the National Courses Examination, which are widely publicised in the media and largely used. Private publishers and magazines (including the Brazilian edition of *Playboy* magazine) offer one student guide and one non-official rank of academic institutions. These are helpful publications, but very incomplete. The media have not, so far, established specialised editors to handle education news and issues. A large sample research carried out in 1997 and 1998 found a dominance of higher education news in the national press and, also, that 83% of all published articles were government-related. There is a national cable television channel (the UTV) run by the universities, which carries a patchwork of individually produced programmes. It does not contribute to academic debate and other system-wise issues of higher education. The Internet is a growing source of non-analytical, descriptive information published in the Ministry and the institutions' sites (Aragón, 1999). Finally, there is no Brazilian equivalent of the *Chronicle of Higher Education* or the *Times Higher Education Supplement*, to provide the public with intelligent discussions and information on higher education issues.

Instead, students are bombarded by marketing strategies of private institutions offering low prices, easy admissions and little academic demands to get degrees. In some cases, this strategy makes sense for the student – when, for instance, they only need a degree to get a promotion in a public job. As the job market gets more competitive, however, this kind of strategy can only backfire.

This market failure could not be solved just through a good information system on the Internet, as intended by the INEP's SIEd-Sup advisory committee. In a society with limited tradition in higher education, where diplomas are often considered more important than the competencies they are supposed to represent, it is necessary to increase public awareness about the benefits, problems and choices for higher education, through public debates on principles, values and analysis, as well as through a better understanding of international experiences.

Brazil has a tradition of sending graduate students to foreign universities, but almost none of international interchange at the undergraduate level. Brazilian universities are not prepared to receive students coming from other countries, and the opportunities for undergraduate students to go abroad are limited to a few non-official interchange programmes for a handful of (wealthy) students. It is interesting to contrast this with the European experience, and particularly, with that of Denmark and of other European Union member countries (Green et al, 2002) for they have adopted a consistent policy of providing its population with an experience of international education.[5]

Inequity

Private higher education only absorbs students who can afford its prices – which are almost invariably full, since, in most countries, private institutions are not eligible for public funds. It is in the interest of society to subsidise those who are willing and prepared to successfully attend higher education programmes, but cannot afford its costs alone. The evidence that higher education creates private benefits has justified in some places the replacement of across-the-board subsidies by subsidies geared to those that really need them. In either case, a primary role of the state with regard to market-derived inequity is financing access to the needy through grants and loans.

In Brazil, policies to reduce inequity in education have been centred on the provision of universal basic education, and in efforts to improve its coverage and quality.[6] In higher education, the very selective entrance examinations for the public sector (which is free of charges, but small) has been a factor of inequity. This has been compensated somewhat by expanding private education, and the creation of the new types of short course programmes. Other mechanisms for admission to higher education institutions, besides the traditional written examinations, are being experimented with, including the consideration of the results of the National Secondary School Voluntary Examination (ENEM), provided by the Ministry of Education, and yearly examinations during secondary school, which have helped students to be prepared and succeed.

A well-established system of student loan is the standard measure to redress this problem. The existing student loans programme has a budget of about $200 million, allowing for 15,000 new loans a year, and 45,000 students with loans at any given time. To be significant, a student loan programme should be around 10 times bigger (Schwartzman & Schwartzman, 2002). Besides its small size, there is no effort to use the programme to induce improvements in higher education institutions, since there are no clear academic criteria for loans assignation and renewal. Additionally, it places on the institutions the burden of establishing a system to monitor every semester both the academic performance and the continuance of the economic need of the students aided by the loan. In Brazil, the government does not offer any merit-based or need-based scholarship programme for students outside the public sector.[7]

Inequity appears also in the large number of students who never complete their degrees. Drop-out, motivated by financial or academic difficulties, is a waste of the student's resources, which affects more those in the worse conditions. While the number of enrolments in the private sector more than doubled between 1990 and 2001 (rising from 962,000 to 2,092, 000), the number of students graduating in 2000 was only 30% of those being admitted. Part of the explanation is that the system was expanding, and the number of entrants four years earlier was smaller. In any case, this 70% loss should be compared with the average of the public sector (50%) and the average of the health sector in public universities (18%) (Schwartzman & Schwartzman, 2002, Table 18).

Economic Squeeze, Wild Markets and Inequity

The inability of most private institutions to provide satisfactory education to their students, as evidenced among other things by the high drop-out rates and low scores in *Provão*, can be explained in part by the economic squeeze they have suffered in recent years. The 1997 change in the legislation on philanthropy, with the abolition of tax privileges for most institutions, meant an increase of 20 to 25% of the expenses for two-thirds of them.[8] Besides, the new education legislation requires that, by 2004, all universities should have at least a third of their faculty with graduate degrees, with full-time contracts, and doing research. They are also required to have at least three accredited graduate programmes, and three established research lines. For the private sector, where there was neither research nor graduate education, and where most lecturers are paid by the hour, this means a very significant increase in costs.[9] These costs are compounded by the fact that about 20-30% of the students fail to pay their monthly tuition fees, and, once enrolled, the institutions cannot stop them from attending classes and getting their grades in the ongoing academic term. Actually, many private institutions are dealing with even higher default rates during their academic terms. For this reason, they have cut in half the standard (10 months) academic regime in order to press students to clear their debts every semester, or otherwise miss the enrolment for the new term. Government authorisation of many new institutions with the very same profile of course programmes increased competition to the point at which competitors plunged into predatory behaviours. New businesses were opened in already crowded markets and it is no wonder that, in the year 2000, about a third of the places offered remained empty (Schwartzman & Schwartzman, 2002). A quite common consequence has been price wars and marketing campaigns aimed at attracting BA degree holders and students already enrolled in competing institutions by offering up to half tuition fee discounts. One can easily guess the impact of such an environment on the quality being offered to the largest part of the Brazilian higher education student population.

In an effort to compensate for their financial problems, private institutions increased the offer of places and courses, in search of economies of scale; and expanded their locations to sites closer to where potential students may live or work. Very few institutions tried to offer a better product. Many turned to cost reduction strategies by hiring law firms and organisational consultants to, respectively, fight the government and re-engineer their organisations.[10] Given the current environment, the best institutional arrangement for the private sector seems to be the 'university centre', which has the autonomy to create new courses, but not the costs of research and graduate education. However, it is necessary to consider whether it would not be better to review the regulatory environment, instead of restricting the country's university system to the non-profit sector alone and leaving the expansion to the least qualified group of institutions: the 'university centres' and the 'non-university institutions'.

Inequities in Brazilian higher education are not just those that derive from market competition. The public sector, which is free from charges, benefits from much higher demand and selectivity, and thus, recruits the very best students. Salaries in public institutions are not very high, but faculty enjoy stability, long academic vacations, generous retirement benefits, academic autonomy and prestige, making this an attractive job for qualified professionals. Most academics in the public sector have full-time contracts, which supposes a light teaching load and time for research. In the public sector, the minimum academic requirement for lecturers is a Master's degree, and, in some institutions, a PhD. Since the 1970s, public universities have benefited from several programmes placing special incentives, including fellowships and long paid leaves of absence for lecturers to get their MA and doctoral degrees or to develop post-doctoral research; support for undergraduate students willing to work as research assistants and start their research careers; scholarships for graduate students; a significant salary supplement attached to undergraduate teaching loads; fellowships for academic departments hiring on a trial basis young PhDs, and others.

Given this quite supportive environment, it is no wonder that academic productivity is rising in public institutions, and their courses get the highest marks in the National Graduation Exam, while private institutions are left behind. While institutions should be responsible for their results, the government is also responsible for where it places its incentives. In this case, the students in the private sector suffer the consequences. Equity would require that private institutions could also compete for these incentives. It is possible to think of other programmes, more adjusted to the peculiarities of each segment (Castro & Levy, 2000). But the criteria for access to public resources should be merit and relevance, not privilege to a specific sector. If the government refuses to provide support and create a policy environment conducive to quality improvement to any of the segments of higher education, especially the larger one, which deals with the students in the direst conditions, one cannot expect the private sector to do so on its own.[11]

In short, the inequities in Brazilian higher education do not come only from market competition, and could not be solved just by an expanded fellowship and student loans programme. There are other factors related to the existing regulations and incentives that aggravate it. In the private sector, as seen, short-term economic and managerial considerations take precedence over academic ones, which should be the institutions' core business. Within the public sector, government incentives for graduate education and research still take precedence over incentives to deliver good quality undergraduate teaching.

Biased and Incomplete Coverage of Higher Education Functions

The third market failure derives from the private sector's avoidance of those higher education functions (in teaching, research and community services) that are less cost-effective, despite their indisputable public relevance. If left alone, the market will leave gaps that are not only undesirable, but can also impair the country's competence in science, engineering and many other fields.

The enforcement of the Brazilian new Law of Education helped diversification of undergraduate course programmes through the introduction of three new kinds of shorter alternatives of vocational studies, whose quality is still to be established. But the government failed to induce differentiation and complementarities in the supply of the main traditional four-year undergraduate course programmes that lead to BA degrees. Instead, new courses and institutions with the very same profile were licensed. According to Schwartzman & Schwartzman (2002), half of the private sector students are enrolled in the applied social sciences, especially in law and business management. Most of the rest are in education and health related fields – not medicine, but in different kinds of 'therapy and rehabilitation' professions. Looking at the whole picture, the enrolments are very concentrated in the so-called 'social professions' (906,961), which is almost three times bigger than the second field, education (319,348). Law schools, alone, absorb 319,059 students, and business management, 287,391. Other imbalances exist within each field of knowledge. For instance, within the sciences area, 70% of the enrolment concerns computer and data processing course programmes.

Graduate schools and scientific research in Brazil encompass all fields of knowledge and are supported, within the public sector, in every state, by the federal and state governments. As we have seen, the private universities face overwhelming difficulties in providing for them without some kind of assistance, being competitive funding programmes or even academic help.

Finally, market competition seems to be unleashing a specialisation trend between public and private higher education supply of undergraduate courses. While the public sector holds on to the more traditional discipline-based four-year undergraduate course programmes, the private sector is experimenting with the new kinds of shorter course formats and new alternatives of vocational-based studies so as to meet new demands, but also, to bypass state control and direct competition with the public universities. The country is witnessing the introduction by the autonomous private universities and 'university centres' of many new curricula, such as in tourism-related professions, fashion, gastronomy, cinema and the media, etc. This can be one of the positive contributions of private higher education: innovation and prompt alignment to new (or potential) social demands. Quality control, though, is needed, as well as policies to ensure that all kinds of competences are formed and that the higher education system will perform all the desirable 'public good' functions.

Toward a New Regulatory Environment

It is clear, from the above, that a new regulatory environment is needed, which could bring Brazilian higher education closer to the self-regulating mode, with a stronger and more effective state, assisted by the higher education community in the exercise of leadership, ruling authority and the provision of appropriate incentives. It is the role of the state to defend the citizen's right to receive the product they pay for. This requires clear rules and standards, permanent assessment, and good information.

A cornerstone of self-regulated systems is their 'quality assurance' systems, which are devised to attain two main goals: a public accountability function and a quality improvement function (Hartingsveld, 1994). Periodical gathering of quantitative data is essential for the public accountability function and is also important to gauge the broad trends. However, it is unfit to understand the complexity of the institutions; the effort they have made to be where they are, or the relevance they have in their communities. Quantitative approach and objective auditing are not adequate to improve quality; nor is any assessment mechanism that brings a threat to the institutions – by being linked to financial or reputation sanctions. This induces dissimulation, and the quality of the information suffers.

To perform both functions, the quality assurance system needs to be composed of independent quantitative and qualitative mechanisms to gather information on course contents, scientific production, finances, social relevance, and general characteristics of the institutions. Quality promotion is being provided through very interactive on-site peer committees' evaluations coupled with long-term monitoring and assistance. It is delicate work, which should be done with the realisation that higher education institutions represent sizeable social investments that not only are important for the nations, but also influence many people's lives. All those who have worked or still work, or have graduated or still study in a higher education institution can benefit or be harmed by oscillations in its reputation (Vught & Kells, 1988). Kells suggests that regulation of higher education in countries like Brazil should be of two types, according to two main goals to be achieved:

> The need for basic protection of the public in systems in which the types of institutions range from research universities to taxi-cab or garage institutions is a primary consideration. Indeed, such a set of conditions requires a regulation approach with two steps, not just one. The first is some kind of culling step – an approval against a basic set of standards, of the institution's right to exist, to use the term university, to offer certain programs and degree levels – usually run by government and backed by a phalanx of lawyers and often called licensing. This step, periodically run, ideally for all institutions, is followed by and, indeed, permits the normal operation of the second, accreditation step. Accreditation is a relatively weak regulation process compared to licensing, but it is also much more subtle and, if relieved of the basic culling and protection responsibilities, can be the mechanism which encourages and supports truly improvement-oriented efforts with respect to teaching, learning, research, and the environment which support them, (Vught & Kells, 1998, pp. 7-8)

Currently, in Brazil, there are two main assessments for undergraduate higher education, besides the regular collection of statistics: the National Graduation Examinations, and the peer review procedures, based on site visits, to assess institutions requiring authorisation to change their status or to start new courses, as well as to supplement the results of the graduation examinations with information on the institution's teaching conditions.

As well as watching the 'gates' (by defining the minimum competences required for BA degrees), the graduation examinations lead to a public acknowledgement of merit, and help the students to choose their courses and institutions. However, they still need many adjustments (Castro, 2001). It is a very traditional and expensive system, requiring all graduating students to take the examinations on the same day in the whole country.[12] Also, it measures final outcomes, and not the value added by education to students entering higher education from very different backgrounds. Since public institutions recruit the best students, they also do better in the examinations, which reproduces the existing systemic inequities. Some adjustments have already been made. For example, the Ministry was caught by surprise by the institutions' inability to use the examination results sent back to them to identify their problems and deal with them. To address that, the government promoted national meetings with course coordinators, field by field, and promoted on-site visits by specialists.

The peer review procedures could produce a more nuanced and detailed view of the institutions, but suffer from lack of clear guidelines and standards. They should also be geared to perform the second step described by Kells, to help the institutions to improve their work, rather than being just an additional instrument of control and oversight, as many of them usually are.

The assessment system in place in Brazil is also misused due to the imbalance between the two mechanisms (examinations and peer reviews). Only the graduation examinations make it through the national media and are used. So far, the public does not discern the different and complementary information that is being produced. This allows for unfairness: institutions' reputations are derived from one single instrument, which only measures one or few of its courses' programmes, and with the problems mentioned above. The graduation examinations are essential to protect consumers' rights and perform the first step, proposed by Kells, the gatekeeping role. What is needed is to balance the specific and somewhat biased information it brings with other independent assessment mechanisms devised to account for other dimensions (excellence, innovation, social relevance, efficiency, effort, etc.) and effective mechanisms to promote institutional and course quality improvement.

Besides information and assessment, it is necessary to develop a proper system of financial incentives. Student loans should be large enough, and designed so as to keep default rates low and allow students to become self-sufficient. Loans can be assigned to students as a voucher, or to institutions.

In any case, this public money must be attached to the right incentives. If given to institutions, it should follow the US example of requiring accountability (disclosure of data) and quality (accreditation by the traditional regional agencies). If given to students, it should be coupled with the provision of information and guidance, stimulating the students to make the best possible decisions, fostering quality and relevance of higher education.

Student grants and loans, however, are not enough. Private institutions should have access to public resources for institutional and academic enhancement. And legislation to stimulate private philanthropy should be improved, allowing the private sector to benefit from it. Private philanthropy leads the institutions to keep contacts with their alumni – which can provide, also, important information about their professional careers, very useful for prospective students. It also requires enhanced levels of transparency, good managerial practices, and close contacts with the community. This is so because private donors, usually, want to choose the specific projects and activities they will support and to learn if their resources are being properly used. There are many benefits in private philanthropy, besides the money itself.

The Higher Education Community

We have seen how the government brings representatives of the higher education community to participate in assessment and advisory bodies, starting with the National Council of Education, and including a large number of peer review committees of different kinds. There is a growing network of higher education umbrella institutions, some of them quite influential. They include the Council of Brazilian Rectors (CRUB), created in the early 1970s, with about 145 public and private universities; the National Association of Leaders of Federal Higher Education Institutions (ANDIFES), bringing together 55 institutions; the Brazilian Association of State and Municipal Universities [13] (ABRUEM), the Brazilian Association of Community Universities (ABRUC), with 36 affiliates; the National Association of Private Universities (ANUP); the National Association of University Centres (ANACEU), with 52 affiliates; and the largest of all, the National Association of Providers of Higher Education (ABMES), with 306 providers and 448 higher education institutions they maintain. Besides, there are regional representative bodies, such as the Association of Higher Education Foundation of Santa Catarina (ACAFE) and the Union of Higher Education Providers of the State of São Paulo (SEMESP), with 330 providers and 380 institutions; and several others.

These associations were created to foster the interests of their constituencies. Some of them are developing meaningful connections with other segments, exchanging experiences and views, and promoting studies and publications, as well as common projects and activities. Few of them stand out in terms of awareness and commitment to the public interest. Besides the Council of Rectors, there are two, out of five Forum of Deans, that have overcome the public–private divide (congregating leaders of both sectors) to assess and devise policies for their areas of concern: the ForProp (Deans of Research and Graduate Schools) and ForGrad (Deans of Undergraduate Schools). Both attained seats at some key policy making arenas and are creating a collaborative and better-informed environment.[14] Two private sector entities have also shown a clear commitment to quality promotion and to negotiated solutions. The huge ABMES has pursued a moderate advocacy and intermediation role between its constituency and the government throughout many crises; was able to attain seats in three government committees, and has maintained a very useful publishing strategy. The Funadesp (National Foundation for the Development of Private Higher Education) is an agency created by ABMES with 69 affiliated institutions that contribute to maintain a fund used to emulate CAPES (Brazilian Agency for Postgraduate Education) programmes to promote research and the quality of graduate studies programmes. A national medical schools association, the CINAEM, set up an assessment system of medical schools during the 1980s. More recently, there is the PROMED programme and other initiatives committed to the quality of teaching and research in this field. The University Television cable channel – the UTV – is another concerted initiative that could easily provide regular forums to disseminate information and promote debate, fostering collaboration and awareness of systemic themes.

The impression, from informal observation of the work of these institutions, is that they may have localised influence in some issues, but not enough to change the dominance of the Ministry of Education over the matters of education policy. The views of the private sector were expressed in a recent document of ABMES, the largest umbrella entity of the private sector:

> A lack of confidence regarding private higher education
> institutions still persists in Brazilian society ... Government has
> strengthened its 'de facto' control through a profusion of norms
> based on new quality indicators, which are in conflict with the
> existing legislation ... The context entails other problems, as well –
> the declining purchasing power of the middle class; ... and the
> entry into tertiary education of new social groups that are
> increasingly less well-off. This calls for a more audacious student
> aid policy from the government. ... Also, it is necessary to gather
> and study proposals to: (a) expand graduate studies and increase
> the volume of resources to better finance them; (b) finance
> research with public funds as well; (c) review the methodology of
> the Provão ...; (d) expand post-secondary education beyond the
> regular undergraduate programs and think of new formats; (e)
> discuss a Professional Master's, particularly for university

teaching; (f) identify the sectors (institutions, course programs) with the best prospects for efficient expansion, as well as their territorial distribution; and (g) discuss ethical standards that should frame the supply of courses and relations between institutions.

The involvement of individual scholars in peer reviews, working groups and assessment activities of different kinds did not lead to more permanent links and channels between the government and the higher education community. Participation was individual, by invitation, and, with a few exceptions, limited to persons from public universities. In the absence of proper channels and of a receptive environment, the private sector reacted defensively, sometimes from ill-informed standings, trying to cut its losses and protect its business. System-wide questions such as the ones mentioned by ABMES above, or of academic interest, like the proper role of private and public institutions, the professional life of their students; the discrepancies between secondary and post-secondary education; the low quality of evening courses, the use of distance education, the comparisons between the Brazilian and other experiences, never had the chance to come to the foreground.

Likewise, for the lack of proper channels and support within the higher education community, the state remained alone and unable to implement several of the policies that it initiated. This did not help to increase the public responsibility of the private and public agents, or to make sure that its achievements would last. Instead of promoting an environment of cooperation and trust, with shared dilemmas and responsibilities, the government allowed for an adversary climate to develop, raising its own costs. In such an environment, its actions were received with suspicion, generating defensive strategies and bypass mechanisms, frustrating many of the government's regulatory efforts. For lack of institutionalisation, what will happen in the future depends on the personal inclinations and preferences of future office holders.

By contrast, in self-regulated systems the management of higher education is no longer contained within ministries. The academic and scientific community, institutional administrators and other core stakeholders make up a set of indispensable partners that must minimally:

- produce, disseminate and improve the quality of information about the higher education system. This means auditing and validating data provided by institutions; processing and analysing information, and formatting it for different audiences and ends. The issues identified by the analyses, in turn, call for surveys or specific research to be undertaken, which must also be designed and subsequently analysed with the help of the community;
- advance knowledge about what is going on. There is a lot of creativity and innovation being introduced at institutional or even course programmes level, as a result of new technologies, education products

and services, and of the internationalisation of all kinds of partnerships. In the UK, there is a debate about the criteria that should be adopted to evaluate the quality of the international partners working with British institutions;

- design, implement, assess, review and adjust auditing and evaluation instruments. The definition and accompaniment of programmes and assessment processes – be it of accounts/finances and management efficiency, or of academic and institutional quality, are overwhelming tasks, which generate inaccuracies and protest and require not just negotiation and even revisions, but also the mobilisation of a lot of people with expertise in different areas, who are to be found within the community and not in the state bureaucracy. Qualitative evaluations involve direct interaction between the evaluated and external evaluators, are laborious, human intensive, and still lack a definitive format. They are in a constant process of revision, as the growth of periodicals and literature on this topic demonstrates;
- elaborate the parameters and criteria for the execution and follow-up of other policies and programmes;
- negotiate and mediate between higher education institutions, associations, and other segments of society, and the government, and likewise contribute to disseminate information and views;
- select projects for a variety of competitive funds, grants and loans, for institutional development, teaching, research, programmes and services focused on highly relevant goals (local and regional development, mitigation of social inequalities, etc.)

Although some of these tasks can be undertaken by bureaucrats and ad hoc consultants, they require supervision by practitioners and specialists. Their participation generates knowledge on what is going on in the sector, informs leaders about their competitors and how their segment is doing compared with others, and so on. Further, it promotes scholarship, the development of the field of studies on higher education, the increase in specialised literature and media, and the variety and public visibility of evaluation results.

It is true that the Cardoso government undertook the thankless task of reorganising the system of higher education, fulfilling what Kells calls a gatekeeper role. It is also true that it missed opportunities to use student aid, and other public monies to foster quality in the private sector, and encourage the realignments called for by the many new regulations it promulgated. Even so, and despite the fact that higher education expanded and became more differentiated, it is now better understood by society.

Is Brazil Ready for a New Contract?

It is not easy to break with immobility and decades-old taboos, as the Ministry of Education did under the last government. It had to deploy all the force of authority and regulatory power. Structural reforms like those undertaken – the re-establishment of the National Education Council, the institution of regular accreditation, the evaluation of undergraduate courses, the revision of philanthropy, etc. – entail adjustments. Many were made and others were under way when the recent change of government took place. As self-regulated systems demonstrate, the management of higher education continues to be a challenge and requires all kinds of revisions, fine-tuning and experimentation. There are no long-lasting or generically valid recipes. It would be out of place to expect the Ministry of Education to get it right the first time round, or for initial positive results to continue for eight years without any adjustments. This is not the issue and, in a way, the intensity with which the government used its regulatory power can be justified.

The problem is that the attainment of the sound and lasting outcomes aimed at by policies and regulations depends, critically, on the administrative (operational) capacity to implement changes, which in turn, depends on adherence to the objectives that such policies hope to achieve. Alone, the state and its bureaucracy are not likely to arrive at the most adequate policies, let alone implement them. As the principal–agent model helps to show, it is particularly difficult to frame the educational area by any of its 'principals'. Various regulations were misused and it was impossible to enforce others. By delegating responsibilities, the state multiplies its capacity to envisage and implement policies, and by involving the community in policy dilemmas and in policy-making, it rapidly widens the stock of information and competences at hand and broadens understanding and adherence to its actions.

The Ministry did not create sufficient conditions for adherence to the new policies and rules. Many of the distortions and evasions of the law occurred because the aims were not properly understood, the means were not adequate (and it was impossible to negotiate other ways to attain them), and/or the costs involved were too high for private institutions to bear. The private sector is not eligible for the government grants and programmes, such as the Recent-Doctor Placement programme of the CNPq, or for the various CAPES quality promotion programmes (scholarships for professors willing to attend graduate school – PICD, PROAP, PRODOC, PROIN, etc.) – all exclusive to the (mostly public) research universities.

Private institutions received no help to identify and hire professors with the required Master's or doctoral degrees in some geographic areas and fields of knowledge in which they were not available. Even more pressing was the need and extreme difficulty of attaining the required accreditation by the CAPES system of the Master's programmes they were obliged to establish. CAPES could have offered assistance, or stimulated a system by which new programmes could evolve with the support of other programmes already established in the country or abroad. This insensitivity not only caused indignation and protest, but also impeded the expansion of graduate education necessary to fulfil the 30% quota of professors with Master's or doctoral degrees in various fields and the minimum of three graduate studies programmes and three 'institutionalised' research programmes. In an attempt to overcome this bottleneck, the private universities moved to the 'inter-institutional Master's degree programmes', wasting efforts and resources on agreements with low prestige institutions in Spain, Portugal and other countries.

The political-institutional engineering of self-regulated systems has different costs depending on the size of countries, the coverage and tradition of their higher education systems and the capacity of the government to exercise leadership in new ways and fulfil new functions. The European countries that have recently adopted this participatory model are small and had homogeneous and well-structured higher education systems. Besides, they all found reinforcement in the concerted and participatory programmes and initiatives of the European Union. In a country of the size of Brazil, with a tradition of bureaucratic centralism and a small, differentiated and recent higher education system, the costs are higher. The main trade-off seems to be between the rhythm of progress and the sustainability of outcomes.

If these arguments seem sensible, it remains to be demonstrated that the needs pointed out can only be met by the participatory solution proposed here. Further, the defence of this proposal must take into account the issue of viability: are we ready to go ahead with the reforms needed to install a self-regulated system in Brazil?

An experience that is quite relevant for this discussion is that of the Institutional Assessment Programme launched by the Council of Rectors of Brazilian Universities (*Conselho de Reitores das Universidades Brasileiras*, CRUB) in 2000. The Programme is a non-governmental initiative aimed at promoting institutional development that was immediately joined by 19 universities in its first and somewhat restricted announcement. It adopted the method of institutional/comprehensive accreditation developed by North American regional agencies, which is also being adopted by the European Union and dozens of countries on all continents. The programme begins by overseeing the preparation of a self-diagnosis, which asks for the information and analysis that any institution with inner quality assurance concerns must have at hand. Based on the self-diagnosis, a peer-review commission is set up to undertake *in loco* validation of the self-study, as well as to discuss problems and define the priorities of each round of evaluation. This commission elaborates a written report, the bases of which have already been discussed with the top-level administration at the end of the visit. The institution must respond in writing to this report. On the basis of this interaction and the three documents – the self-diagnosis, the report written by the external assessors, and the response of the institution – a commitment is defined and signed whereby the institution commits itself to complying with the recommendations within a pre-defined time period, and benefits from the advice and accompaniment provided by the CRUB.

This initiative was well received, with strong support coming from former rectors, evaluation specialists and leaders of the best univesities in the country, who spent considerable effort participating in the external evaluation committees.

The significant acceptance of the Programme can be attributed to the concern of universities with the upcoming implementation by the Ministry of Education of institutional re-accreditation as provided by the Education Law (LDB). As the universities could not predict the quality and efficacy of the evaluation to be offered or provided by the CRUB programme, they actually seem to be taking advantage of a rare opportunity to prepare for another threatening action by the Ministry of Education.

Although it is too early to gain a consistent picture, the self-analyses that have been submitted, as well as the visits already undertaken, suggest that the universities are driven by outside influences. On one hand, they are more concerned with market strategies and with anticipating the Ministry's next steps than with their own priorities, strengths and potentials. On the other, a common feature is the influence of organisational management consultancies that are cutting down costs by eliminating academic departments and even the academic institutes and schools that group departments and courses according to areas of study. Directly connected to vice-rectors, course coordinators are treated like managers and held responsible for financial and administrative matters, such as for students' payments.

The most positive aspect is the frankness with which these evaluations have taken place – so much so that both parties have experienced them as a precious opportunity for learning about their differences and commonalities, and to uncover a readiness to collaborate. The CRUB has invited external assessors from public and private, and even from 'for-profit' universities, without meeting any resistance from the private institutions that have already been visited. This kind of programme generates a completely new mode of communication that evolves with unexpected ease. There is the space, interest and openness for a genuine exchange of experiences and for an open debate about the rather intractable issues faced by universities.

As noted above, the representative bodies of the higher education community gained density in the last years. Evidences of 'public responsibility' and system-wide perspectives, though, do not abound among them. The few significant examples we singled out may be enough to steer the realignment of other segments, even though, this will not happen without a significant change in the government's attitude.

The harder task required for orienting Brazilian higher education towards a self-regulated system concerns the government, and it does so in three regards: it concerns its administrative culture, its institutional framework and its university network. New competences have to be attained and an adequate, more complex and diverse institutional framework has to be devised if the government wishes to conduct a more collaborative and sustainable reform process. New forums and institutional settings will be used to host work teams of representatives of both government and the community. And, effective institutional channels must be established between the government and the academic community.

The role of governments in self-regulated systems is much more subtle and has more to do with social adaptation than with technical expertise. Instead of providing answers, decisions, strength, and a map of the future – that is, instead of knowing where we ought to be – the leadership needed is one that challenges the community to face problems for which there are no simple, technical solutions – problems that require us to learn new ways (Heifetz, 1994). Regulations, for instance, become, for the government, a matter of coordination of collaborative efforts (studies and debate), and of negotiation.

Since self-regulating systems, under remote administration by the state, only make sense if its main components are aware and ready to respond to the incentives and constraints administered by the government, the Brazilian federal universities must be incorporated into the self-regulating condition already shared by the other institutions in Brazil (as well as by their western European counterparts). The resistance to accepting autonomy from state direct control, still voiced by the federal universities' representative bodies, might be disguising reality. There are signs that a voluntary programme with negotiated transition agreements will get the prompt acceptance of some leading federal universities that are ripe for autonomy. As the first stages are grasped, other universities will voluntarily join the programme.

The prescriptions, laid out above, compose a huge agenda and what we do not need now is another experience of overloaded agendas and the 'too much, too fast' mood. The good news is that self-regulation is a flexible process of mutual adaptation that may progress better through consensus-building and controlled experimentation, than through encompassing reforms, plans and regulations.

Notes

[1] They are: University of Oslo, of Bergen, and Trondheim (Norway); University of Edinburgh, University of Ulster, and Essex (UK); Utrecht and Twente (Netherlands); Lulea and Umea (Sweden), and University of Joensuu (Finland).

[2] 'The recent *Der Spiegel* review placed British universities at the top of a European league table with the Netherlands second – the two European university systems, it pointed out, that had substantially been restructured by external pressure. A recent Council for Industry and Higher Education report shows that corporate spending on British higher education is high and growing, a sign that industry continues to support the system; Higher Education Statistics Agency figures show that the proportion of non-government money flowing into higher education is rising. The number of overseas students choosing to study full time in British higher education is three times as large as 15 years ago' (Shattock, 1999, p. 3).

[3] There are, however, important exceptions, and observers in Latin America have distinguished two main types of private institutions in the region, the elite *university-like* institutions and the *excess-demand accommodating* institutions (Balán & Fanelli, in Castro & Navarro, 1999, pp. 51-72).

[4] The potential for the expansion of private higher education should be huge, because of the high returns higher education brings to the students, and the public sector will not be able to grow within the very expensive structure it currently entails. Unfortunately, two serious obstacles preclude such growth: the bottleneck of secondary education and, more importantly, income concentration. Secondary education is expanding rapidly; but does so in public schools that struggle with lack of teachers and of quality, all over the country. Also, it is growing through the incorporation of lower social strata; that is to say, of students unable to afford private higher education.

[5] 'Danish students, since 1992, can take their government grant support with them abroad for up to three years, because increased international mobility would in itself influence the national education market, contributing towards an integrated quality measurement of higher education. It would give users better possibilities to assess teaching methods and standards. Danish students with experience from abroad would become better-informed users and observers of their educational system. Therefore, the various sectors of the national higher education system would be committed to proving internationally that the necessary quality objectives are met' (Thune, 1994, p. 165). For a European picture, see Green et al (2002, p. 3).

[6] See the articles of Francisco Soares and João Batista de Araujo e Oliveira, in this volume, about the limitations of these efforts.

[7] Personal information obtained through informal contacts with one Finance Director and some other owners.

[8] Personal information from interviews.

[9] University centres, however, need only 10% of full-time staff, and do not have to show research, just good quality undergraduate education.

[10] Typically costs have been reduced by extinguishing the academic departments and including institutes and schools. Course coordinators are turned into 'academic managers' and directly linked to the higher administration.

[11] Public money can be saved when the private institution is filling up niches of excellence for an elite public; that is to say, when it already holds quality and sustainability. Even in these cases, as Charles Cook (former head of the American NEASC) notes, there are always improvements to be pursued for which incentives are needed.

[12] In 2003, the examination was held in 704 municipalities, for 435,810 students, accounting for more than 92% of the graduates in the 26 areas of studies covered (Newspaper *O Globo*, 10 June 2003, p. 10).

[13] Within this group, there are associations by religious denominations: Catholics, Methodists, Baptists and Presbyterians.

[14] ForProp is represented in the CAPES CTC, and CNPq Scientific Committee.

References

Altbach, P.G. (1999) *Private Prometheus: private higher education and development in the 21st century.* Westport: Greenwood Press.

Altbach, P.G. (2001) The Rise of Pseudouniversities. Available at: www.bc.edu/cihe

Aragón, V. (Coord.) (1999) *Mídia e Educação: Perspectivas para a Qualidade da Informação.* Brasilia: NEMP–CEAM/UnB.

Balán, J. & Fanelli, A.M.G.d. (1993) *El sector privado de la educación superior políticas públicas y sus resultados recientes en cinco países de América Latina.* Buenos Aires: Centro de Estudios de Estado y Sociedad.

Bauer, M. (1994) Changing Quality Assessment in Sweden, in D.F. Westerheijden, J. Brennan & P.A.M. Maassen (Eds) *Changing Contexts of Quality Assessment: recent trends in European higher education,* pp. 135-148. Utrecht: LEMMA.

Castro, C.d.M. & Levy, D.C. (2000) *Myth, Reality, and Reform: higher education policy in Latin America.* Washington, DC: Johns Hopkins University Press for the IDB.

Castro, C.d.M. & Navarro, J.C. (1999) Will the Invisible Hand Fix Latin American Private Higher Education? in P.G. Altbach (Ed.) *Private Prometheus: private higher education and development in the 21st century,* pp. 51-72. Westport: Greenwood Press.

Castro, M.H.d.M. (2001) Tomando o pulso: o que buscar no credenciamento institucional das universidades brasileiras? in *Série Documental – Textos para Discussão.* Brasília: Ministério da Educacão, Instituto Nacional de Estudos e Pesquisas Educacionais.

Clark, B.R. (1998) *Creating Entrepreneurial Universities Organizational Pathways of Transformation.* Oxford: Published for the IAU Press by Pergamon Press.

de Wit, H. (2001) The Long and Winding Road to a European Higher Education Area, *International Higher Education,* 25, pp. 4-5.

Green, M., Eckel, P. & Barblan, A. (2002) The Brave New (and Smaller) World of Higher Education: a transatlantic view, *International Higher Education,* 29, pp. 3-4.

Hartingsveld, L.M. van (1994) Looking Inside the Black Box: aspects of quality assessment in higher vocational education in the Netherlands, in D.F. Westerheijden, J. Brennan & P.A.M. Maassen (Eds) *Changing Contexts of Quality Assessment: recent trends in European higher education,* pp. 111-121. Utrecht: LEMMA.

Heifetz, R.A. (1994) *Leadership without Easy Answers.* Cambridge MA: Harvard University Press.

Holtta, S. & Nuotio, J. (1995) Academic Leadership in a Self-regulative Environment: a challenge for Finnish universities, *Tertiary Education and Management,* 1, pp. 12-20.

INEP (2001) Relatório da missão à Washington. Instituto Nacional de Estudos e Pesquisas Educacionais: Brasilia.

La Belle, T.J. (2002) More on the Pseudouniversity and its Consequences, *International Higher Education,* 28, p. 22.

Schwartzman, J. & Schwartzman, S. (2002) O ensino superior privado como setor econômico, *Ensaio – Avaliação e Políticas Públicas em Educação*, 10, pp. 411-440. Available at: http://www.schwartzman.org.br/simon/suppriv.pdf

Shattock, M. (1999) The Challenge Ahead: British universities in the 21st century, *International Higher Education*, 15, pp. 24-26. Available at: http://www.bc.edu/bc_org/avp/soe/cihe/newsletter/News15/text14.html

Task Force on Higher Education and Society (2000) *Peril and Promise: higher education in developing countries*. Washington, DC: World Bank.

Thune, C. (1994) The Evaluation Center in Denmark, in D.F. Westerheijden, J. Brennan, & P.A.M. Maassen (Eds) *Changing Contexts in Quality Management: recent trends in European higher education*, pp. 163-178. Utrecht: Lemma.

Trow, M. (1993) Managerialism and the Academic Profession: the case of England, *Studies of Higher Education and Research*, 4, pp. 2-23.

Vargas, J. (2002) Indo além da dicotomia público-privado: relações entre agente e principal, in L. Wolff, P. Gonzáles, & J.C. Navarro (Eds) *Educación privada y política pública en América Latina*, pp. 87-103. Santiago, Chile: PREAL/BID.

Vught, F. v. & Kells, H.R. (1988) Stepping Back to Examine National Higher Education Evaluation Systems: an analysis and some propositions for the research and policy void. Paper presented at the 11th Annual Consortium of Higher Education Researchers Conference, Kassel, Germany, 3-5 September.

Graduate Education: emerging challenges to a successful policy

ELIZABETH BALBACHEVSKY

Higher education in Brazil is known for its many problems, but the graduate segment is still a place for pride among Brazilian faculty and policy makers.[1] The figures are impressive: in the year 2000, more than 57,000 students were enrolled in Master's programmes and a further 30,000 were enrolled in doctoral programmes. In the same year, more than 18,000 Master's and 5,000 doctors graduated in Brazilian higher education institutions (see Table I).These figures place Brazilian graduate education among the most impressive in developing countries.

The achievements of Brazilian graduate education are not only associated with its size. There is quality also. Since the late 1960s this sector has been subjected to a consistent set of policies aiming at assuring both growth and quality. In the mid-1970s, The *Fundação Coordenação de Aperfeiçoamento de Pessoal de Nível Superior* (CAPES), the Ministry of Education's agency in charge of graduate education, created a sophisticated peer-review evaluation that successfully links performance with support. This evaluation system has had a decisive impact on Brazilian graduate education development. It successfully limited growth without quality and imposed threshold performance standards for the graduate programmes nationwide.

Nonetheless, despite its success, graduate education in Brazil faces important challenges in the present. In this chapter, a portrait of Brazilian graduate education will be presented, summarising its trajectory, presenting new data about its students, and pointing out the most relevant challenges it faces in the new environment created by the 1990s reforms.

Brazilian Graduate Education: a brief history

The origins of graduate studies in Brazil can be traced to early experiences with the chair model adopted by the Brazilian universities in the 1930s. In those years Brazil attracted a significant number of foreign scholars: some of them came in special missions organised by the Brazilian authorities in collaboration with foreign governments, while others entered Brazil as refugees from the European turmoil of the 1930s. With the foreign scholars came the first institutional model for graduate training. Pursuant to that model, graduate studies were conceived of as an apprenticeship. Central to this model was the tutorial relationship between a full professor and a few students who were supposed to support the professor as teaching and/or research assistants. Training was mostly informal and centred on the student's dissertation. The authority of the professor was almost absolute, having sole responsibility to assign the assistant's academic workload, to determine the acceptable content and methodology, and to establish the standard of quality for the dissertations.

	Master's programmes		Doctorate programmes	
	Enrolled	Graduated	Enrolled	Graduated
Physical sciences	9.3	9.8	13.6	13.6
Biological sciences	6.7	8.3	11.8	12.5
Engineering	16.6	14.7	16.7	13.2
Health professions	13.9	15.7	15.3	19.5
Agricultural sciences	8.7	10.9	9.7	10.3
Administrative and legal professions	17.8	14.8	8.7	8.3
Humanities	16.9	16.8	17.1	16.7
Arts and Literature	6.6	6.0	5.7	4.8
Multidisciplinary	3.3	2.9	1.4	1.1
Total (100%)	(57,059)	(18,132)	(30,272)	(5,335)

Table I. Brazilian graduate education: students enrolled and graduated by academic field and degree – year 2000.
Source: CAPES, Coordenadoria de Estudos e Divulgação Científica.

However, these earlier experiences in graduate education had little impact on the higher education system as a whole. It was a small enterprise more or less tolerated by the academic authorities. The Master's or doctoral degree had no currency outside the academy. In most cases, graduate activities were supposed to be one of the thresholds (but not the only one) to the institution's academic career.

Only in 1965 did the Ministry of Education take the first steps to recognise and regulate this experience as a new educational level. Its main organisational features were sketched by the Report 977, enacted by the Federal Council of Education (known in Brazil as *Parecer Sucupira*). This Report created the two-level format for graduate studies, where students were supposed to conclude a Master's programme successfully prior to being accepted in a doctorate programme.

At that time Brazil was under an authoritarian regime with important and particular nationalistic orientations. The regulation of the graduate sector illustrates the government's awareness of the potentialities of advanced training. Its role as a domestic alternative to qualify academics for the growing federal network of universities was, most probably, the chief motivation for the growing interest shown by the governmental authorities.

After the 1968 reform [2] graduate studies in the most prestigious universities became semi-autonomous programmes to be overviewed by the newly organised departments, which were supposed to replace the old Chairs. In the new institutional framework, graduate studies incorporated new features, which represented a compromise between the old Chair model and the new American model adopted by the 1968 reform. In the new format, the tutorship was preserved but relations between the candidate and his/her tutor were now to be supervised by the board of the graduate programme. To conclude the graduate studies successfully, candidates were supposed to follow a specialised curriculum to be complemented by the public defence of a thesis before a board of examiners – three in the case of a Master's degree and five for the doctorate.

But the decisive change emerged when the graduate programmes came to be defined as a privileged focus for policies adopted for science and technology in the early 1970s (Schwartzman, 1991). In those years science and technology policies were on the threshold of a major change. For the first time, the Brazilian government was attempting to place science and technology as a means to attain economic development. This initiative can be best understood if one takes into account the consensus then built between influential scientists (some of them with well-known leftist orientations) and the nationalist sector in the Brazilian army, both supporting the idea of building an important sector of science and technology as an instrument for the country's economic development. From the science elite's point of view, the assumption was that with adequate economic incentives private investors would change their attitude from technology consumers to technology developers. This transformation would enable the country to break away from technological dependency, then perceived as one of the most important sources of economic underdevelopment. From the armed forces' perspective, this objective was important also as a means to ensure access to sensitive technology in strategic fields such as information technology, aeronautics and nuclear energy. In these convergent perspectives, investments should be concentrated in a few large strategic projects from which scientific and technological competence were supposed to *trickle down* to the economy and society.

Graduate education was then perceived as an important tool to fulfil this goal. It was supposed to deliver the sophisticated human capital deemed necessary for implementing these projects. Accordingly, the Brazilian government also launched an important programme of scholarships for Master's and doctorate students abroad. This programme greatly expanded the number of fellowships offered by foreign foundations such as the Ford Foundation and the Rockefeller Foundation, which were, until the end of the 1960s, the most important alternative for those aiming for a postgraduate

211

education abroad. It was this new generation of scientists, graduated abroad, that gave substance to the new graduate sector that was being developed in Brazil. These young researchers came back to Brazil with a well-defined picture of what a graduate programme should be by international standards and were an important instrument for the dynamism one could find in these developments even in the earlier stages.

To achieve these objectives the main Brazilian investment bank – the government-owned *Banco Nacional de Desenvolvimento Econômico* (BNDES) – established an initiative to support technological development in 1964. The success of the fund created pressures which moved it into a new specialised agency, the *Financiadora de Estudos e Projetos* (FINEP), which was in charge of a national fund for the development of science and technology, entitled to a permanent item of the Federal Budget. In 1975 the old and small *Conselho Nacional de Pesquisa* (National Research Council) was reformed and transformed into a new and larger *Conselho Nacional de Desenvolvimento Científico e tecnológico* (National Council for Scientific and Technological Development – CNPq), placed under the control of the Ministry of Planning, then an important arm of the Brazilian government.

The 1970s were years of economic expansion, in which the Brazilian economy grew at annual rates of 7-10%. As such, these new agencies had funds to spend, and to create a flexible and modern bureaucracy, unfettered by the rigid controls found in other governmental offices. Their first attempts were directed towards stimulating private and public firms to invest in technological development. But these initiatives were mostly doomed to fail due the firms' lack of interest in investing in such a risky enterprise, being placed, as they were, in a highly protected environment created by the macro-economic import substitution policies. Then they turned their attention towards the informal research environments to be found in some of the most prestigious universities, where some scientific tradition was already in place. The new roles assigned to science and technology were acclaimed with enthusiasm by the research leaders. As stated by the founder of one of the country's most prestigious graduate programmes in engineering, Alberto Luis Coimbra:

> [The Programme] was created to form a kind of new professional Brazil did not have at the time. One at the Master's and doctoral levels. We believed that people with these qualifications were necessary to the country's technological development ... We lacked graduate people who could create new technology ... (as quoted by Schwartzman, 1991, p. 229)

The strategy adopted by the science and technology agencies was to search for talented people in the academic institutions and provide them with the necessary direct support in research infrastructure and staff. Often, the agencies preferred to deal directly with the research leaders, bypassing the university's institutional procedures and bureaucratic controls. This strategy assured that resources were spent where they were deemed necessary. But it also meant that the universities as a whole were unable to benefit from the new investments. A two-tier and unequal system began to develop inside the public universities: well-staffed and equipped graduate programmes and departments were to be found side by side with poorer counterparts, the latter oriented toward the more traditional role as teaching faculty of undergraduate courses (Schwartzman, 1991).

With such support, graduate education in Brazil grew at a great pace. In 1965, when the graduate studies were recognised, the National Education Council had accredited 38 graduate programmes: 27 as Master's degrees and 11 as doctorates. Ten years later, in 1975, there were already 429 MA and 149 doctoral programmes. As one can see in Figure 1, these numbers have grown continuously since then, so that by 2000, there were in Brazil 1420 accredited MAs and 865 doctorates.

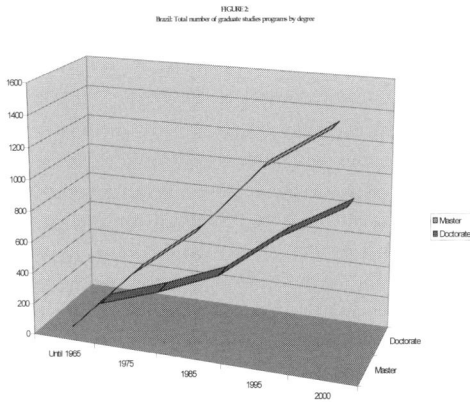

Figure 1. Brazil: total number of graduate studies programmes by degree

While FINEP and CNPq favoured hard science and engineering; the Ministry of Education tended to support a broader range of fields, being focused on faculty qualification. Since the majority of the undergraduate courses were in soft science, its policy tended to favour programmes in these areas. In the end, with the overlap of policies of these two stakeholders, graduate education in Brazil became fairly well distributed among the major academic fields. As one can see in Table I, in 2000, while 32.6% of the students enrolled in Master's studies were attending programmes in biological and physical sciences, and engineering, another 41.3% were enrolled in the humanities, legal and administrative professions or literature and arts. Then, 13.9% were attending Master's programmes in health professions, and agricultural sciences accounted for 8.7% of the enrolments. The pattern of enrolment for the doctoral level is more or less the same.

213

Here, hard science has a small advantage, with 42.1% of the students attending programmes in physical and biological sciences or engineering, while only 31.5% of the students were enrolled in humanities, legal and administrative professions or literature and arts. The difference is associated with a sharp decrease in enrolments at the doctoral level in the soft professions (legal and administrative professions) and a smaller increase in the enrolments in physical and biological sciences.

The Quest for Quality and Evaluation

The 1965 Graduate Report conferred on the Ministry of Education's *Conselho Federal de Educação* (Federal Education Council) [3] the responsibility for the accreditation and evaluation of programmes. However, its earlier attempts to fulfil this role failed due to the lack of appropriate mechanisms and procedures. New graduate programmes were being created very rapidly, while the Council was slow in providing the necessary guidelines for accreditation and evaluation.

Lacking general standards, the science and technology agencies had little expertise in choosing to support or dismiss initiatives. While CNPq had some experience in peer review procedures, they were mostly employed in rating individual projects, not programmes as a whole. For the research groups to attain high quality standards was crucial: it meant independence from the internal struggles of the agencies and was perceived as an alternative for preserving the prestige associated with graduate education. The solution to this impasse was reached when CAPES – a Ministry of Education agency originally in charge of providing scholarships for faculty and graduate students – organised the first general evaluation of graduate programmes in 1976. The procedure was supposed to serve as a guideline for allocating student scholarships (Castro & Soares, 1986). In order to assure credibility, CAPES opted for extending the peer review procedures in evaluating the collective outputs of the programme's faculty. In each academic field, prestigious scholars were hired as consultants to work in committees, which were in charge of evaluating and ranking graduate programmes. The work of these committees had a major impact on the institutionalisation of academic research in Brazil. They became a major forum for establishing quality standards for research and academic careers, and for legitimising subjects of study, theories and methodologies, as well as evaluating international links and publishing trends (Coutinho, 1996). As such, the work of the evaluation committees was very helpful in expediting the institutionalisation of all fields of knowledge and in building the foundations of the Brazilian scientific community.

Eventually, the CAPES evaluation was accepted by all stakeholders as a quality reference for graduate programmes. As it successfully connected performance with reward, the better the evaluation, and the greater its chances for accrued support as expressed in student scholarships, research infrastructure and funds. Such a situation stands in clear contrast with all other policies regarding higher education in Brazil, where until now the government has not succeeded in relating performance to rewards.

In spite of its positive aspects, CAPES evaluation had some deficiencies that became more and more apparent as time went by. The small size of the Brazilian scientific community and the visibility of the peer-committee work created unavoidable parochial pressures. One consequence was grade inflation (Castro & Soares, 1986; CAPES, 1998). In 1996, four in every five programmes were placed in the two highest ranks, A or B. It meant that CAPES evaluation was quickly losing credibility.

Reacting to this situation, the CAPES authorities established in 1998 a new model for programme evaluation. This new model preserves the authority of the peer committees, but adopts more formal rules for evaluation. It reinforces the adoption of international standards for all fields of knowledge; imposes a set of parameters for faculty evaluation stressing their academic background and research performance as measured by their publishing patterns; extends the periodicity of evaluation from two to three years; adopts a more comprehensive procedure, evaluating Master's and doctoral programmes together, instead of evaluating each programme per se; and adopts a scale of seven points (instead of five), where the ranks of 6 and 7 are restricted to programmes offering doctoral degrees that could be qualified as good or excellent by international standards, and establishing that 3 was the lowest acceptable rank for attaining graduate programme accreditation. The 1998 evaluation round proceeded under these new rules. The results were satisfactory from the agency's point of view. Using the new criteria, only three out of ten programmes were ranked in the three highest positions (CAPES, 1999).

As indicated above, the whole process gave rise to a growing dynamic graduate tier inside the Brazilian higher education system. Nevertheless, hopes of a big impact on the country's capabilities for technological innovation have not been fulfilled. The new professionals formed by this system were, most often, absorbed in the academic area, and few created solid links with the outside world. As also stated by Professor Coimbra:

> We created the graduate programs for a Brazil that did not exist
> and still does not exist, which did not correspond to what we
> expected to happen. We were throwing into the market a
> sophisticated product for the country's technological development
> ... But it never happened. (Quoted in Schwartzman, 1991,
> p. 229)

Thus, the graduate section is the pride of all Brazilian scholars, but it is facing some important challenges in the new century, as the next sections will show.

Regional Inequalities

The direct support provided by CAPES and other science and technology agencies to the high-quality programmes allowed them to engage and secure the best researchers as faculty. So, the success of universities in developing a broad graduate sector became an important source of stratification inside the public sector in Brazil.[4] At the top, one finds a small number of universities strongly motivated by academic standards, where academic research is permanent and fully institutionalised. These institutions provide a superior working environment, which in turn allows them to attract and secure better-qualified faculty as well as financial support for research. These institutions confer the majority of the doctoral degrees granted domestically.

However, many public institutions were still unable to develop a strong graduate section. As a consequence, they have problems in attracting and retaining doctorate holders among their faculty. As a result they reinforced their previous orientation towards undergraduate education. In such institutions, research environments can only be found in isolation in what has been described as small 'isles of excellence' (Oliveira, 1984). These environments are usually big enough to support small Master's programmes but only rarely are they offering doctoral opportunity. So by the new CAPES evaluations rules, such programmes are by definition placed in the middle rank, whatever their performance, since the two highest positions are reserved for programmes that confer doctoral degrees. In spite of all these constraints, the institutions placed in this stratum are responsible for more than 50% of all enrolments at MA level in Brazil (Balbachevsky & Quinteiro, 2003).

Predictably, this stratification has also a regional component. As one can see in Table II, the South-east – the more modern, industrialised and urbanised region in the country – contains 65% of all students enrolled at the Master's level and 80.5% of those enrolled at doctoral level. At the other extreme, the northern region has only 1.1% of all graduate students. But the most expressive indicator of inequality is illustrated in the last column of Table II. Here the size of the graduate sector is shown as a proportion of each region's population. As one can see, in 2000 there were 8.5 graduate students per 10,000 habitants in the south-eastern region. The southern states, with modern industries located in a network of small, dynamic urban centres and a fairly well-educated population, had 5.6 graduate students per 10,000 habitants. The centre-western region is not so badly positioned: here there were 2.7 graduate students per 10,000 habitants. Here, the presence of the country's capital, Brasília, and the academic profile of its federal university, the *Universidade de Brasília*, explains this figure. The worst results are to be found in the densely populated but poor states of the north-eastern region, where one could find only 0.2 graduate students per 10,000 habitants. The situation found at the sparsely populated northern region was not much better, there being only 0.7 graduate students per 10,000 habitants.

	Enrolments by degree level		Total	Total enrolments per 10,000 habitants
	Master	Doctorate		
Centre-western	4.3	2.2	3.8	2.7
North-western	10.8	4.8	9.2	0.2
Northern	1.3	0.6	1.1	0.7
South-eastern	65.2	80.5	75.1	8.5
Southern	18.4	11.9	17.1	5.6
Total (100%)	(57,059)	(30,272)	(82,331)	(Brazil: 4.8)

Table II. Brazil: total of graduate enrolments by degree and enrolments per 10,000 habitants by region – 2000.
Sources: CAPES, Coordenadoria de Estudos e Divulgação Científica and IBGE.

These regional disparities are perceived by Brazilian society as unfair, and are a source of complaint for politicians with regional constituencies. Programmes and policies specially designed to deal with regional inequalities have been proposed since the late 1970s, but little success has been achieved. Most of these initiatives fail because of their paternalistic approach: they earmark small portions of the science and technology resources, including fellowships, to be distributed only among researchers from the North-east or the North. Such policies create reserved markets with lower thresholds open only to researchers from these regions, while supporting the ideal of a unitarian system where all universities should, in the end, follow the same model (the great research-oriented university) regardless of its costs. As this model is unreachable for most institutions, especially those from the poorer states, it damages faculty's morale, while, at the same time, creating a vicious circle, rewarding poor performance and poor academic standards, as long as the research group is placed in a poor region.

What is more important, these regional policies adopted by the science and technology agencies fail to recognise and reward special traits of the research community in these regions. In a recent survey with research leaders from the biotechnology community in Brazil, it was discovered that research groups from these peripheral regions are more prone to open their research agenda to societal needs and demands than those belonging to the more academically oriented central universities (Coutinho et al, 2003). This observation corroborates the hypothesis that, besides resources, a more flexible set of standards – one that recognised and rewarded differentiation, while supporting quality – could be an important tool in reducing sharp disparities between regions in Brazil.

Institutional Challenges

Other special challenges faced by graduate education refer to its potential for differentiation and diversification, especially regarding multidisciplinarity and transdisciplinarity. As one can see in Table I, multidisciplinary programmes are seldom found in Brazil. In the year 2000, such programmes attained only 3% of the Master's students and 1% of doctoral students. The reasons for this situation are diverse. First, in many cases, departments lack the academic capacity to offer more than one graduate programme. Since Brazilian universities are rigidly organised in disciplinary departments, anything placed outside (or in between) the departments suffers chronically from lack of resources, autonomy, support and prestige. Second, there is a bureaucratic impediment. In the public sector, faculty contracts are based on a standard teaching load. Greater loads do not entitle the faculty to additional material or even symbolic rewards. Finally, but not least important, for the departments, programme diversification does not warrant any reward; neither does the lack of diversification attract any penalty.[5]

Furthermore, the evaluation process implemented by CAPES seems to fail in facing the special demands and challenges posed by multidisciplinary programmes. CAPES evaluation assumes a unique disciplinary affiliation for each programme. So its officials, having trouble in classifying the multidisciplinary programmes, chose to subordinate them to the committee that seems the best proxy. Such choices rarely prove positive in outcome. Committees' members, lacking experience with multidisciplinary research, tend to fail to perceive, or simply disregard the special needs inherent in such programmes. It is not a surprise to find that 94% of all multidisciplinary programmes accredited by CAPES were ranked between 4 and 3 in a scale of seven positions, where 7 is the highest rank (CAPES, 1999).

The Serial Model and Overextended Completion Time

Another challenge faced by graduate education in Brazil is its assumption and toleration of an unusually long completion time. CAPES officials estimate that in order to conclude the Master's degree, a student would spend 34 months [6] on average (almost three years). To achieve the doctoral degree, it takes an additional 53 moths (four and half years). Since Master's programmes in Brazil are regarded as an intermediate stage, an almost mandatory prerequisite for obtaining a doctorate, students spend, on average, more than seven years to reach that ultimate objective.

A fairly recent survey made of graduate students suggests that the average student reaches the graduate level at 30 years of age (Velloso & Velho, 2001), five years after finishing his/her undergraduate studies. Braga (2002) agrees with this conclusion, showing that this span of time is growing. Students who were admitted to Master's programmes in the late 1990s spent, on average, more years between finishing their undergraduate courses and beginning the Master's programme than those who were admitted in the early 1990s. Between graduating at the Master level and being accepted at the doctoral level, there is also a gap of 2.5 and 3.5 years. With all those delays, the average student is likely to finish his/her training at around 37 to 42 years of age.

This is a very large span of time from an international perspective and represents a huge investment from the government's point of view. CAPES estimates that, in 2002, almost 40% of all Master's students and 50% of all doctoral students were supported by fellowships provided by public funding.[7] Additionally, such excessively long training paths result in a shorter productive research life, when the academic should be contributing to training new researchers.

A number of measures have been taken by the Brazilian science and technology agencies to counteract this trend. First, the span of time covered by fellowships has been reduced from the original four to two years in the case of Master's degrees and from six to four years in the case of the doctorate. At the time this measure was taken in the early 1990s it aroused considerable concern among Brazilian academics, but nowadays is accepted by almost all stakeholders. Second, evaluation procedures have emphasised this requirement, penalising programmes where students take more than the desirable span of time for achieving their degree (two years in the case of Master's programmes and four years in the case of doctorates). There were even some incentives for by-passing the Master's level, but until now this rarely happens, even in the hard sciences, where this alternative is more likely to be accepted in principle.

Follow-up studies [8] made with masters and doctors graduated in Brazil since the early 1990s (Velloso, 2002b) clearly suggest that, at the Master's level, in the fields included by the studies, such policies have been successful. The average time to achieve a degree in the 1990s fell by approximately 15%, varying from about 10% to more than 20%, depending on the field of studies involved. Concerning doctorates, the information collected is less conclusive. While in some fields the average time to graduate did shorten, in others the changes are not significant. Nevertheless, the widely accepted sequential model, requiring that the student first finishes the Master's level before being accepted for doctoral studies, is still a real barrier to reaching international norms and standards. Resistance to accepting the bypassing of the Master's level is very strong among Brazilian academics. One important source of this resistance is the assumed academic orientation and utility of the Master's programmes in Brazil. For example, if a Master's degree has academic credibility and utility, why can it be circumvented? After all, could it be true that most of the Brazilian public universities and the faculty they employed were wasting their time teaching and advising pupils in second-best programmes that cannot be improved?

The Prospects for Master's Studies in Brazil: academic orientation and market pressures

As stated above, both Master's and doctoral programmes in Brazil are supposed to be academically oriented. But the data gathered by follow-up studies show a very different picture. Most holders of Master's degrees are working outside academia, such as in firms (mostly private), in public administration or in professional offices. Of course, these figures vary a great deal, according to the field under consideration, as shown in Table III. Masters in professionally oriented fields are heavily concentrated in jobs outside academia, in a proportion ranging from 60% (Business and Public Administration, Economics and Engineering) to 80% (Law and Medicine), while nearly two-thirds of those in more basic fields hold academic jobs such as in Chemistry, Physics and Sociology (Velloso & Balbachevsky, 2002).

Disciplinary field of the programme	Academic oriented market (%)	Non-academic oriented market (%)
Agronomy	51.3	48.7
Biotechnology	45.4	54.6
Business Studies	36.7	63.3
Chemistry	60.2	39.8
Civil Engineering	39.3	60.7
Dentistry	32.7	67.3
Economy	39.1	60.9
Electrical Engineering	33.9	66.1
Geology	34.6	65.4
Law Studies	19.7	80.3
Mechanical Engineering	32.4	67.6
Medicine (General Practice)	22.0	78.0
Physics	66.7	33.3
Psychology	45.6	54.4
Sociology	64.5	35.5

Table III. Brazilian Master's holders: patterns of employment in academic and non-academic markets by field of knowledge.
Source: Velloso, 2002b, my tabulations.

Also, in spite of the sequential model, a significant number of Master's holders are not looking to continue their studies. Working with the data collected with the follow-up studies, Weber found out that little more than one-third of all interviewed did enter a doctoral programme after graduating at the master level (Weber, 2002).

The professional perspectives for doctorate holders are much more homogeneous: more than 60% of them work in academic institutions, either in public universities or in public research institutions. The proportion of academic employment is not significantly diverse among doctors, whether in hard or soft sciences, or in fields professionally or academically oriented. While 90% of all doctors in Physics and Biochemistry are in academia, 86% of those in Electrical Engineering hold faculty positions or work at research institutes. While 60% of chemists and sociologists found employment in the academic market place, about 75% of economists, civil and mechanical engineers, and psychologists have the same kind of jobs.

These findings are quite impressive, revealing remarkable proportions of academics among doctors graduated in professionally oriented fields, vis-à-vis the figures found for masters in similar fields. They raise important questions about changes that are taking place in Brazilian graduate education. In fact, while the academic community and governmental agencies tend to view training at the Master's level as a meaningful intermediate step toward the doctorate, this is not how the students perceive it. For an important portion of them, this training is a terminal stage preparing them for the job market outside academia.

This situation poses important dilemmas for policy making, as argued above. Acknowledging that the Master's degrees are not always primarily academically oriented could imply a step towards drastically shortening the length of time spent by postgraduate scholars in Brazil. Braga, using the data collected with doctorate holders without a Master's degree, discovered that they were three or four years younger than their colleagues when they finished their studies (Braga, 2002). But this trend generates another set of questions: is the training received by our masters relevant to the needs of non-academic jobs? Does the portfolio of academic fields covered by the Brazilian Master's education fit the demands of the non-academic job-market? Is the schedule adopted by the Master's programmes adequate to the needs of part-time students? These issues pose more difficult challenges: to recognise and incorporate the interests of another stakeholder until now ignored in all decisions made about graduate studies in Brazil: – the private firms. This is a great step forward that neither the Brazilian academic community (at least those employed in the public sector) nor the governmental agencies are prepared to take.

Up to the present, the sole response to this challenge has come from CAPES. In 1996, this agency proposed a diversification at Master's level, offering the alternative of a new kind of Master's programme – the so-called 'professional Master's degree', oriented toward the demands of the non-academic job market. In the CAPES proposal, this kind of programme should include faculty from outside academia and should be self-sustaining – meaning that the public funds should, in time, be replaced by revenues from the tuition fees that it would be allowed to charge. Nevertheless, this proposal generated considerable resistance among academics. The main argument against such programmes is that they would open up the public sector to market pressures, an anathema to be avoided at all costs. In 2001, after seven years from its regulation, only 64 professional Master's programmes had been accredited by CAPES, and 60% of them were ranked at level 3 or 4 in the last evaluation.

Even for Master's holders employed in the academic workplace, the survey highlighted another relevant tendency. While most of the masters graduated in the early 1990s found employment in public universities, many of those graduated at the end of 1990s found placement at private institutions. This new pattern of employment is probably created by the new requirements posed by the Education Act (*Lei de Diretrizes e Bases da Educação*) of 1997, which demands at least one-third of any institution's faculty to hold a Master's or other higher degree if it is to be officially accredited as a university. Being accredited as a university entails not only prestige, but also a number of important prerogatives for the institution, such as autonomy in creating new undergraduate and graduate programmes. It is not surprising to see the new interest revealed by the private sector in employing post professionals. This tendency had been reinforced by procedures adopted by the last government for evaluating the quality of undergraduate programmes. In those evaluations, one important requisite taken into account by the Ministry of Education was the proportion of graduate holders among the faculty.

In Brazil, the private sector comprises a huge number of institutions and accounts for more than 60% of the enrolments at undergraduate level. These institutions are mostly teaching institutions with no real commitment to academic research, which Master's studies are supposed to train for. Institutions in the private sector claim that they are very successful in meeting labour market demands for rapid training. Thus, from their point of view the quality of teaching should be measured by the employability generated by the credentials they provide. As such, the professional profile they are in search of is not the one produced by the training offered by Master's studies in Brazil. Currently this question is not being posed. Nevertheless, one can expect that this new pattern of employment for the Brazilian Master's holders in Brazil will create new pressures sooner or later. Once again, it seems that the Brazilian academic community and agencies' officials are not willing to face such a debate, or envisage the likely reform that would ensue.

The International Dimensions of Graduate Education

Internationalisation of graduate education is a hot issue abroad but seldom heard of in Brazil. To most stakeholders, the Brazilian graduate system is perceived as a domestic alternative to graduate studies in foreign countries. In fact, since the mid-1990s, when the Brazilian doctoral programmes were deemed sufficient to supply the domestic demand, science and technology agencies adopted a policy oriented to limit the number of fellowships for doctoral studies abroad, which resulted in a drastically reduced number of doctorate holders graduated in programmes outside the country. A recent analysis shows that while among Brazilian scholars graduated until 1985 almost 50% had concluded their doctoral training abroad, among those graduated between 1986 to 1996 this proportion had declined to 30%. For those graduated after 1996, only 20% hold international degrees (Guimarães et al, 2001).

On the other hand, there is no policy oriented for the internationalisation of the Brazilian domestic graduate section. On the contrary, decisions taken until now go in the opposite direction. As an example, early in 2002 the country's allegedly 'top' university – the University of São Paulo – issued new regulations under which Portuguese becomes the only and exclusive mandatory language for all graduate theses. Foreign candidates are required to prove their proficiency in Portuguese prior to being accepted as regular students and are supposed to present their dissertation written in the same language. This decision was taken in order to counteract the tendency found in some programmes to regard Spanish along with English as an acceptable language for the student's thesis.[9]

Of course, this situation does not mean that Brazil has an isolationist science policy. In fact, one could argue that even if Brazil did opt for training its doctors domestically, there is enough support for academics interested in doing post-doctorates abroad (at least for academics employed by the public sector) and for doctoral students going abroad for short internship periods.[10] What we are arguing is that policies related to the Brazilian graduate system seldom take into account its potential for internationalisation. Interchange with its counterparts abroad is deemed as a one-way flux; which greatly limits the international dimensions of Brazilian graduate studies, at least in those programmes that are acknowledged as good by international standards.

The Challenges from Abroad

Graduate education in Brazil has always been confined to the public sector.[11] Nevertheless, in recent years one can witness a growing interest in this kind of programme from private, for profit, institutions. This awareness has many sources: first, there are the pressures imposed by the 1997 Education Act. Second, there is the new job market value attached to the Master's degree, which creates new niches for the more enterprising institutions in the private sector.

Lacking experience and support for this enterprise, a number of these institutions turned their attention to the offers of partnership made by institutions abroad. The opportunities opened by the new technologies applied in distance learning, and the interest of foreign entrepreneurial institutions in the Brazilian graduate market greatly facilitated the implementing of partnerships between private for-profit Brazilian institutions and their counterparts abroad. Since the end of the 1990s, an unknown number of such partnerships have been settled, most of them in 'soft' fields like business studies.

In general, the official reaction to these initiatives has been very negative. The Ministry of Education stressed the dubious quality of such programmes and expressed concerns about the unfair competition that could arise between those with international connections and those offered by the public universities in Brazil. From the CAPES perspective, these initiatives pose sharp questions about evaluation and open important breaches in the quality control instruments that have been built up in the past years. Accordingly, CAPES has resisted accrediting these programmes, imposing a number of requirements that virtually deny accreditation to almost all initiatives.

In spite of all resistance, the presence of such programmes has been growing in the Brazilian academic scenery. From the student's point of view, the credentials acquired in such programmes appear to have a real market value. Even if not officially accredited, they are accepted by the job market. What is more, these programmes appear to have important marketing implications for the Brazilian institutions. In fact, advertising partnerships with foreign institutions seems to be an important piece of publicity for those institutions. They add appeal and credit to the institution which has extended to its undergraduate programmes and their enrolment.

With such appeal and the lack of clear policies regarding the presence of the private sector in the graduate layer, it is not difficult to envisage the growth of the number of such initiatives in the near future. Ignoring their inconvenience by denying any legitimacy will not solve the problems posed by the increasing presence of these internationally shared programmes.

Concluding Remarks

The 1990s were a decade of major change and reform in Brazil. Changes in the economy's framework had powerful impacts over Brazilian higher education's demand figures. Public demand in Brazil is moving away from an elite formation perspective and toward a general workforce qualification perspective. This decision implies an evaluation of the quality of undergraduate programmes, the employability of their alumni, general science and mathematics literacy and the quality of teachers' training. By the time the graduate section was organised in Brazil, the concerns of Brazilian society about higher education were in open contrast to those predominating nowadays, as highlighted in Table IV.

Brazilian higher education's ability to respond to the new demands rests, to a considerable extent, on the graduate system's ability to self-reform. It is in this layer that the new generation of academics will be formed. In order to partake of the new globalised knowledge economy, Brazil needs urgently to upgrade the quality of education at all levels. Graduate education plays an important role in this process. In the format it operates in the present-day it will not fulfil the society's expectations for a more dynamic, diverse and inclusive education.

In the past, graduate education was deemed responsible for creating and reproducing the country's intellectual and scientific elite. In the present, while this task has not been discarded, new demands have been introduced. It is now supposed to bring forth a more polyvalent professional, one who could provide strong connections between academic research and the external world. New demands pose new requirements, among which the most important one is training a new, modern generation of higher education teachers, who could operate the new learning tools that have been developed around the world.

Concerns	1970s	1990s
University institutional autonomy	Low	Low
Control of public spending in HE	Low	High
Quality of undergraduate programs at public sector	Low	High
Quality of HE private sector (undergraduate)	Low	High
Quality of graduate courses	High	High
Diversity of science and technology human resources	High	High
General science and mathematics literacy	Low	Medium
Outputs of scientists	Medium	High
Elite formation and enlightenment	High	Low
University-productive sector interface	Low	High
Teacher education	Medium	High
Employability of alumni	Low	Medium
Faculty and alumni entrepreneurship	Low	High
Regional equity	High	High

Table IV. Brazil: changes in national concerns about higher education.
Source: Balbachevsky & Quinteiro, 2003, p. 89.

Until now, these needs have been poorly addressed by short-term training programmes organised mostly by schools and universities in the private sector. They are the so-called 'specialising' programmes (*cursos de especialização*). We have few data about these programmes. They are placed outside the mainstream graduate system and, as such, have no official support, no scholarships and weak international ties.

As a tool for elite enlightenment, Brazilian graduate education is still a very expensive, exclusive and self-indulgent system. In 1999, public support for the graduate system consumed almost 54% of all the public investment in research and development (Ministério da Ciência e Tecnologia, 1999). Requirements for granting public support to graduate programmes include a high proportion of full-time teachers with a high performance in both research projects and publication while discarding less expensive and more diverse contributions from part-time teachers. Class schedules and tight deadlines for achieving degrees all but exclude non-full-time students, which, in turn, requires a very extensive and expensive programme of scholarships. Besides, while entitled to publicly funded scholarships, postgraduate students are not required to participate in teaching or research assistance tasks or in any tasks outside their own education for that matter.

Another issue is that its decision-making process only admits internal stakeholders: the academic community and the science and technology governmental agencies, and even though not all academy. The whole postgraduate layer in the private sector is poorly represented, if at all. The remaining governmental agencies, the business community and the public at large have no part in designing and evaluating the system's policies and achievements. Now these actors are knocking at the door. It is still too early to predict whether or not or how far the door will open. But the quality of the system's response will shape Brazilian graduate education's future as well as the country's competitiveness on the international stage in the emerging era of the knowledge economy.

Notes

[1] In this text, we use the expression 'graduate education' to refer to the Master's and doctoral level of studies. In Brazil, however, there is no undergraduate education in the American sense, and the term 'graduate' is used to refer to the first level of higher education, which lasts around four years, and leads to a professional degree, while the MA and doctoral level is called 'postgraduate'.

[2] In 1968 the federal government enacted a bill seeking to reorganise the Brazilian universities after the US model. This reform replaced the old chair system with the department model, adopted the full-time contract for faculty and substituted the traditional sequential course system for the credit system.

[3] The *Conselho Nacional de Educação* is a special assembly of education stakeholder representatives that works as an auxiliary body of the Ministry of Education, dating from the 1930s. It overviews curricular contents at all education levels, accredits new undergraduate programmes proposed by non-university institutions and supervises schools and universities nationwide.

[4] Graduate education in Brazil is limited mostly to public universities, with private institutions playing a minor role. In 1998, only 10% of the MA and 9.3% of the PhD programmes were to be found in the private sector.

[5] See Albuquerque & Balbachevsky (2002). Evidences that this situation is widespread in Brazilian universities were collected by the author when doing the field research for the article about the Brazilian academic market place. See Balbachevsky & Quinteiro (2003).

[6] CAPES, www.capes.gov.br

[7] A survey with graduate students in Brazil in 1995 found out that 80% of all graduate students received a fellowship at least once while enrolled in graduate programmes (Velloso & Velho 2001). Since the length of time covered by the standard fellowship is two years for Master's students and four

years for doctorate students, it is easy to see why Brazilian science and technology agencies are concerned with this situation.

[8] The three follow-up studies, carried out in the past five years, involved graduates from Master's and doctoral programmes who were trained in Brazil and obtained their degrees since 1990, in 15 fields: Agronomy, Biochemistry, Business and Public Administration, Chemistry, Civil Engineering, Electrical Engineering, Internal Medicine, Physics, Sociology, Economics, Dentistry, Geology, Mechanical Engineering, Law and Psychology.

[9] One should not forget that the Brazilian graduate system is the biggest in Latin America and thus attracts students from other Latin American countries.

[10] If such experiences result in similar patterns of research, internationalisation is an issue open to the debate. For arguments sustaining this conclusion, see Meneghini (1995). For arguments to the contrary, see Velho (2001) and Velloso (2002a).

[11] The only important exception in this picture is the network of Pontifical Catholic Universities which started graduate education programmes at the end of 1960s. These universities, although private, have always received important public support and have an institutional framework very similar to the public ones.

References

Albuquerque, J.A.G. & Balbachevsky, E. (2002) Public Policy Analysis at the Graduate Level in Brazil: a case of institutional underdevelopment, in J. Dassin, J.S. Tulchin, & A. Brown (Eds) *Training a New Generation of Leaders*, pp. 147-168. Washington: Woodrow Wilson International Center for Scholars, Latin American Program.

Balbachevsky, E. & Quinteiro, M.C. (2003) The Changing Academic Workplace in Brazil, in P.G. Altbach (Ed.) *The Decline of the Guru: the academic profession in developing and middle-income countries*, pp. 75-106. New York: Palgrave Macmillan.

Braga, M.M. (2002) Características da trajetória acadêmica de mestres e doutores formados no pais em seis areas, in J. Velloso (Ed.) *A pós-graduação no Brasil: formação e trabalho de mestres e doutores no país*, vol. II, pp. 245-264. Brasília: CAPES, UNESCO.

CAPES (1998) *Uma década de pós-graduação -1987-1997*. Brasília: Ministério da Educação, CAPES/DAV.

CAPES (1999) *Avaliação da pós-graduação: síntese dos resultados*. Brasília: Ministério da Educação, CAPES/DAV.

Castro, C.d.M. & Soares, G.A.D. (1986) As avaliações da Capes, in S. Schwartzman & C.d.M. Castro (Eds) *Pesquisa universitária em questão*, pp. 190-224. São Paulo: Editora da UNICAMP.

Coutinho, M. (1996) Ecology and Environmental Science in Brazilian Higher Education; graduate programs, research and intellectual identity, *Documentos de Trabalho*, 6.

Coutinho, M., Balbachevsky, E. & Holzhacker, D. (2003) Intellectual Property and Public Research in Biotechnology in Brazil: the scientists' opinion, 19th Congress of International Political Science Association, Durban, South Africa.

Guimarães, R., Lourenço, R. & Cosac, S. (2001) O perfil dos doutores ativos em pesquisa no Brasil, *Parcerias Estratégicas*, 13, pp. 122-150.

Meneghini, R. (1995) Performance of Brazilian Scientists and the Pattern of Scientific Training: a comparison between physicists and chemists, *Ciência e Cultura*, 47(5), pp. 343-346.

Ministério da Ciência e Tecnologia (1999) Indicadores de Ciência e Tecnologia, Esforços em Ciência e Tecnologia (C&T) e Dispêndios em Pesquisa e Desenvolvimento (P&D) – Dados Preliminares. Available at: www.mct.gov.br/estat/ascavpp/portugues/2_Recursos_Aplicados/tabelas/tab2_5_1.htm

Oliveira, J.B.A. (1984) *Ilhas de competência: carreiras científicas no Brasil*. São Paulo: Editora Melhoramentos.

Schwartzman, S. (1991) *A Space for Science: the development of the scientific community in Brazil*. University Park: Pennsylvania State University Press. Available at: http://www.schwartzman.org.br/simon/space/summary.htm

Velho, L. (2001) Formação de doutores no país e no exterior: estratégias alternativas ou complentares? *Dados – Revista de Ciências Sociais*, 44, pp. 609-631.

Velloso, J. (2002a) *Formação no Brasil ou no exterior? doutores na pós-graduação de excelência*. Brasília: CAPES, UNESCO.

Velloso, J. (2002b) *A pós-graduação no Brasil formação e trabalho de mestres e doutores no país*. Brasilia: CAPES.

Velloso, J. & Balbachevsky, E. (2002) Graduate Training and Employment in Brazil, *International Higher Education*, 29, pp. 19-20.

Velloso, J. & Velho, L. (2001) *Mestrandos e Doutorandos no País – Trajetórias de Formação*. Brasília: Fundação Coordenação de Aperfeiçoamento de Pessoal de Nível Superior (CAPES).

Weber, S. (2002) Estudo e situação de trabalho de mestres titulados no período 1990-1999, in J. Velloso (Ed.) *A pós-graduação no Brasil: formação e trabalho de mestres e doutores no país*, vol. II, pp. 265-276. Brasília: CAPES, UNESCO.

Notes on Contributors

Elizabeth Balbachevsky (balbasky@usp.br) is Assistant Professor at the Department of Political Science of the University of São Paulo, and senior researcher at the research centres for Higher Education (NUPES) and International Relations in the same university. She is currently directing a national survey on the Brazilian academic profession. She has written on the Brazilian academic profession and science and technology policies. Recent publications include 'The Changing Academic Workplace in Brazil', in *The Decline of the Guru: the academic profession in developing and middle-income countries*, edited by Phillip Altbach (Palgrave Macmillan, 2003) and 'From Encirclement to Globalization: evolving patterns of higher education in Brazil', in *The Emerging Markets and Higher Education*, edited by Matthew McMullen and others (RoutledgeFalmer, 2000).

Colin Brock (drcbrock@hotmail.com) is Senior Research Fellow in the Department of Educational Studies at the University of Oxford, where he has worked since 1992 in the field of Comparative and International Education. A graduate in Geography and Anthropology, he has been involved in international educational development for 35 years, working in various locations in Africa, Asia and the tropical island zones as well as in Latin America, and for most of the major agencies such as the World Bank, United Nations Development Programme and the European Commission. He has published in the field of Latin American education, and has been co-organiser of the UK Seminar on Latin American Education for the past 15 years.

Cláudio de Moura Castro (claudioc@pitagoras.com.br) is a Brazilian economist, with a PhD in Economics from Vanderbilt University. He taught at the Catholic University of Rio de Janeiro, the Vargas Foundation, the University of Chicago, the University of Brasilia, the University of Geneva and the University of Burgundy (Dijon). He was the director of CAPES (Brazilian Agency for Postgraduate Education) and Chief of the Training Policies Branch of the International Labour Office (Geneva) between 1986 and 1992. He worked in the World Bank as Senior Human Resource Economist and was Chief Educational Advisor of the Inter-American Development Bank. Presently, he is President of the Advisory Council of Faculdade Pitágoras. He has published over 35 books and around 300 scholarly articles.

Maria Helena de Magalhães Castro (necastro@globo.com) holds a PhD in Political Science from Duke University, USA (1993) and is Professor of the Department of Sociology at the Federal University in Rio de Janeiro. She worked at the Research Group on Higher Education of the University of São Paulo from 1990 to 1994; participated in the Harvard Fellowship Programme on Latin American Higher Education during the spring of 1995, and made a study on Higher Education in Nicaragua for the Inter-American Development Bank in 2000. She was a member of the Advisory Committee on Higher Education Statistics for the National Institute of Education Research in Brazil, for the development of Brazil's national information system for higher education; and has been a member of the Coordinating Committee on Institutional Evaluation for the Brazilian National Council of Rectors since 2000.

Maria Helena Guimarães de Castro (helenaca@uol.com.br) is currently the State Secretary for Social Development of the Government of São Paulo. From January 1995 to April 2002, she acted as President of the National Institute for Educational Studies and Research (INEP), the government agency in charge of education statistics and evaluation in Brazil. Some of the most important projects implemented by INEP under her coordination are: the School Census, the Higher Education Census, the National Basic Education Evaluation System (SAEB), the National Secondary Education Examination (ENEM), and the National Course Examination (Provão). Also, she took part in the formulation and implementation of several important educational policies and reforms implemented during Fernando Henrique Cardoso's administration (school grants curricular reforms, funding decentralization, etc.)

Robert Cowen (r.cowen@ioe.ac.uk) is Emeritus Professor of Education at the Institute of Education, University of London, and President of the Comparative Education Society in Europe and a Senior Visiting Research Fellow at the University of Oxford. He has been a Visiting Professor at the University of Brasília, in Brazil, the Catholic University of Leuven in Belgium, the University of La Trobe in Melbourne, and the State University of New York, at Buffalo, New York, USA. His publications include *Latin America and Educational Transfer* (ed.), Special Issue of *Comparative Education* (2002); *Education in Times of Transition: The World Yearbook of Education 2000* (ed., with David Coulby & Crispin Jones) (Kogan Page, 2000). His recent articles include: 'Moments of Time: a comparative note', in *History of Education*, 31(5), 2002; 'In the Minds of Men: the shifting contexts of interculturality', in *Interculturel: Balance y Perspectivas* (UNESCO, 2002); and, on teacher education, 'Socrates was Right? Teacher Education Systems and the State', in Elwyn Thomas (Ed.) *Teacher Education: dilemmas and prospects, World Yearbook of Education 2002* (Kogan Page, 2002).

Eunice Durham (nupes@usp.br) is Professor of Anthropology at the University of São Paulo. She is the founder and director of the Research Group of Higher Education in that University since 1989. She was the director for the Brazilian Agency for Graduate Education (CAPES), National Secretary for Higher Education and National Secretary for Educational Policy for the Brazilian Ministry of Education between 1991 and 1995. Her earlier studies dealt with issues of culture and social mobility; more recently, she has written extensively on questions related to higher education policy and assessment.

Maria C.M. Figueiredo (m.cowen@ioe.ac.uk) started her career as a lecturer and senior administrator in the State University of Montes Claros, in Brazil. She was also a regional adviser to CAPES, a research and funding agency of the Ministry of Education. She studied at the Sorbonne, in Paris. She undertook her MSc in University Planning and Administration at the University of Wisconsin, USA. Later she obtained her PhD from the Institute of Education, University of London where she became the Brazilian Lektor, appointed by the Institute of Education in partnership with the Brazilian Ministry of Foreign Affairs. Her publications include *Paulo Freire at the Institute* (with Denise Gastaldo) (Institute of Education, University of London, 1995); 'Latin American Universities, Academic Freedom and Autonomy: a long-term myth?' in *Comparative Education*, 38(4), 2002; 'Educational Excellence: the case of Brazil' (with Robert Cowen) in *Higher Education Policy*, 2(3), 1989.

João Batista Araujo e Oliveira (jm@terra.com.br) worked on academic, professional, consulting and managerial positions throughout his career in Brazil and abroad. In the last eight years he has been involved in the development of large-scale educational interventions for at-risk students as well as for teaching children how to read and write (www.alfaebeto.com.br). He also published a number of papers and books based on the results of these projects. His most recent books are *A Pedagogia do Sucesso, Aprender e Ensinar, A Escola Vista por Dentro* (with Simon Schwartzman) and *ABC do Alfabetizador* (Belo Horizonte: Alfa Educativa, 2004).

Simon Schwartzman (simon@schwartzman.org.br) is the President of the Institute for Studies and Labour and Society (IETS) in Rio de Janeiro. He is Brazilian, with a PhD in political science from the University of California, Berkeley. He has worked in the areas of comparative politics, science and technology, higher education and social policy. Between 1994 and 1998, he was the President of Brazil's Statistical and Geographical Institute (Fundação Instituto Brasileiro e Geografia e Estatística, IBGE). His books include *Bases do Autoritarismo Brasileiro* (Editora Campus e Editora da Universidade de Brasília, 1982); *A Space for Science: the development of the scientific community* *in Brazil* (Pennsylvania State University Press, 1991 and 2001 in Portuguese); *The New Production of Knowledge* (with Michael Gibbons, Camille Limoges, Helga Nowotny, Peter Scott & Martin Trow) (Sage, 1994); and *El futuro de la educación superior en America Latina* (Washington, DC, Organization of American States, 1996); and *As Causas da Pobreza* (Rio de Janeiro, Fundação Getúlio Vargas, 2004).

Francisco Soares (francisco-soares@ufmg.br) is Professor of Statistics at the Federal University of Minas Gerais, where he studied mathematics before obtaining his MA in statistics from the Institute of Pure and Applied Mathematics in Rio de Janeiro, and his PhD from the University of Wisconsin at Madison, USA. He coordinates the Group of Educational Assessment and Measurements at the University, and works on statistical models used to identify and assess intra- and extra-school factors associated with student achievement. He has worked in the planning and analysis of the Brazilian National Assessment of Basic Education (SAEB) and in education assessment for the state of Minas Gerais, Brazil.

Sergio Tiezzi (sergio.tiezzi@ig.com.br) holds a degree in History from the University of São Paulo, and an MA in Urban Planning from the University of Brasilia. From 1995 through 2002, he has occupied different staff positions in the Brazilian government: special advisor to the Minister of Education; Director in the Ministry of Planning, Budget and Management, and in the President's Chief of Staff Office. Throughout, he has worked with special policies in general, and education in particular. He is currently technical advisor in the Brazilian Senate.